BIPOLAR
or
ADHD

Strategies for Bipolar Disorder, ADHD and other Co-existing Conditions

Educational &
Home Based
Strategies for
Bipolar Disorder,
ADHD and other
Co-existing
Conditions

- Types of Bipolar Disorder

- Strategies for Elementary & Secondary Students

- How to Reduce Mood Swings and Rage States

- How to Teach Students to Self-Monitor

- Co-existing Conditions and Strategies to Deal with Them

- Disciplinary Model for Home and School

F. Russell Crites, Jr.

Published by EXCEL Digital Press Dallas, Texas.
www.exceldigitalpress.com/pages/1/index.htm

Printed in the United States of America

Library of Congress Cataloging-in-Publication Data
Crites, F. Russell

Bipolar or ADHD: Educational & Home Based Strategies for Bipolar Disorder, ADHD and other Co-existing Conditions / F. Russell Crites, Jr.

Manic-Depressive Illness in children -- Popular works
Manic-Depressive Illness in adolescents – Popular works

ISBN 0-9786376-1-5

First Edition

Table of Contents

Charts, Checklists and Appendices

Charts

Checklists

Appendices

Preface

This book was written with two objectives in mind. The first objective was to help educators obtain a better understanding of Bipolar Disorder as it relates to school aged children and the strategies that may be used to help them function more effectively at school. The second objective was to identify co-existing disorders and provide educational strategies and modifications that can be readily applied in a school setting (or home in some cases) for each co-existing disorder. In addition to providing helpful information for educators, this book was intended to be parent friendly. It provides parents with needed information as to what strategies and modifications can be used at school to help their child, as well as some strategies that can be used in the home that will reduce bipolar or co-existing conditions. Many of the school strategies can be adapted for use at home.

This book is not intended to be a complete collection of all the strategies and modifications that could be used either at home, or in the school for any of the conditions listed. However, the recommendations, strategies and modifications that are within this work will be of some benefit to teachers, parents and students who are dealing with Bipolar Disorder and related conditions. It is important to note that many of the strategies listed in this book can be taught by parents, counselors, teachers, and other staff to help the student learn how to self-monitor and self-manage issues related to Bipolar Disorder.

In addition, this book is not intended to take the place of a Psychiatrist, Physician, Psychologist, Counselor, Psychotherapist, Social Worker, etc. It is merely intended to be a resource for those who work or live with bipolar kids. Please note the following important points in regards to dealing with Bipolar Disorder, as well as many of the co-existing conditions.

- It is important to note that there are numerous other 'disorders' that can mimic Bipolar Disorder, e.g., Attention Deficit/Hyperactivity Disorder (ADHD), Asperger, Obsessive-Compulsive Disorder, Traumatic Brain Injury, and Tourette Syndrome.
- Before any treatment begins a professional should collect data in order to determine what can be done to help the child. This data includes information from parents, and teachers, as well as individual testing and evaluation of the student. A fifteen minute to an hour interview is not enough to obtain a true picture of a child. The myriad of possible conditions require a thorough evaluation in order to determine true causality and condition.
- As part of the data collection it is vital to obtain sound medical/psychological assessment in order to determine the true underlying disorder (or disorders) in order to properly treat the condition.
- Keep in mind that when medication is called for, the wrong medication can have significant negative effects on the individual. On the other hand, the proper medication can literally save the life of the child and help him become a fully functional human being.
- Medication should always be accompanied by some form of counseling, including behavior management strategies. Over time inappropriate behaviors are internalized and become part of the person. Medication does not correct learned behaviors.....counseling and/or social skill development is needed.

For grammatical consistency and clarity, the pronouns "he", "his" and "him" have been used throughout most of this work instead of "she or he", "his or her" and "her and him." No sexual bias or insensitivity is intended.

Thanks to many teachers who have contributed to information
found in this work. Special thanks goes to Debbie and Sarah for all the wonderful
strategies they shared from working with students who have special needs.

I'd like to dedicate this book to Pamela, Derek and Terri.
Without their patience and support it would never have been finished.

x

An Overview of Bipolar Disorder

Chapter One

ADHD has become one of the most widely diagnosed conditions in the United States. Although there are in reality many children who have this condition, it is sad to say that many who have been diagnosed with ADHD actually have Bipolar Disorder. With this thought in mind, it is important for parents and educators to develop a better understanding of Bipolar Disorder as it relates to children. Bipolar disorder has been a debilitating problem for adults for years. Children and adolescents have rarely been diagnosed with this disorder until recently. Numerous researchers have identified that children and adolescents can indeed have Bipolar Disorder. As a result, more and more students are being given that diagnosis. Of interest, especially in the school systems, is that ADHD should not be diagnosed until Bipolar Disorder has been ruled out. New knowledge has made it easier to identify Bipolar Disorder, which is in itself very helpful, since bipolar students have some very specific needs that go beyond what is seen in ADHD students. However, there is still a need for ongoing education in the area of Bipolar Disorder. Numerous studies by Geller, Miklowitz, Papolos & Papolos, CABF, the American Academy of Child and Adolescent Psychiatry and other individuals or agencies have provided information that can help us understand Bipolar Disorder as it relates to children and adolescents.

Here are some of the results of a few studies that can give needed information regarding Bipolar Disorder and children.

- Bipolar disorder has been investigated by federally funded teams in children as young as age 6.
- Approximately 7% of children seen at psychiatric facilities meet criteria for the diagnosis of Bipolar Disorder using research standards (Carlson, G.A., 1998).
- Based on one large scale study, 5.7% of the adolescent population had some form of Bipolar disorder (Strober, M. 1990).

- Over 80% of children with a Bipolar Disorder will meet full criteria for attention-deficit disorder with hyperactivity, ***ADHD should be diagnosed only after Bipolar Disorder is ruled out.***
- Stimulants unopposed by a mood stabilizer can have an adverse effect on the bipolar condition.
- 65% of the children in a study done by Papolos had hypomanic, manic and aggressive reactions to stimulant medications (Papolos & Papolos, 1999).
- According to the Child & Adolescent Bipolar Foundation (CABF), 15% of U.S. children diagnosed with ADHD may actually be suffering early-onset Bipolar Disorder instead.
- According to the American Academy of Child and Adolescent Psychiatry up to 33% of the 3.4 million children and adolescents with depression in the United States may actually be experiencing early-onset Bipolar disorder.
- Bipolar disorder appears to be genetic. If one parent has the disorder, the risk to each child is 15-30%. If both parents have the disorder, the risk increases to 50-75%.
- If Bipolar Disorder is caused entirely by genes, then the identical twin of someone with the illness would *always* develop the illness, and research has shown that this is not the case. However, if one twin has Bipolar Disorder, the other twin is more likely to develop the illness than is another sibling.
- If the Bipolar Disorder is untreated, the suicide rate can be as high as 20%.
- Dr. Miklowitz tailored his therapy to address the special needs of kids, including learning to understand changes in school functions and recognizing normal adolescence from pathological behavior, working at regulating sleeping, and addressing mood disturbances in other family members (Miklowitz, 2002).
- Studies using positron emission tomography (PET), a technique that measures brain function in terms of blood flow or glucose metabolism, have found abnormal activity in specific brain regions including the prefrontal cortex, basal ganglia, and temporal lobes during manic and depressive cycles.
- Bipolar children can have night terrors. Their dreams are filled with blood and gore.
- In one study 43% of the study sample who had Bipolar Disorder were also hypersexual.
- Those with Bipolar Disorder who present with a mixed state take the longest to recover, and are the most vulnerable to experience recurrences.
- Studies suggest that Bipolar Disorder beginning in childhood or early adolescence may be a different, possibly more severe form of the illness than older adolescent and adult-onset Bipolar Disorder (Carlson, 1998; Geller, 1997).

Geller has completed many studies on child/adolescent Bipolar Disorder. She has found that children/adolescents do not exhibit many of the manifestations of bipolar symptoms described in adults. However, they do have five symptoms that are specific to their condition. These symptoms are elation, grandiosity, flight of ideas/racing thoughts, decreased need for sleep, and hyper-sexuality (in the absence of abuse or over-stimulation). Based on her studies she has determined that these five symptoms provide the best discrimination of childhood/early adolescent Bipolar Disorder from uncomplicated ADHD (Geller, 1998).

Additional studies are ongoing by numerous authors regarding Bipolar Disorder and children. As time goes on a more clear picture of what Bipolar Disorder is and what can be done about it in children will emerge.

Reasons for Not Diagnosing Bipolar Disorder

In the scheme of things the diagnosis of Bipolar Disorder in children and adolescents is relatively new. Due to this, and the fact that there are many co-existing conditions that look like Bipolar Disorder, there have been few children who have actually been given the diagnosis. In addition, it is not always an easy disorder to diagnose. There are many reasons why a child or adolescent may not have been properly diagnosed as having Bipolar Disorder. Some of these reasons include:

- A parent may be scared, or in denial about what the symptoms suggest.
- Some believe that it is better to wait and see before you place such a diagnosis on a child. The rationale for this is that the child is still developing and he may grow out of it as he develops.
- Even without professional help the parents believe that the symptoms are not too bad, and that they can be managed with loving care at home. The school may or may not agree.
- Someone in the family is convinced that drugs are not in the best interest of the child, so they don't take him to the doctor to address the issue.
- If the student is an adolescent who is going through puberty, the behaviors may be a result of hormonal changes in his body. This may or may not be true.
- The parent is convinced that the child has another disorder, e.g., ADHD, Asperger, or Tourette.
- The parent is concerned that the stigmatization of having such a disorder will cause damage to the child's ability to live a normal life.

Regardless of the reason a student has not been identified, it is important that either school personnel, other professionals, or the parent take a closer look at the child who may be experiencing bipolar symptoms. Untreated Bipolar Disorder can produce deadly results. The remainder of this chapter will help both parents and educators identify if a student has the symptoms of Bipolar Disorder. It will also identify the various types of Bipolar Disorder that the student may possibly have.

Medically Related Mood Disorders

In the DSM there is a section that addresses the possibility that Bipolar Disorder may be caused by a medically related condition. The title is, 'Mood Disorder Due to a General Medical Condition'. This should be considered as a possible diagnosis if it appears that the depressive, manic or mixed-episode state is being caused by a medical condition. Some of the most common medical conditions that would suggest a need for this diagnosis are:

- Cancer
- AIDS
- Stroke
- Endocrine conditions
- Severe infections

For children who have difficulty communicating, it is vital that medically related issues be ruled out before a mood disorder is diagnosed.

Signs that a Student May Have Bipolar Disorder

There are a number of signs or symptoms that indicate a student may be experiencing mood swings. Here are some of them:

- Problems with sleep
- Laughing for no apparent reason
- Teasing or joking that seems to be excessive
- Extreme temper tantrums that last long periods of time
- Physically aggressive
- Being unusually quiet...sometimes withdrawing from others
- Failing grades
- Reports of inappropriate behavior or bullying at school

Bipolar Disorder: The Mood Spectrum

There are many aspects of the mood spectrum. Although children and adolescents do not often have Bipolar I or II they do experience other forms of Bipolar Disorder. This section will describe the following in greater detail.

- Bipolar I
- Bipolar II
- Hypomania
- Cyclothymia
- Bipolar Disorder: Mixed type

- Rapid Cycling Bipolar Disorder
- Ultrarapid & Ultradian Bipolar Disorder
- Bipolar Disorder & Children
- Bipolar Disorder & Adolescents

Bipolar I

There are actually six different variations of Bipolar I disorder. Because of the complexity of diagnosing each of these, data for each is not found in this work. Due to the number of variables that need to be addressed, it would take a trained professional to accurately identify which type of Bipolar I disorder is present. Bipolar I in this work is identified as Bipolar I single manic episode and is the first type found in the DSM-IV – TR. Bipolar I is found predominantly in adults. To be identified with Bipolar I the individual must have at least one lifetime episode of mania, or a mixed disorder with elated mood, and three other associated symptoms of mania that lasted a week or more and required hospitalization.

Clarification

- The student must have at least one lifetime episode of manic or mixed disorder with elated mood and three other associated symptoms of mania (see manic symptoms in Chapter 3), that lasted a week or more and required hospitalization.
- If the student's mood was irritable and not elated four or more symptoms are required for diagnosis.
- One lifetime episode of major depression is often seen (not required for diagnosis).

> *Must have at least one lifetime episode of mania, or a mixed disorder with elated mood, and three other associated symptoms of mania, that lasted a week or more and required hospitalization to be diagnosed Bipolar I.*

Bipolar I will often have the following mood states:

- Severe Depression: At least two weeks of hopelessness, apathy, decreased appetite, and insomnia.
- Mild/Moderate Depression: Similar to severe depression, but not as long lasting or debilitating.
- Normal: Moods may change from day to day, but not in a way that interferes with life.
- Hypomania: Days of unusually elevated mood, less need for sleep, distractibility, inflated self-esteem.
- Mania or Mixed Mania: At least a week of mania; mixed states show signs of both mania and depression.

Bipolar II

To be Bipolar II the individual must have or experienced at least one lifetime episode of hypomania that lasts four days and at least one episode of major depression.

Clarification

- The student must have at least one lifetime episode of hypomania that lasts four days.
- The student must have at least one episode of major depression.
- If the student's mood was irritable and not elated, four or more symptoms of hypomania are required for diagnosis (see hypomania).
- The student alternates between hypomania and major depressive episodes.

Bipolar II will often have the following mood states:

- Severe Depression: At least two weeks of hopelessness, apathy, decreased appetite, and insomnia.
- Mild/Moderate Depression: Similar to severe depression, but not as long lasting or debilitating.
- Normal: Moods may change from day to day, but not in a way that interferes with life.
- Hypomania: Days of unusually elevated mood, less need for sleep, distractibility, inflated self-esteem.

> *To be Bipolar II the individual must have at least one lifetime episode of hypomania that lasts four days and at least one episode of major depression.*

Hypomania

Hypomania is similar to mania except that the symptoms are less intense. It affects a students functioning much less than a manic episode. In some cases hypomania actually helps a student's concentration, focus, socialization and actually seems to help with creativity. Here is a checklist that will help determine if a student may have some characteristics of hypomania. Only check the symptom if there has been a period of at least four days in which the student has experienced the problem.

Hypomania Checklist

	Yes	No
1. The student's mood is elevated, overly outgoing, or irritable.	___	___
And three or more of the following symptoms (four if mood is irritable) have been present to a significant degree!		
2. The student has an inflated self-esteem or grandiosity.	___	___
3. The student has a decreased need for sleep.	___	___
4. The student is more talkative than usual, or feels pressured to keep talking.	___	___
5. The student has racing thoughts or a continuous stream of thoughts, ideas or images.	___	___
6. The student is easily distracted by unimportant things.	___	___
7. The student has an increase in goal-directed activity, feeling compelled to obtain a goal.	___	___
8. The student has excessive involvement in pleasurable activities that have potential for painful consequences (such as spending sprees, risky behaviors).	___	___

If you answer yes to some of the above symptoms the student may have Hypomania. Adapted from the Diagnostic and Statistical Book of Mental Disorders IV – TR. Copyright 2000, American Psychiatric Association.

Clarification

- Hypomanic episodes usually do not cause big problems for school, family or friends; however, more arguments or disagreements may occur.
- Hypomanic episodes can be very satisfying or enjoyable for the individual. He may feel energized and driven to do things that are important to him.
- The primary symptoms that are often seen in hypomania are sleep problems (sleep less), increased activity, hyper-sexuality, irritability, and an inflated sense of self (this is not to a dangerous level like seen in mania).

> *With hypomania there is an absence of the more severe mania. It may feel good to the person who experiences it, and may even be associated with good functioning and enhanced productivity.*

Cyclothymia

Cyclothymia is characterized by periods of hypomania followed by periods of mild depression. Here is a checklist that will help determine if a student may have some characteristics of cyclothymia. Check the symptom if the student has alternated between high and low periods for at least two consecutive years and has had mood disorder symptoms for more than two months at a time.

Cyclothymia Checklist   Yes   No

1. The student has had numerous periods with depressive symptoms that do not meet full criteria for a major depressive episode (see 'Symptoms of Depression' in Chapter 4). ___ ___

2. The student has had numerous periods with hypomanic symptoms (see 'Symptoms of Hypomania' in Chapter 1). ___ ___

3. The student has not been without symptoms for more than two months at a time. ___ ___

4. The student's symptoms are not caused by a substance (drug, alcohol, medication), or a medical condition. ___ ___

6. The student's symptoms have caused significant problems in daily functioning. ___ ___

If you answer yes to some of the above symptoms the student may have Cyclothymia. Adapted from the Diagnostic and Statistical Book of Mental Disorders IV – TR. Copyright 2000, American Psychiatric Association.

Clarification

- About one in three people who have cyclothymia progress to bipolar I or bipolar II disorder over a period of two to three years.
- Individuals with cyclothymia can look normal and be relatively functional. Their highs are not high enough to cause problems and their lows are not significant enough to keep them from functioning.

Cyclothymia has the following mood states:

- Mild/Moderate Depression: Similar to severe depression, but not as long lasting or debilitating.
- Normal: Moods may change from day to day, but not in a way that interferes with life.
- Hypomania: Days of unusually elevated mood, less need for sleep, distractibility, inflated self-esteem.

With Cyclothymia there is an absence of the more severe mania and the more severe depression.

Bipolar Disorder: Mixed Type

Adolescent Bipolar Disorder often begins as a mixed disorder...both mania and/or irritability and depression. When Bipolar Disorder begins before or soon after puberty, it is often characterized by a continuous, rapid-cycling, irritable, and mixed symptom state that may co-exist with disruptive behavior disorders, particularly attention deficit hyperactivity disorder (ADHD), or conduct disorder (CD), or may have features of these disorders as initial symptoms. Students who experience mixed states describe a feeling of being agitated or manic while also feeling anguish and despair. Check the symptom if the student has experienced both mania and depression at the same time for at least four days.

Bipolar Disorder: Mixed Type	Yes	No
1. The student experiences depression & mania at the same time.	___	___
2. The student is manic on outside (happy, agitated, laughing hysterically) while internally suicidal, frustrated, etc.	___	___
3. The student is experiencing psychosis.	___	___
4. The student is experiencing trouble sleeping.	___	___
5. The student is experiencing agitation.	___	___
6. The student is experiencing a significant change in appetite.	___	___
7. The student is experiencing suicidal thinking.	___	___

If you answered yes to a few of the above symptoms the student may have Bipolar Disorder: Mixed Type. Adapted from the Diagnostic and Statistical Book of Mental Disorders IV – TR. Copyright 2000, American Psychiatric Association.

Clarification

- A mixed state Bipolar Disorder occurs when the student meets the criteria for both a manic episode as well as a major depressive episode nearly every day for at least four days.
- Students with mixed disorder are more likely to commit suicide than those with pure mania.

When Bipolar Disorder begins before, or soon after puberty, it is often characterized by a continuous, rapid-cycling, irritable, and mixed symptom state.

Rapid Cycling Bipolar Disorder

When four or more episodes of illness occur within a 12-month period, a person is said to have rapid-cycling Bipolar Disorder. Children tend to rapid cycle and have less level time between each episode.

Clarification

- Students who experience four or more depressive, manic, or hypomanic symptoms within a single year are said to rapid cycle. Rapid cycling occurs when manic and depressive symptoms alternate several times a year.
- When rapid cycling occurs, students switch back and forth between mania and depression.
- Studies have suggested that rapid cycling is not a life time condition.
- Up to half of bipolar patients experience rapid cycling temporarily, often when their illness begins.

Ultrarapid & Ultradian Bipolar Disorder

Geller has continued to study how both children and adolescents respond to Bipolar Disorder. One of her studies found that children have a more severe, chronic course of illness than the typical bipolar adult. She believes that, "Many children will be both manic and depressed at the same time, will often stay ill for years without intervening well periods, and will frequently have multiple daily cycles of highs and lows." Based on her research there appears to be two relatively new types of Bipolar Disorder. They are, 1) Ultrarapid Bipolar Disorder, and 2) Ultradian Bipolar Disorder (Geller, 1997).

- Ultrarapid: Children who have Ultrarapid Bipolar Disorder will have mood cycles every few days, i.e., they will have manic highs during the week and will also have depressive moods during the week.
- Ultradian: Children who have Ultradian Bipolar Disorder will have multiple mood cycles every day, i.e., they will have multiple manic highs and depressive episodes during each day. Schools have children who do this every day, and most have been diagnosed as being ADHD. However, it appears that some of these students actually have Ultradian Bipolar Disorder.

> *Children may have a more severe, chronic course of illness than the typical bipolar adult.*

Bipolar Disorder & Children

Children with Bipolar Disorder have episodes that are much less clearly defined than those in adolescence and adulthood. The following information better defines how Bipolar Disorder is seen in younger children (Geller, 1997; Carlson, 1998).

- When in a manic or hypomanic state younger children seem to exhibit a pervasive irritability more than elation.
- They also seem to throw destructive temper tantrums when in the hypomanic or manic state.
- When in a manic or hypomanic state, children may also have an inflated self-esteem, exhibit grandiose behavior, be talkative, distractible, have decreased need for sleep, exhibit inattentive behaviors, pleasure seeking behaviors, and has an increased goal directedness.
- These children also experience depression. However, it appears that with these younger children the depression seems to be chronic and less cyclical.
- According to Geller, "Many children will be both manic and depressed at the same time, will often stay ill for years without intervening well periods...".
- Geller also stated that, children with Bipolar Disorder will frequently have weekly or multiple daily cycles of highs and lows.
- In addition, Geller's group found that the children involved in her study had a more severe, chronic course of illness than the typical bipolar adult.
- Depression and dysphoria are an almost constant part of the presentation of pediatric Bipolar Disorder.
- The most common mistaken diagnoses for children and early adolescents who are bipolar is attention deficit/hyperactivity disorder.
- When the illness begins before or soon after puberty, it is often characterized by a continuous, rapid-cycling, irritable, and mixed symptom state that may co-exist with disruptive behavior disorders, particularly attention deficit hyperactivity disorder (ADHD) or conduct disorder (CD), and may have features of these disorders as initial symptoms (Geller, 1997).

> *When the illness (Bipolar Disorder) begins before or soon after puberty, it is often characterized by a continuous, rapid-cycling, irritable, and mixed symptom state.*

Bipolar Disorder & Adolescents

Adolescent Bipolar Disorder is a bit more specific in nature. Teens with Bipolar Disorder and those with sub-clinical symptoms had greater functional impairment and higher rates of co-existing illnesses, especially anxiety and disruptive behavior disorders, suicide attempts, and mental health services utilization.

- Later adolescent or adult-onset Bipolar Disorder tends to begin suddenly, often with a classic manic episode. In addition, adolescents usually have more episodic patterns with relatively stable periods between episodes. There is also less co-existing ADHD and CD among those with later onset illness (Geller, 1997).
- The most common mistaken diagnoses for adolescents who are bipolar is schizophrenia (in up to 50% of cases), and conduct disorder. Attention deficit hyperactivity disorder has been the main differential problem in pre-pubertal and early adolescent patients.
- Up to 80% of children and adolescents who have Bipolar Disorder show complex cycling patterns, characterized by brief manic periods lasting four or more hours.
- Psychosis is uncommon with children who have major depressive disorder, but delusions are a predictor of switching to mania in adolescent major depressive disorder.

Treating Bipolar Disorder at Home and at School

Chapter Two

Bipolar Disorder can take on many faces and produce a multitude of problems for the student and his family.   Whether it be predominantly a depressive state, an agitated state, a hypomanic or manic state, or a combination of all of the above it produces ongoing problems for the student. Many students exhibit multiple mood shifts during the week and sometimes during the day. This poses significant problems for teachers and administrators as they scramble to identify what should be done to help these students. Many of these characteristics are similar to that found in ADHD students. As a result, many students who have Bipolar Disorder are misdiagnosed as being ADHD. Regardless, of the diagnosis there are multiple strategies that need to be implemented to assist the student as he struggles to function both at home and at school.

This chapter provides a listing of the different types of strategies, techniques, etc. that can be utilized for the problems that are associated with Bipolar Disorder and its co-existing conditions. Co-existing simply means that the student has Bipolar Disorder, and also has one or more of the other conditions listed below at the same time.   Some people use the terms co-morbid or co-occurring to explain this phenomena. Regardless of the term used, any co-existing condition is problematic for the student and the adults working with him. Techniques and educational strategies are provided for the following:

- Mania
- Depression
- ADHD
- Anxiety
- Social Anxiety
- Obsessive-Compulsive Disorder
- Post Traumatic Stress Disorder
- Oppositional Defiant Disorder
- Conduct Disorder
- Psychotic Issues
- Substance Abuse Issues

This work is not intended to be a complete work on each of the disorders listed above. However, it is important that each co-existing issue be addressed that is causing the student problems. Even the slightest problem not addressed can become a major problem for the bipolar child. Each co-existing issue that is present can trigger manic, depressive, or rage states that obviously cause the student significant problems. As a result, it is important to identify which co-existing issues the student is struggling with. Once identified, each identified condition must be addressed at least at a cursory level in order to avoid inadvertent triggering of bipolar problems.

The remainder of this book was developed to assist educators, counselors and parents as they seek to identify how to better support these students. Strategies for school counselors, private therapists, parents, teachers and school administrators are included specific to each aspect of Bipolar Disorder that is causing the student difficulty.

> *Co-existing issues can trigger manic, depressive or rage states in the bipolar child.*

Strategy System

The strategy system that is found in the next few pages is meant to provide the teacher, counselor, administrator and parent with a quick reference tool that will help determine what strategies or techniques might be helpful in addressing specific issues. Each strategy found in this book is listed. Many of the strategies can be used for Bipolar Disorder as well as many of the co-existing conditions. The page number is listed for each strategy. Some strategies are condition specific. However, there are many strategies that may be adapted for use with other conditions. Once you identify the strategy or technique that you may want to use for a specific situation, go to the page and read about it. Many of the worksheets are found in the appendices.

	Basics fro Dealing with mania	Mania Reduction	To Play or Not To Play	Peaceful Heart technique	General Guidelines for Mania	Strategies for the Agitation State	Strategies for the Verbal Stage	Strategies for the Explosion Stage	Classroom Clear	Strategies for the Recovery Stage	Contract	Educational Strategies for Mania
Mania	25	26	26	27	28	32	33	34	35	36	39	41
Depression												
ADHD												
General Anxiety												
Obsessive Compulsive												
Social Anxiety												
PTSD												
ODD												
CD												
Psychotic Disorder												
Substance Abuse												

	Depression Reduction	Dissecting Cognitive Distortions	Negative vs Positive Thoughts	Negative Thought Tracking	Thought Interruption Techniques	The Balloon Exercise	Selecting Fun Activities	Healthy Social Support System	Quick Reward Menu	Daily or Weekly Rewards List	Fun Activities Form	Visualizing a Fun Activity
Mania												
Depression	46	48	49	50	51	52	53	55	56	56	57	59
ADHD												
General Anxiety												
Obsessive Compulsive												
Social Anxiety												
PTSD												
ODD												
CD												
Psychotic Disorder												
Substance Abuse												

	Took Box for Depression	Tips for Suicidal Issues	Educational Strategies for Dep.	Strategies for ADHD or BP	Modifications for ADHD/BP	Quick Stress Busters	Basic Abdominal Breathing	Meditation for Relaxation & Health	Quick Relaxation Technique	Progressive Muscle Relaxation	Positive Imagery & Relaxation	Deflating Anxiety
Mania				68-80	80-81							
Depression	59	60	61									
ADHD				68-80	80-81							
General Anxiety						87	88	89	90	90	91	92
Obsessive Compulsive							88				91	
Social Anxiety						87	88	89	90	90	91	92
PTSD						87	88	89	90	90	91	
ODD												
CD												
Psychotic Disorder												
Substance Abuse												

	Stress monitoring	Stress Innoculation Training	Anger Reduction	Student St. for Social Anxiety	Identifying Obsessive Thoughts	Obsessive Thoughts	ERP Techniques	Quick Strategies for OCD	OCD Strategies for Home	Classroom St. for OCD	Psycho-education & PTSD	Coping with PTSD
Mania												
Depression												
ADHD												
General Anxiety	92	93										
Obsessive Compulsive	92	93			100	101	102-104	105	105	106		
Social Anxiety	92	93		96								
PTSD											110	111
ODD			95									
CD			95									
Psychotic Disorder												
Substance Abuse												

	Ed. St. for ODD	Ed. St. for CD	St. for Dealing w/ Psych. Epi.	St. for Dealing with S.A.	Ed. St. for Bipolar Disorder	Personal Warning Signs for Mood Swit.	Daily Mood Diary	Warning Signs for Depression	Warning Signs for Mania	Self-Monitoring	Behavior Monitoring	Monitoring Communication
Mania					125 - 134	139	140		142	143	144	145
Depression					125 - 134	139	140	141		143	144	145
ADHD										143	144	
General Anxiety												145
Obsessive Compulsive										143	144	
Social Anxiety										143	144	145
PTSD												
ODD	115									143	144	145
CD		118								143	144	145
Psychotic Disorder			119									
Substance Abuse				123								

19

	Personal Time Outs	Monthly Medication Management	Daily Activity and Mood Chart	Reasons To Exercise	Types of Exercise	Self-Defeating Thoughts and Exercise	Exercise Journal	Student Initiated Proactive Strategies	The Rage Freeze Technique	Somatic Precursors to a Rage State	Covert Modeling and Bipolar Disorder	Cue Card
Mania	145	160	163	166	166	167	168	173	173	175	176	178
Depression	145	160	163	166	166	167	168	173				178
ADHD	145	160		166	166	167	168					178
General Anxiety	145	160		166	166	167	168				176	178
Obsessive Compulsive	145	160									176	178
Social Anxiety	145	160									176	178
PTSD		160										
ODD												178
CD												178
Psychotic Disorder	145	160										178
Substance Abuse		160										178

	Proactive St. for Behavior Change	Auditory Strategies	Visual Strategies	Altering Antecedents	Reinforcement Survey	School Reward Survey	Proactive Reinforcement Schedule	Daily/Weekly Rewards Menu	Reinforcement Board	Restraint		
Mania	178	179	180	180	182	182	183	184	185	186		
Depression	178	179	180	180	182	182	183	184	185			
ADHD					182	182	183	184	185			
General Anxiety	178	179	180	180								
Obsessive Compulsive												
Social Anxiety	178			180								
PTSD		179	180	180								
ODD					182	182	183	184	185			
CD					182	182	183	184	185	186		
Psychotic Disorder		179	180							186		
Substance Abuse										186		

Mania and Bipolar Disorder

Chapter Three

Mania can take on many faces when a student has Bipolar Disorder. Specifically, when children and adolescents are manic, they are more likely to be irritable, angry, and prone to destructive outbursts (Carlson, 1998; Geller, 1997). In addition, when a child is in a manic state he may experience elation, be extremely cheerful, be grandiose in his thinking, and may also believe that he has powers that are superior to others. This student may have an ongoing issue with being overly energetic which may look like hyperactivity. In the evening he may have little need for sleep. His thoughts may race, and he may speak fast and be highly distractible. Some bipolar children and adolescents become risk takers and will engage in dangerous behavior. They also have a tendency to be hypersexual at an early age. In some cases these children will have psychotic symptoms. These symptoms usually show up as auditory hallucinations or delusional thinking. This distorted type of thinking often consists of the student believing that he is hearing voices that instruct him to do a special task.

Students who experience the manic side of Bipolar Disorder are impacted in a very negative way in their relationships, ability to work, do school work, and in every other aspect of their lives. Studies have identified various symptoms that can be observed by teachers, parents, counselors, and administrators. The list of manic symptoms shown in this chapter are based on numerous studies that have been conducted by multiple individuals.

Manic Symptoms

The following symptoms have been identified in children and adolescents who are experiencing either mania or hypomania (Geller, 1997; Carlson, 1998; Miklowizt, 2002; Papolos & Papolos, 2002).

Mania Checklist for Children and Adolescents

		Yes	No

1. **Irritable Mood:** The student is irritable. The first major symptom of mania and depression is irritable mood. ___ ___

2. **Severe Changes in Mood:** The student may be overly silly and elated. An elated child may laugh hysterically and act infectiously happy without any reason at home, school, church, etc. ___ ___

3. **Overly-inflated Self-Esteem or Grandiosity:** A grandiose student may believe that stealing is illegal for other people, but not for him. ___ ___

4. **Increased energy:** The student seems to have more energy than usual. ___ ___

5. **Decreased Need for Sleep:** The student may have very little or no sleep for days without tiring. This student may have a high activity level in the bedroom prior to sleep. He will stay up and rearrange furniture, play games, watch TV, etc. When he is sure his parents are asleep, he may go out to party with friends. ___ ___

6. **Increased Talking:** The student talks too much, too fast; changes topics too quickly and cannot be interrupted. ___ ___

7. **Distractibility:** The student's attention moves constantly from one thing to the next. ___ ___

8. **Hyper-sexuality:** The student may have increased sexual thoughts, feelings, or behaviors, or use sexually explicit language. Sexually based profanity occurs and the student may tell his teacher to "f--- herself" and/or give her the finger. He may also masturbate frequently. If he can't do it openly he will simply make frequent trips to the bathroom. In addition, he may try to touch the private areas of his teachers and classmates. The student may also proposition teachers, and make overt sexual comments to classmates. 1-900 numbers are often used for sexual thrills. ___ ___

9. **Increased Goal-Directed Activity or Physical Agitation.** The student may set high or multiple goals, and work extremely hard to attain them...more so than is normal. ___ ___

10. **Disregard of Risk:** The student may have excessive involvement in risky behavior or activities. He may drive wildly, and fast. He may also receive more speeding and driving under the influence tickets than his peers. A younger child may exhibit risk via grandiose delusions. For instance, he may believe that he can fly, and will jump from roof to roof, or limb to limb believing that he is above the possibility of danger. ___ ___

11. **Spending Money:** Even though this student may not have access to a lot of money, he may find a way to spend it. He will often begin to order multiple items on line, and borrow money to get things he wants from the store. ___ ___

12. **Flight of Ideas:** This student has racing thoughts and often says that he can't stop his brain from thinking. He may jump from topic to topic in rapid succession when he talks. ___ ___

If you answer yes to some of the above symptoms the student may have manic tendencies.

If manic symptoms are situational they may not be a result of mania. For instance, some students can have a false manic high. Specifically, an adrenaline rush can mimic a manic state. It can also look like the student is on drugs. However, if he calms in 15-20 minutes after going into a manic state, it may have been a result of an adrenaline rush due to trauma or anxiety.

> *An adrenaline rush can mimic a manic state. It can also look like the student is on drugs. However, if he calms in 15-20 minutes after going into a manic state, it may have been a result of an adrenaline rush due to trauma or anxiety.*

Basics for Dealing with Mania

There are some very important preventive strategies that should be considered when you are dealing with a bipolar student. Some of these must be addressed in the home, and some can be addressed in either the home or at school. Here are a few strategies to keep in mind.

- Make sure that the student's sleep rhythm is not disturbed. This is obviously a home issue.
- Turn off the fluorescent lights and use soft light in the classrooms where possible.
- Address Post Traumatic Stress Disorder (PTSD) issues if there are any. PTSD can trigger manic attacks.
- Keep the classroom doors closed to reduce the noise from the hallways between classes.
- Reduce stress and anxiety. Both can trigger manic episodes.
- Teach coping skills to reduce reaction to conflict.
- Make sure the child is taking his medication daily. Missing one dose can cause problems. Schools can volunteer to give morning medications to help with this issue.
- Reduce the volume of bells, music, announcements in the school if at all possible. Call for quiet to make sure that your students can hear what you (teacher) are saying.
- Give the student advance notice of tornado drills, fire drills, etc. Any time there is a change in his routine, let him know in advance. Structure is extremely important for bipolar students.
- Provide a safe, sensory reduced location where the student can go to when he needs to self calm or receive assistance.

Mania Reduction

The Mania Reduction form is intended to help the student work through symptoms of hypomania/mania as they occur. If the symptoms can be identified and strategies implemented as soon as is possible, there is a chance that the student can avoid a manic state and reduce the hypomania. There are four steps to using the Mania Reduction Form: The student must:

1) Identify a specific symptom of hypomania.
2) Determine how hypomanic he is at the moment.
3) Utilize a strategy that would help reduce the hypomanic symptom.
4) Reevaluate how much he feels hypomanic after using the mania reduction strategy.

In addition to the Mania Reduction form, additional mania reduction techniques can be found in Chapter Six. These strategies, or some like them, must be taught and practiced so that the student will be able to effectively use them when he has need. Here is an example of how the Mania Reduction Form can be used.

Mania Reduction

Name: *Johnny* **Date:** *3/11*

Instructions:
1) Write down the hypomanic symptom.
2) Using a 1-5 scale, mark the number that describes your current mood.
3) Use a strategy that will help control the manic tendency.
4) Using a 1-5 scale, mark the number that describes your mood after using the strategy.

1 = Normal for me		3 = Very Agitated		5 = About ready to go manic
Date/ Time	Symptom	How hypomanic initially?	Strategy Used	How hypomanic after strategy?
Mon 10:00am	*Agitated*	1 2 3 4 5	*Deep breathing*	1 2 3 4 5
Mon 10:45am	*Talking a lot*	1 2 3 4 5	*Muscle Relaxation*	1 2 3 4 5

If needed, copy the Mania Reduction form from the appendices and have the student complete it.

To Play or Not to Play Technique

This is a simple technique that calls for the teacher/parent to take direct action when a student is escalating. Some bipolar children live on the edge and will attempt to escalate you as you spend time with them. It is important that you not react to the students attempt to incite you, or escalate the situation. Here is a simple technique that may help you counter such attempts.

- If the student appears to be escalating and looking for a verbal or physical fight you need to be directive. Consider that his behavior may be a cry for help.
- Say, "I have the feeling that you are trying to get a rise out of me for the fun of it. But I don't want to play that game. What can we come up with that would be more interesting for both of us?" (Lynn, 2000).

As simple as this technique appears to be it can be very powerful when you are working with a student who has Bipolar Disorder. He needs to know that you are not going to simply accept that he cannot control his behavior and that you want to help him avoid mania or rage attacks as much as you can.

Peaceful Heart Technique

When a Bipolar student loses control you may want to use the Peaceful Heart Technique. This emotional state often occurs when something has triggered bipolar behavior in the student. In other words, there is probably an antecedent (see Chapter Twelve) that leads to the out of control behavior.

- Make sure there is nothing around him that he can use to hurt himself or others.
- Sit as closely as is safe and listen to his anger or frustration.
- Speak only when you are convinced that you should say something...be supportive, not punitive (punitive will only exacerbate the problem).
- Let him calm. When he is relatively calm, speak to him about how he can start fresh...begin again....start the day over, etc. Assure him that everything will be o.k. Be calm.
- Encourage him to pick up where he left off.

This statement will be made on more than one occasion as you read this book. If a bipolar student is triggered, and as a result exhibits inappropriate behavior, he should not be disciplined. It would be the same as giving a consequence to a blind person for accidentally running into another individual in the hallway. Instead, it is our responsibility to identify the trigger and remove it in order to reduce anger, and limit the manic or rage states (see chapter 12).

> *If a bipolar student is triggered, and as a result exhibits inappropriate behavior, he should not be disciplined.*

General Guidelines for Mania

Although there are innumerable suggestions and guidelines that could be listed, there are five that should be considered when you are dealing with a student who is experiencing a manic episode. They are as follows:

- When a student is manic there is a very good chance that he will become violent, or go into a rage state. If the student is going into a manic or rage state, and has previously been aggressive, call for help, e.g., crisis team, police, administration.
- Some studies have indicated that over 50% of students with Bipolar Disorder have a substance abuse disorder. If substance abuse is an issue for the student, the likelihood of violence increases significantly. Obviously, treatment for substance abuse is extremely important for students who have this disorder. Bipolar students will often self-medicate to deal with their internal distress (see Chapter Seven for specific drugs that are often used to self-medicate).
- There are two specific goals that should be considered when a student is in the acute phase of mania. First, the teacher, counselor, parent, etc. must attempt to decrease the symptomatology. This may be done by decreasing sensory input, or by implementing a stress reduction technique. Second, safety for all involved (student and staff) must be established as best as possible, e.g., if possible move the student to a safe location, remove possible dangerous items, keep distance from student, etc.
- Attempt verbal interventions first. If the manic state becomes too severe and it is obvious that you cannot safely deal with the student, you have to consider physical interventions depending on the size of the student. Many 7-12 grade students are as big as teachers and parents. These students should not be restrained. Many students this age are too strong to be held. However, you can take dangerous items away, or hold a hand briefly to reduce danger or damage.
- If the student becomes aggressive, the school crisis team, Student Resource Officers (SRO), or local police may need to be called to assist. Physical restraints should be used only as a last resort. The student may need to be taken to the hospital by the police, or the parents can take him for treatment/hospitalization.

Rage or Meltdown

It's hard to describe the difference between bipolar rage and a meltdown. However, there are some factors that appear to differentiate the two. This is important because you should not give a consequence to a student for going into a bipolar rage. However, if it is an emotional meltdown, where the student to some degree chooses to become angry, he should be given a consequence.

Rage or Meltdown	
Bipolar Rage	**Emotional Meltdown**
Is not a meltdown. It is an expression of the manic-depressive condition.	Is a meltdown.
Explodes as a result of a biochemical imbalance in the brain. Bipolar rage appears to come out of nowhere and suddenly strikes.	Explodes as a result of being overwhelmed, frustrated and out of control. Is often a result of anxiety that leads to and explosion.
Bipolar rage can last hours.	A meltdown will usually not last much longer than fifteen to thirty minutes.
Bipolar rage is based on the 'fight' response. The student will be aggressive, destructive and often demanding.	In the meltdown the student usually will want to flee (flight) to get away from the anxiety or stressor.
Bipolar rage will cause students to attack others...sometimes with objects.	Ineffectual temper tantrums or screaming fits.

Regardless if the student is in a rage state or a meltdown, he will need support when he loses control. There are a number of strategies that should be considered.

- If the student is in a classroom with other students and he melts down, or goes into a rage state, 1) get him out of the classroom, or 2) send the other students to another location.
- Restraint should be considered for a younger student if he appears to be in danger of hurting himself, others, or if it appears that significant property damage may occur.
- For older students, do what can be done to protect the child, other children, or property. You may not be able to restrain, but you can remove objects that might cause damage.
- Send for help (crisis response team or SRO) as soon as a student goes into a rage state or a meltdown.

Characteristics of Rage in the Bipolar Student

There a number of characteristics that can identify a student who is going through a rage state. Some of these characteristics are as follows:

- Rage can occur at any time and for no apparent reason. It may be the result of the student having been denied something, or as a result of some limitation that has been placed on him.
- Some students report visual fuzziness, sensitivity to smell and generally feel a bit strange prior to a rage state. If he can catch it as these symptoms occur he may be able to stop himself from going into a rage state.

- Rage escalates from agitation to major trauma very quickly and gradually returns to normal as the student's tension reduces. Once the cycle is complete the student may have a headache, be exhausted, and/or want to sleep.
- The intensity of a rage is extreme. Raving, crying, obscenities being shouted, and threats are at a fever pitch. Statements that are gory in nature are often included.
- The student will destroy things that are important to him. This happens more at home where he may destroy his favorite teddy bear or video game, etc. However, he may destroy anything that may be of value to him if he has it at school.
- Often parents, teachers, and staff are seen as the enemy when the student is in a rage state. He perceives that everyone is out to get him, and he will trust no one.
- Reward Deficiency Syndrome is a term coined by Kenneth Blum and David Comings (Blum and Comings, 1996). This suggests that students who are bipolar may have difficulty experiencing a sense of satisfaction in their lives. Rage causes the student's body to release a rush of adrenaline which produces a degree of pleasure in the brain. Bipolar students may periodically enjoy a good fight that leads to a rage state simply because it produces a pleasurable sensation.

> *Bipolar students may periodically enjoy a good fight that leads to a rage state simply because it produces a pleasurable sensation.*

Rage and the Bipolar Student

Rage goes beyond manic behavior and also produces extremely unacceptable and inappropriate behaviors. It is not something that the student can always control. As a result, it is important to treat this condition with love and patience at home and at school. This type of rage is usually manifested as a result of the depressive aggression that is part of Bipolar Disorder. These sudden and wild expressions of rage can be extremely difficult for teachers and parents to handle. Rages appear to be a result of a chemical imbalance that occurs in the brain and can be controlled to an extent by seizure medications such as Depakote, Tegretal, or Neurontin as well as some other medications that help control the overall problem of Bipolar Disorder. The point that must be kept in mind is that the bipolar rage state can be positively impacted by various medications. Finding a psychiatrist who truly understands this rage disorder is essential in order to get the most effective medications.

One theory suggests that something akin to seizure activity occurs when a bipolar child goes into a rage state. The effects include:

- A loss of awareness that may be severe enough to stop a child in his tracks. The child may not know who he is or what he is doing.
- There may be dilation of the pupils as the rage state begins.
- He may have amnesia about what happened during the rage event.

Many writers have written about cycles of behavior for students. Most can easily build a case for how students can go from one stage to the next as their behavior escalates. However, there is a problem with this concept when you are addressing the needs of bipolar students. Strategies for bipolar students must be different than what you may use for students who do not have Bipolar Disorder. If the student's behavior is a result of the bipolar condition, he simply may have little if any ability to control it. It is not that he wants to misbehave. He may simply be triggered by sensory over-stimulation, mental overload, stress, etc. As a result, when a teacher or parent attempts to manage a rage state for bipolar students, she must consider what is triggering the student's behavior in order to determine how it can be best managed.

The Rage Cycle

Most children go through stages when they become angry, oppositional, defensive, etc. Many writers have identified various stages. Some start with 'normal' and show each stage until the student returns to 'normal' again. The problem with bipolar kids is that normal is never normal. Bipolar students are rarely if ever at the same level of emotional control that most kids function at on a daily basis. They live in a perpetual stressed state. In other words their anxiety level is 'normally' higher than most other kids even when they do not appear to be having any problems. As a result, it takes less stress to elevate a bipolar student's anxiety and/or trigger hypomanic, manic or rage states. When a student who is bipolar goes into a rage, there are two important points that should be considered.

- First, you must realize that you are dealing with a student who is in a chemically induced primitive state of mind…he is not thinking rationally.
- Second, you must not attempt to punish a student who is in a rage state….it is counter productive. Rather, you must learn to utilize proactive techniques, reduction techniques, or skills training to help the student better cope with his bipolar issues (see chapter 12).

The rage cycle is a bit different from normal cycles of behavior that is seen in students who do not have Bipolar Disorder. There are stages, but bipolar students do not always conform to these stages and often rise to a rage state in seconds, simply bypassing every stage before it. Regardless, there are some emotional states or stages that this child may go through.

Stage One: Agitation Stage
Stage Two: Verbal Stage
Stage Three: Explosive Stage
Stage Four: De-escalation Stage
Stage Five: Recovery Stage

Agitation Stage

The Agitation Stage is the 'normal' state for most bipolar students. In other words, the bipolar student lives at a level of stress that is above what is normal for most people on a day by day basis. That's why the bipolar student is so easily overwhelmed or triggered into meltdowns or rage states. This heightened level of agitation keeps the student a heartbeat away from mania, rage, or a meltdown. If you are lucky, this increased stress and agitation will lead to the Verbal Stage. If you are unlucky, it may cause the student to escalate into a manic, rage state, or a meltdown immediately. Students can exhibit agitation either by increasing behavior or by decreasing behavior. Here are some basic signs of agitation that you may see in a bipolar student.

Increase in Behavior
- Makes disruptive verbal noises
- There is an increase in body language
- Hands are 'busy'
- Eyes dart around
- May go in and out of group
- May go on and off task

Decrease in Behavior
- May have his head on his desk
- May stare into space
- Language may become subdued
- Hands may not move much
- May withdraw from peers or groups
- May be off task

Staff Strategies for the Agitation Stage

There are a number of things that can be done to keep the student from progressing into mania, rage state or meltdown. Reducing stress is one of the most powerful methods that can be utilized to help the child. When the student is starting to get upset, it is important to provide him with an opportunity to de-escalate. Here are some things that can be attempted to help the student.

1. Give the student space.
2. Give the student choices.
3. Give the student a preferred activity.
4. Provide independent activities.
5. Show empathy to the student.

6. Have the student practice stress reducing strategies (must be taught and practiced in advance).
7. Provide a cool down place.
8. Remove the student from triggering social situations.
9. Redirect him to a satisfying physical activity.
10. Give the student something to eat.
11. Encourage the student to use the Rage Freeze technique (must also be taught and practiced in advance).
12. Encourage the student to use Covert Modeling, or any other strategy that helps with conflict, crisis, stress, etc. (also must be taught in advance).
13. If the student is attempting to maintain control over his feelings or rage… back off, give him some space and time. Don't talk with him until he instigates a communication.

Verbal Stage

If this student does not immediately escalate into a rage state he may move into the Verbal Stage. The Verbal Stage occurs when the student progresses from agitation and begins to get mad, angry, etc. He may yell, threaten, and exhibit other inappropriate verbal behaviors. Characteristics of the Verbal Stage are as follows:

- May exhibit angry facial expressions
- Volume level increases
- May scream, yell and threaten
- Tonal quality suggests anger, frustration, etc.

Staff Strategies for the Verbal Stage

Once a student escalates into the Verbal Stage it is up to the adults in his life to find ways to help him calm down. The utilization of stress management strategies along with gentle redirection can be helpful at this stage. Here are some things that can be attempted to help the student at this stage.

1. Establish eye level position for communication.
2. Maintain a calm demeanor.
3. Keep in mind what you would need to do if the student escalates.
4. Keep your communication simple and brief…back off, give him time.
5. Allow the student to express emotion.
6. Minimize the number of persons interacting with the student.
7. Avoid power struggles.
8. Provide even more space than usual.
9. Remind student of the Rage Freeze technique or other techniques that have been helpful.
10. Give the student the option of going to a safe, sensory reduced, structured environment.
11. Utilize stress reduction techniques.
12. Assess the need for additional assistance.
13. Be gently directive…if you push to hard it may trigger the student.

Explosive Stage

The Explosive Stage is often the first thing that most teachers and parents see when a student is triggered into a rage or meltdown. He will often bypass the verbal stage and go directly to the Explosive Stage. This stage is predominantly physical in nature. As the student verbally expresses his anger or rage towards others, he also becomes destructive or harmful to self, others, or may cause property damage. Characteristics of the Explosive Stage include what is seen in the Verbal Stage, plus he will exhibit one or more of the following behaviors:

- Hit, kick, grab, bite or throw things at others
- Be self-abusive
- Break whatever is around him
- Scream, run around, and be violent
- Exhibit severe tantrums
- Hyperventilate

Staff Strategies for the Explosive Stage

Once a student escalates into the Explosive Stage the primary concern is safety for all people involved. He is beyond stress management or talking. He may be allowed to ventilate. However, it is important that he not be allowed to hurt himself, others or do significant property damage. Here are some things that can be attempted to help the student at this stage.

1. **Safety:** The safety of the student and the staff must be of greatest importance when a student is in the explosive stage.
2. **Calm:** Stay calm when you communicate with the student.
3. **Property Damage:** If property damage is occurring, or about to occur, it is up to the staff to determine if it is significant enough to warrant using restraint on the student.
4. **Location:** Attempt to get the student out of the class (or away from other students).
5. **Other Students:** If the student cannot be removed from the class, do a classroom clear (get the other students out of the classroom).
6. **Monitor:** Monitor for the health and safety of all involved.
7. **Get Help:** Call for the School Crisis Response Team, campus police, or 911 if he is at home.
8. **Communication:** If communication is necessary, use only clear, short and positive statements. Chances are the student will not hear what you say. He will be perceiving non-verbal language at a much greater degree. Utilize non-threatening, nonverbal communication as much as possible. If there is no danger to self, others or property, back off....give him space and time. Stop talking to him and let him work through things in his head.
9. **Restraint:** If the student is violent to the point that he is dangerous to self, other or property it may be important to restrain him. Restraint should be used primarily for elementary or smaller middle school/junior high students. In addition, it should only be used as long as it is necessary.

Classroom Clear

This is an important strategy to use when any student becomes angry and has an episode. Obviously, it is important to keep the other students safe. If the student refuses to leave the classroom you may want to attempt to do a Classroom Clear.

- Teach the students what a Classroom Clear is and what they must do if you call for one.
- Select two responsible students (and an alternate in case someone is sick) who will help you when you do the Classroom Clear.
    o When you call for a Classroom Clear the first helper will immediately go to the office and report what you are doing. This will tell the office staff that you need support from an administrator, the Crisis team, or the SRO immediately.
    o The second student will lead the class out of the room and to the library or other designated location. The job of this student is to tell the librarian, or who ever is in charge of the room, what has happened.

De-escalation Stage

When the student gets to the De-escalation Stage he will often be extremely tired or exhausted. Let him sleep if necessary. If he is not sleepy he will still need to go to, or stay in a safe place where he can cool down. Characteristics of the De-escalation Stage are as follows:

- Becomes extremely tired
- May sleep
- Will be very agitated
- May cry and communicate remorse

Staff Strategies for the De-escalation Stage

As the student begins to de-escalate it is extremely important to remember that he is not ready to address the problem behavior. To do so, would very possibly cause him to escalate his behavior again. Allow the student time to calm down. Here are some things that can be attempted to help the student at this stage.

1. Monitor student for re-escalation of behavior.
2. Allow the student to sleep in a safe, structured place where he can be monitored.
3. Encourage the student to use stress reduction techniques to help him calm.
4. Restore the environment to its previous state.
5. Allow time and space for the student to calm.
6. Provide easy, concrete tasks to help him normalize.

NOTE: Do not attempt to discuss the event at this stage. It may trigger him back into a rage state. He is still too close to the event to discuss it. Wait until you are sure he is in the Recovery Stage before you talk about what happened.

Recovery Stage

When the student is in the Recovery Stage he begins to return to his 'normal' state. However, it must be kept in mind that for bipolar students this state is still a state of agitation with heightened stress. Characteristics of the Recovery Stage are as follows:

- Has calmed down
- Returns to his normal agitated state

Staff Strategies for the Recovery Stage

The student has returned to the state he was in prior to the incident. He is still agitated, but that is his normal condition. Now is the time to debrief the student and help him figure out how he could avoid a similar incident in the future. Here are some things that can be attempted to help the student at this stage.

1. Determine appropriate time to de-brief with student and staff.
2. The counselor or staff member should conduct a debriefing session with the student.
3. Is there an antecedent that could be changed? If so, discuss what could have been done to avoid the antecedent (see Chapter Twelve).
4. Consider practicing the Covert Modeling technique for the trigger that set off the rage state (see Chapter Twelve).
5. Discuss how he could have identified the trigger more quickly and used self-management by asking to go to a safe place where he could, 1) avoid additional triggers, 2) reduce sensory load, and 3) where he can do stress reduction techniques.
6. If he is not using a monitoring system for hypomania or mania he may need to do so. He can monitor his symptoms and do a periodic check regarding his mood state throughout the day.
7. Provide opportunity for non-judgmental discussion.

Debriefing Model

If a student has gone into a rage, or has had a meltdown, it is important to debrief him after the event and after he has calmed down. There are four specific areas that should be addressed when you are debriefing the student. They are:

- **Event:** Identify the event...what happened?
- **Trigger:** Identify the trigger. What caused the rage state?
- **Patterns:** Is the trigger something that has happened before? Look for patterns.
- **Training:** Train the student in multiple strategies that will help him learn to better handle triggers as they occur.

Debriefing the Student

The student has just gone through a rage state or a meltdown that is usually much more severe than what is normally experienced with children who do not have such a disability. After a rage state the student will be exhausted and often upset with himself. He will need time to rest. It is important for the staff to do all they can to help the student work through this process in a way that will help him deal more effectively with similar states in the future. Remember that this student may not remember the event. You must not push him to remember. Accept what he has to say or not say. If he cannot remember, you may want to explain to him that you have documentation and that you simply want to help him try to determine if there would be a way for him to avoid the rage next time around. Be sensitive....empathetic and warm. Make sure that he knows you are not angry or upset. You are there to help him figure out how to better control his bipolar rage. The areas to be covered in the debriefing are as follows:

Event: If he can remember the event discuss what happened. Tell him what he did during the rage. He needs to understand how the rage can be dangerous to him, others, and property. If he emotionally struggles with hearing about the episode, take your time. If he can remember, let him tell what happened during the rage. Once he has worked through what happened during the rage he is ready to go to the second step.

Trigger: Explore what triggered the rage state. Was there an antecedent? If so, what was it? Help him determine what seemed to cause the rage state. There will be times when you will not be able to identify the cause. Often such times will be a result of built up stress that wasn't dealt with. See if you can identify stressful situations that had caused a buildup of anxiety over a period of time. If there were a number of things causing the buildup of stress and anxiety you may need to help the student work through the past events that produced the stress.

Patterns: As you look at what triggered the rage state you should also look to see if there has been a pattern. Is the antecedent a person who consistently triggers the rage state? If so, help the student initially avoid the triggering student. Is the antecedent a location that has too much sensory overload? Keep the student away from the location where the overload is too great. Is the antecendent pressure from too much work? Reduce the work. Consider all possibilities as you seek to determine both antecedent and any patterns that may be present.

Training: Identify the method that would best handle the triggering event. You may want to desensitize the antecedent so that it is no longer a trigger. Consider doing desensitization training (adapt Exposure and Response Prevention Techniques). You should also teach the student additional coping skills that will help him effectively deal with specific stress provoking situations, e.g., conflict management skills, assertive skills, etc. Training also requires that you have an ongoing program of stress management in place. The student should practice a chosen stress management method daily or at least on multiple occasions during the week. Ongoing stress management practice will reduce overall stress level, which in turn will make it more difficult for him to be triggered by daily stressors. See Debriefing Worksheet in appendices.

Tips for Teachers and Staff

When a teacher or staff member is debriefing a student who has been in crisis or a rage state there are a few guidelines that should be considered. Following these will reduce the possibility of exacerbating the situation.

Tips for Speaking

- Speak Calmly
- Speak Respectfully
- Use Simple Language
- Speak Privately

Tips for Movement

- Move Slowly and Deliberately
- Keep Reasonable Distance
- Minimize Body Language

Miscellaneous

- Acknowledge Student Cooperation
- Withdraw if Problems Start to Escalate

Contract for Rage Reduction

When a student begins to go into a rage state it is usually too late to offer a reward or negotiate. However, if a reward has already been established via a contract, it can, and does help a bipolar student control his behavior. The control occurs prior to the manic/rage event. When the student realizes that he is about to go 'out of control' and has some degree of rationality in which he can make a decision, he can decide to go to a time out room or safe zone where he can sit down and do a relaxation technique that would help him stabilize. See an example of the contract below.

Contract

Name: *Johnny*

Situation: *When I get angry and am about to go into a meltdown or rage.*

Condition: *I must go to my safe spot before I yell, hit, throw things, or get out of control. I will stay there and relax until I have control of my emotions.*

Reward: *For every day that I don't have a meltdown or rage I will receive either a short term reward, or be allowed to accumulate credit so that I can receive a larger reward at the end of the week as pre-determined. See Reward List.*

Johnny Sample .
Child/Adolescent

Mrs Mary Sample .
Parent or Teacher

*If needed, copy the Contract from the appendices
and have the student complete it.*

If the student knows that he has a reward for keeping his behavior under control, it gives him motivation to stop himself before the actual rage state or meltdown occurs. When writing such a contract, keep the following guidelines in mind:

1. Make sure the contract is simple and specific.
2. Make sure the wording uses developmental language that the student understands.
3. Discuss it in advance with the student. He has to buy into the contract, or he won't work it.
4. Define a reward that the student may want. Consider using both a daily and a weekly reward. He can accumulate daily rewards to obtain one weekly reward (see Daily or Weekly Reward List found in the appendix).
5. Periodically change the reward to assure that the student is more apt to work for it. The end goal is for him to take initiative so that he can control manic/rage states or meltdowns as much as is possible.

NOTE: In Chapter Four and Twelve there are multiple methods to identify rewards that can be used with the contract.

Parent/Teacher Response to a Rage Event

The student has just raged for two or more hours. He has finally calmed down and seems to be doing fine. However, you are overwhelmed, fatigued, frustrated and desperately need a break. Whether you are a teacher, counselor, administrator or parent, it is important to take care of yourself after you have dealt with an explosive episode with a bipolar student. Here are some things that you should and need to do to take care of yourself regardless of your role.

Document

It is important to write down exactly what happened, what/who seemed to trigger the incident, and any other related information that might be helpful when you discuss the incident with the student after he has calmed down. The goal must be to help identify antecedents or other factors that could be altered in order to reduce the amount of episodes. This documentation will help the person who is debriefing the student (see Debriefing Model in this Chapter).

Detoxify

Once the event is over you may need to speak with someone about it. If you are a teacher you may need to document what occurred and discuss it with a counselor, another staff member or the principal (or assistant principal). If you are a parent you may need to talk to a friend, spouse, or therapist.

Regenerate

Find a way to regenerate, e.g., work out, take a long bath, read, watch a humorous movie, or do something else that helps you reenergize. It is important that you reenergize so that you will be ready to deal with the next episode that may very well happen the next day.

Discuss

Once you have regenerated and once the student has recovered from the episode it is important to discuss it with him. If he starts to get upset when you bring up the event, drop it and try again later. If he is willing, ask him what seemed to trigger it. Would the Rage Freeze technique have helped if he had used it? Was there an antecedent that triggered the event? If so, what could be done to change the antecedent? Seek a solution with him...find something that could be done that would slow down or stop the rage the next time he is in a similar situation.

- See Chapter Twelve, Discipline & Management of Bipolar Children for a description of the Antecedent Modification Form.
- You should also review the Debriefing Model in this chapter.

Educational Strategies for Mania

When a student is hypomanic, or starts to become manic there are some basic strategies that should be considered as you deal with him in the classroom, or in the office. Here are some basic strategies that might be helpful.

- If a student starts to become agitated, speaks in sexually inappropriate ways, etc. it is important to get him to the counselor, or another safe location where he can start relaxing.
- During the acute phase of a manic attack, treatment is aimed at decreasing symptomatology and promoting safety for all concerned.
- If time relaxing in a safe, less intense environment does not reduce hypomanic behavior, the parent should be called. Medication may need to be adjusted.
- The parent should also be called if a student starts to go into a manic state. He may very well need to go to the hospital, or at the very least see his doctor.
- Keep classroom doorways closed to reduce noise in classroom.
- Do what is possible to help the bipolar child avoid all forms of over-stimulation.

Depression and Bipolar Disorder

Chapter Four

When a bipolar student experiences the depressive aspect of his disorder he is often sad and/or very irritable. As a result, he will often cease to enjoy activities that he normally finds enjoyable. This student may not openly complain about being sad. However, he will often be tearful, whiny and will complain of being bored. He may also experience a lack of motivation, have a tendency to be inattentive, and be off task. He may experience many physical symptoms, e.g., headaches, muscle aches, stomachaches or tiredness. He may also have frequent absences from school, and have poor school performance. At home he may talk about, or actually run away from home. He will often complain, have irritability, experience unexplained crying, social isolation, poor communication, and be extremely sensitive to rejection or failure (Carlson, 1998; Geller, 1997). Keep in mind that depression can occur without mania (unipolar), but mania rarely occurs without depression. Here are some statistics regarding depression and bipolar students.

- A number of studies have reported that up to 2.5 percent of children, and up to 8.3 percent of adolescents in the United States suffer from depression (Carlson, 1998).
- In childhood, boys and girls appear to be at equal risk for depressive disorders. However, during adolescence, girls are twice as likely as boys to develop depression (Carlson, 1998).
- Depressive disorders confer an increased risk for illness and interpersonal and psychosocial difficulties that persist long after the depressive episode is resolved for both children and adolescents. In adolescents there is also an increased risk for substance abuse and suicidal behavior.
- Cognitive-behavioral therapy and relaxation therapy resulted in significant clinical improvements in children and adolescents with depression. As a result, it is important to utilize stress management techniques with these students when they are in either the manic or depressive mood state.

- The brain is inflamed when it is under stress, or when negative input is being internalized. This inflammation is obviously stressful and can produce mania or depressive symptomotology. When used on an ongoing basis, stress management techniques will reduce, or get rid of the inflammation and allow the student to have a better chance at normalcy.
- Depressive symptoms in adolescence have been found to be the most significant predictor for depressive symptoms in adulthood.
- In one study, prevalence for major depression was 7.4 percent for boys and 13.9 percent for girls, and prevalence for substance abuse/dependence during the year prior to the study was 8.2 percent for boys and 6.2 percent for girls. Nearly three fourths of all the adolescents who met the criteria for PTSD also met the criteria for major depression, substance abuse/dependence or both (Strakowski, 2000).
- Six years after the study mentioned above 42% of the diagnosed depressed students were found to have Bipolar Disorder.

> *Internationally, depression has nearly doubled with each successive generation since the 1920's.*

Depressive Symptoms of Children and Adolescents

Being blind to depression is a common characteristic of both educators and parents. When a student is not exhibiting any behavior problems, we all want to sit back and say, "Finally, one student who is not taking all my time. What a good kid." This student may not cause any problems at home, and may sit in the back of a classroom and not cause one disturbance. McKnew, Cytryn and Yahraes (1983) identified a potential problem with this viewpoint. In summary, they stated that many depressed students are often seen as the nicest kids on the block and the best behaved students at school. They went on to say that unless you really understood depression and knew your child and what to look for, you probably won't even notice that there is something dreadfully wrong. Dr. Carl Malmquist of the University of Minnesota and others suggest the following symptom list:

Depression Checklist for Children and Adolescents   Yes   No

1. **Persistent Sadness:** The student has low energy, lack of interest, etc.   ___   ___
2. **Low Self-Concept:** This student is overly-sensitive to comments, criticism, or correction.   ___   ___
3. **Irritable Mood:** This student is easily angered and will often lash out at others when upset.   ___   ___

4. **Loss of interest:** This student may lose interest in activities ___ ___
    once enjoyed.
5. **Change in Appetite or Body Weight:** This student has had a ___ ___
    significant change in appetite or body weight. He may be eating
    less or more.
6. **Sleep Disorders:**   This student has difficulty sleeping or ___ ___
    oversleeps. If the depression gets severe, he will have little
    energy or desire to get up, go to school, or deal with daily life
    activities.
7. **Physical Agitation or Slowing:** This student may be physically ___ ___
    agitated, or could slow down.
8. **Easily Disappointed:**   This student may be prone to being ___ ___
    disappointed easily when things do not go exactly as planned.
    There is a low tolerance for frustration.
9. **Loss of Energy:** This student may have a loss of energy and ___ ___
    feels fatigued.
10. **Physical Complaints:** This student has physical complaints, ___ ___
    e.g., headaches, stomach aches, fatigue, or sleep problems.
11. **Low Self-Concept**: This student has feelings of worthlessness, ___ ___
    or inappropriate guilt. He often has a lack of success, which in
    turn magnifies his low self-concept.
12. **Difficulty Concentrating:**   This student looks like an ADHD ___ ___
    inattentive child, e.g., can't concentrate, focus, stay on task.
13. **Fear of Rejection:**   This student exhibits provocative, ___ ___
    aggressive behavior, or other behavior that leads educators
    and/or peers to reject or avoid him. The behaviors cause the
    student to experience the rejection that he fears.
14. **May Have Recurrent Thoughts of Death or Suicide:** See ___ ___
    'Risk Signs for Suicide' in this chapter. This student has
    thoughts of death, and thinks about committing suicide.

If you answer yes to some of the above symptoms the student may have depression.

Overcoming Depression

There are no simple solutions to overcoming depression. However, there are a multitude of methods, strategies, etc. that can be used to minimize or reduce depression. There are two basic areas that are addressed in this book that will aid a student in reducing or minimizing depression:

- Thoughts: Negative thoughts and images must be reduced and positive thoughts images must be increased.
- Actions: Actions are broken down into two areas.

    - First, the student must improve communication, problem solving, social skills, and learn to relax. When these skills are utilized it causes positive brain & body changes.
    - Second, he must learn to have fun or enjoy life both by himself and with others.

Depression Reduction

The Depression Reduction form is intended to help the student work through symptoms of depression as they occur. If the symptoms can be identified and strategies implemented as soon as it is possible, there is a chance that he can avoid going into a deeper depressive state and possibly reverse the depressive tendencies. There are four steps to using the Depression Reduction form. The student must:

1) Identify the specific symptom of depression
2) Determine how depressed he is at the moment
3) Utilize a strategy that would help reduce the depressive symptom
4) Reevaluate how much he feels depressed after using a depression reduction strategy

Depression reduction techniques found in this chapter must be taught and practiced so that the student will be able to use the strategies when he is in need of them. The sample Depression Reduction form will give you an idea as to how it would help a student work through depressive symptoms.

Depression Reduction

Name: *Johnny*   **Date:** *2/13*

Instructions:
1) Identify the depressive symptom.
2) Using a 1-5 scale, mark the number that describes your current mood.
3) Use a strategy that will help control the depressive tendency.
4) Using a 1-5 scale, mark the number that describes your mood after using the strategy.

| 1 = Normal for me | 3 = Moderate Depression | | 5 = Depressed |

Date/ Time	Symptom	How depressed initially?	Strategy Used	How depressed after strategy?
Mon 10:00am	*Low energy*	1 2 ~~3~~ 4 5	*Exercise..walked around building*	~~1~~ 2 3 4 5
Mon 10:45am	*Negative thoughts*	1 2 ~~3~~ 4 5	*Thought stopping technique*	1 ~~2~~ 3 4 5

If needed, copy the Depression Reduction form from the appendices and have the student complete it.

Cognitive Distortions and Your Brain

Research by Mark George, MD and colleagues at the National Institute of Health demonstrated that happy, hopeful thoughts had an overall calming effect on the brain, while negative thoughts or distortions inflamed brain areas often involved with depression and anxiety. Burns (1980), in his book entitled, 'Feeling Good', identified numerous mental distortions that can produce negative thoughts. Here are some distortions that have been identified:

- **All or Nothing Thinking** --- Events are really only black or white, good or bad. There is no middle ground. This distortion often leads to perfectionism and ongoing frustration. For instance, if the student is turned down for a date, he may feel that no one will ever say, 'Yes.' If he fails his Language Arts test, he is convinced that he will not pass any test. This distortion leads to negative thinking which in turn has a negative impact on the brain.
- **Mind Reading or Jumping to Conclusions** --- Illogic is the key problem with this distortion. The student may predict what another person thinks without having evidence or information that would support his conclusions. For instance, the student may feel bad because he believes a fellow student is thinking something negative about him, even though nothing has been said or done to suggest it.
- **Maximization or Minimization** --- These distortions occur when the student blows things out of proportion, or when he minimizes things, e.g., he may minimize/maximize qualities, or characteristics about himself. Both distortions cause problems for the student in how he feels about himself and in how he relates to others.
- **Fortune Telling** --- This distortion occurs when the student predicts a bad outcome to a situation before it has even happened. The mind is a very powerful organ. If the student feeds his mind enough information suggesting that there will be a bad outcome, it will go out of the way to assure that it happens. For example, the student may say, "I know I will fail my math test." His mind will then do what it can to help him accomplish that belief. One way it might accomplish this is by making him believe that since he is going to fail anyway, there is no use in studying hard.
- **Emotional Reasoning** --- This distortion calls for the student to believe what he feels. In other words if he feels something is true, it is true. It doesn't matter what the facts say, his feelings rule. For instance, if he feels that others don't care, then it is true. Emotional reasoning can easily produce depression.
- **Shoulds or Musts** --- This distortion calls for the student to set strict rules or expectations that are not always realistic. He feels guilty if he doesn't live up to the rules or expectations. When others don't live up to his 'shoulds' or 'musts' he feels angry, upset.
- **Personalization** --- This distortion occurs when he believes that the things that people do or say are a direct reaction to him. He may assume the responsibility for something negative that happens even though he had nothing to do with it. For instance, he notices the girl he's sitting next to takes a look at her watch. As a result, the student believes that he is boring.
- **Negative Filtering** --- This distortion occurs when the student focuses on the negative, while he ignores the positive. The student may seem to be a negative person because he finds something negative about everything he looks at.
- **Catastrophizing** --- This distortion occurs when the student expects things to turn out badly. For instance, if he asks a teacher to help, he believes that she will make things hard on him. So he doesn't ask and as a result, he doesn't get help.

If needed copy the Thought Distortion Checklist from the appendices and have the student complete it to identify specific distortions that he is currently using.

This is not a complete list of distortions, but it does include some of the more common ones. Undue stress, partially produced by the above mentioned distortions, damages the brains ability to function effectively......it decreases the student's ability to learn and may trigger a bipolar state.

Dissecting Cognitive Distortions

Cognitive Distortions can cause untold grief and emotional frustration for anyone. This is especially true for bipolar students. Not dealt with, these distortions can contribute to a buildup of stress that can in turn trigger depression.

This technique calls for the student to identify the basic distortions that he often uses in his daily life. Have the student take the cognitive distortion checklist in the appendices in order to identify the specific distortions that he has difficulties with. Once they are identified, and the student sees how they are in fact distortions, he will have a chance at identifying negative thoughts that are connected to the distortions. Most important, he will be encouraged to find a rational response that counters the distortion. Here are some examples of how a student might dissect cognitive distortions and in turn identify rational responses.

Dissecting Cognitive Distortions		
Name: Mary		**Date:** 2/19
Negative Thought	**Cognitive Distortion**	**Rational Response**
Johnny doesn't like me. He is ignoring me every time I pass him in the hallway.	Emotional Reasoning	I can't know what Johnny is thinking. He may simply be busy. I should talk to him.
I'm going to fail this test. I know I just can't do well enough.	Fortune Telling	I can't know that I'm going to fail. However, I can control how hard I study.
Sam turned me down for a date. He will never go out with me.	Always or Never Thinking	Ask him again, he may just have been busy. If he doesn't want to go out, ask someone else.

If needed, copy the Dissecting Cognitive Distortions form from the appendices and have the student use it to reduce ongoing distortions.

Negative vs Positive Thoughts

Another method of reducing or getting rid of negative thoughts is to identify, 1) negative thoughts, and 2) positive counters. To do this you must have the student list any negative thoughts that he currently has in the negative thoughts column. Next have him identify a positive counter for each of the negative thoughts that he has identified. Often the negative thought is in reality not true. There is one important point that must be kept in mind when positive counters are being developed. Do not use a negative statement to counter a negative thought. For instance, if the negative thought is 'I'm ugly.' Don't use a positive counter that says, 'I am not ugly.' The student must replace the negative thought with a positive counter that he would prefer to use instead. A good example would be, 'I'm attractive.' Or 'I look good.' Some students may say, "But that's not true. I really am ugly." The student must believe that he can improve himself. Goal setting calls for the individual to see what he wants to achieve. When the mind sees what the student wants, it will help him achieve it. So, it is important that the student understand that he may have to 'fake it, until he makes it' for a while. Here are some examples.

Negative vs Positive Thoughts	
Name: Jerry	**Date:** 2/14
Negative thoughts	**Positive Counters**
I have a bad temper.	I can control my emotions.
I'm confused.	I know what's going on around me.
I am worthless.	I am a worthwhile person.
I'm ugly.	I'm attractive.
I'll never make any good friends.	I have friends who like me.
Nobody loves me.	I know my parents love me.
I'll never be successful.	I can be successful.
I can't get close to people.	I have some close friends.
Life is unfair.	Life is fair.

If needed, copy the Negative vs Positive Thoughts form from the appendices and have the student use it to reduce ongoing negative thoughts.

When you have helped the student identify the negative thoughts that often come into his mind, and found a positive counter for each one, go to the next step. Help the student pick the top five negative thoughts that cause him the most trouble. Get a tape/digital recorder and have him say the positive counters twenty five times each. If he identifies three negative thoughts, he would say each positive counter twenty-five times equaling to 75 positive statements (counters). The parent, counselor or staff member working with the student could also say the counter 25 times. This gives the student a different perspective when he listens to the tape. Have him sit down and relax. When he is relaxed, turn on the tape/digital recorder and have him listen. It would be beneficial if he could use the recording of the positive counters at home and at school. He could listen to them when he gets up and when he goes to bed each night. He could listen to them when he feels down and needs a boost. The more he listens to this tape the more effective it becomes.

> *If the student is clinically depressed he will most likely need to be on an anti-depressant until his brain chemistry 'normalizes'.*

Negative Thought Tracking Form

Parents and educators may want to encourage the student to use the following tracking form to identify how often negative thoughts occur during a school day. It will tell him which thoughts are causing the most difficulties. If something shows up to be an ongoing problem it can be added to the recording, or another recording can be made once the first few negative thoughts have been overcome. There are two steps to using this form. First, he will need to pick the top three to five thoughts that he wants to monitor. Second, when the selected thought occurs, mark off a number up to ten. If it goes over ten for a day, it is certainly something that needs to be addressed. Follow the directions for the Negative vs Positive Thoughts form shown above, and utilize the recording to help deal with the negative thought.

Negative Thought Tracking	
Name: Josey	**Date:** 2/5
Negative Thought	**Number of Times**
I have a bad temper.	1 2 3 4 5 6 7 8 9 10
I'm ugly.	1 2 3 4 5 6 7 8 9 10
I'm worthless.	1 2 3 4 5 6 7 8 9 10
Nobody loves me.	1 2 3 4 5 6 7 8 9 10
I'll never be successful.	1 2 3 4 5 6 7 8 9 10

If needed, copy the Negative Thought Tracking form from the appendices and have the student use it to keep track of negative thoughts.

Thought Interruption Techniques

Sometimes, even though a student may have worked on getting rid of an unwanted negative thought, it still creeps back into his mind. There are numerous techniques that can help the student interrupt such unwanted thoughts. The following techniques have proven to be helpful for many people. Teach these to the student so that he can have some additional tools to rid his mind of unwanted negative thoughts. The last technique may be used by the teacher to help the student stop unwanted thoughts.

The Rubber Band Technique

Have him wear a rubber band on his wrist and snap it every time he catches himself thinking one of the negative thoughts. This will help to control or prevent many negative thoughts. Some students begin to get a 'high' from the mild pain that occurs when he snaps the rubber band. If this occurs he must discontinue the technique.

Thought Stopping

When he is alone and catches himself thinking a negative thought such as, I'm stupid, have him yell "STOP" as loud as he can. He should immediately say his positive counter, e.g., "I am a unique learner." Or "I'm a smart person." Have him gradually change from yelling out loud to thinking "Stop" to himself. When he can do this without yelling out loud he can utilize the technique at any time.

Stop Sign Technique

This technique is similar to the thought stopping technique described above. The only difference is that the student uses a visual image instead of an auditory cue. All the student needs to do is visualize a stop sign in his mind to stop unwanted thoughts. For those who are more visual in nature this method may work best.

Worry Time

Sometimes the student believes that the problem, thought, etc. is so important or overwhelming that he needs to worry about it. If that is the case, the student needs to do two things. First, he needs to write down the problem or thought that he needs to worry about. When he is finished he must set it aside until it is time to worry. Second, he needs to schedule a time when he can worry. It could be during lunch period, at the end of the day, at the end of the week, etc. depending on how often he needs to worry. Fifteen minutes should be more than enough time for the worry session. Tell him that if he starts worrying at other times during the day, he must tell himself, "I'll think about that later, during my worry time." He needs to add the item to his worry list. When he is in his worry time he should not be doing anything else. For instance he should not be talking, eating, drinking, working, or playing.

Salad Technique

This teacher developed technique is used by the teacher when she perceives that that the student is experiencing negative thinking, seems worried, or seems stuck in some way (it may be used to alter behavior also). When a student is struggling with thoughts that are unhealthy, unproductive, etc. she simply asks the student a question like this, "Is a bowl of lettuce a salad, or is it a bowl of lettuce?" The question often totally confuses the student as he ponders the possible answer. As the student tries to find the answer, he obviously is distracted from the thought, or behavior in some cases. The teacher redirects the student as he ponders the question and the unwanted though/behavior is often forgotten.

The Balloon Exercise: Finding the Negative Thought

The Balloon Exercise is another technique that can be used to help eliminate negative thoughts from the student's mind. The Counselor or staff member who is working with the student should teach him the following:

Step I: Have him pick one of the negative thoughts that he wants to work on reducing or getting rid of, and the positive counter that will replace it.

Step II: Have the student get comfortable. A bean bag, comfortable chair or even laying on the floor would be good choices.

Step III: Have him close his eyes and slowly breathe deeply in and out (see Basic Abdominal Breathing in chapter Six).

Step IV: Tell him to focus his attention inward where he can see images, or thoughts.

Step V: Have him think about the negative thought he has chosen.

Step VI: Have him raise his finger when he is to that point. When he is, ask him the following questions. Give him time to process each question in his mind.

A. What happens to your body when you think this negative thought?
B. What feelings do you have when you have this thought?
C. How much room does it take up, in your life or your mind?
D. How heavy is it? Does it have sound, or color? What does it look like?

Eliminating the Negative Thought

Once the student understands the exercise the counselor, parent, etc. can walk him through this technique using the information below.

I. Pretend you have a balloon that you can blow up.
II. Now, take three deep breaths. With each breath move this negative thought toward your lungs until your lungs are completely full of it.
III. When you can't hold it any longer in your lungs, put your balloon to your lips and blow the negative thought into it. Do whatever it takes to empty your lungs. Blow the thought completely into your balloon!

IV. Tie the end of the balloon and hold it in your hand. Let it go and watch as it floats into the air and up into the sky. Watch as it fades away, never to come back to you again. The farther away the thought gets, the less likely it will ever come back again.

V. Know in your mind that you have let the negative thought go.

VI. Now that you've let the negative thought go, replace it with the positive counter that you previously chose. Hold it in your mind for a moment and see how it actually feels better when you use the counter.

Selecting Fun Activities

The bipolar student must be able to identify fun activities that may be reinforcing to him in some way. Such fun activities can help him enjoy life, reduce depression, bring happiness to his daily existence, and be motivational. The following should be considered as the student attempts to identify activities. They should:

- Be activities that he has complete control over (at least some of them)
- Be something that he can do frequently - at least once a week
- Be inexpensive
- Be positive activities
- Be legal (can't smoke cigarettes, for example!)
- Be activities that he knows he can do without upsetting his parents, teachers, or friends
- Be activities that won't take more free time than he has
- Parents should be involved when the activity is more expensive, e.g., baseball games, football games, etc.

> *If the activity is being utilized as a reward, the student and his teacher/counselor must determine what is a daily reward, or a weekly reward. This applies at home also.*

Fun Outdoor Activities

The depressive side of Bipolar Disorder can be overwhelming to the student. To help with depression, the student should identify outdoor activities that can get him out of his tendency to isolate, withdraw, or be emotionally flat. Help the student identify fun outdoor activities. Here are some examples.

- Playing baseball or softball
- Going to the beach
- Rock climbing or mountaineering

- Playing golf
- Going to a sports event
- Going to the races (horse, car, boat, etc.)

- Boating (canoeing, Kayaking, motor-boating, sailing, etc.)
- Camping
- Playing tennis
- Being with animals
- Exploring (hiking away from known routes, etc.)
- Snow skiing
- Driving
- Driving go carts
- Watching the sky, clouds, or a storm
- Going on outings (to the park, a picnic, a barbecue, etc.)
- Playing basketball
- Gathering natural objects
- (rocks, driftwood, etc.)
- Being in the mountains
- Seeing beautiful scenery
- Water skiing
- Hiking
- Going to a museum or exhibit
- Doing yard work
- Going to a beach/water park
- Sitting/laying in the sun
- Riding a motorcycle
- Going to a fair, carnival, circus, zoo, or amusement park
- Playing miniature golf

If needed, copy the Fun Outdoors Activities form from the appendices and have the student complete it.

Fun Indoor Activities

Identifying fun indoor activities is also important. Help the student identify specific activities that he is interested in. Here are some examples of fun outdoor activities.

- Going to a concert
- Planning trips or vacations
- Doing art work (painting, drawing, movie-making, etc.)
- Rearranging or redecorating your room
- Going to a sports event
- Going to a fun party
- Going to lectures or hearing speakers
- Thinking up or arranging songs or music
- Playing a musical instrument
- Taking pictures
- Hearing or telling jokes
- Going to a museum or exhibit
- Playing a video game
- Watching humorous videos
- Playing a game with friends
- Watching television
- Playing cards
- Having lunch with friends
- Having a party
- Playing pool or billiards
- Being with relatives
- Playing chess or checkers
- Doing craft work (pottery, jewelry, beads, weaving, etc.)
- Lifting weights
- Putting on makeup, fixing hair, etc.
- Drawing
- Bowling
- Listening to the radio/cd
- Having friends come to visit

If needed, copy the Fun Indoors Activities form from the appendices and have the student complete it.

Have the student identify five preferred activities from the fun outdoor and indoor activities lists. After the student has identified his top five preferences for both outdoor and indoor activities, educators and parents will have a good list of enjoyable activities that can be used as motivational tools to help the student work through his depression. This list of activities should be used to help get the student active and moving. He needs to be involved doing things that he enjoys, or he may slip further into depression.

Building a Healthy Social Support System

A form is provided that can be used to help identify how a student can strengthen or improve social relationships. Depressed students have a tendency to withdraw or isolate. This in and of itself contributes to, and can produce depression. It is important that the student stay busy doing things with people that he believes is fun or enjoyable. Have him fill out this form. When complete, he can pick at least one thing from each group that he is willing to do to build or improve his Social Support System. The supports identified by the student can also be used as activities on the Fun Activities Form.

List four things you could do to improve or strengthen your current social support system.

1. *Get more involved with youth group* .
2. *Play pick up basketball at gym* .
3. *Join a bowling league* .
4. *Have friends over to play cards, dance, etc.* .

List activities where you currently enjoy what you do and get to meet other people.

1. *Going to church and being with youth group.* .
2. *Football at school* .
3. *Dances at school* .
4. *Bowling with friends* .

List other activities that you enjoy doing that might offer an opportunity to meet other people.

1. *Hanging out at the mall* .
2. *Go the lake and ski or tube* .
3. *Go swimming at pool* .
4. *Join a karate class* .

If needed, copy the Building a Healthy Social Support System form
from the appendices and have the student complete it.

Quick Reward Menu

Another way to identify some rewarding things for a student is to complete a quick reward menu. If the student is still struggling to determine what is rewarding to him have him complete the Quick Reward Menu. This menu calls for the student to identify:

- Two Peers that he would like to spend more time with each week.
- Two adults that he would like to spend more time with each week.
- Two places he would like to go to.
- Two things the student doesn't own that he would really like to have. Make sure they are things the parent or school can afford (for example, a book, a tape or CD, clothes, etc.).
- Four favorite foods and drinks. He may also want to include items that he hasn't tried very often.
- Two activities he would like to do more often.

If needed, copy the Quick Rewards Menu Form from the appendices and have the student complete it.

Optionally, the Fun Outdoor and Indoor Activity list can be used as motivational tools to help the student work through his depression (see Fun Activities Form in appendices). When you are finished completing the fun activities and reward forms, copy the Daily or Weekly Reward List Form from the appendix and have the student fill out the ten daily rewards and six weekly rewards. Once completed, you will have a list of rewards that you can give the student when he participates in activities that will help him pull out of his depression. These rewards may also be used for any Contract that is made, or for any other motivational system. An example of this form is shown below.

Daily or Weekly Rewards List

As previously stated, it is important that you do not use the fun activities that you want the student to do to help him feel better as a reward. Actually, if he participates in fun activities (that are free so to speak), he can get a reward.

There are numerous rewards that can be given if he fulfills his goal of participating in at least one fun activity each day. In the appendices there are reward questionnaires that can be used to help define a variety of rewards that the student may actually prefer. The rewards are broken down into five specific types. They are:

- Adult approval
- Peer Approval
- Consumables
- Tangibles
- Activities

Daily or Weekly Rewards List	
Name: _Terry_	**Date:** _6/23_

List ten daily rewards that you would really like.

1. _Strawberry Cake_	6. _Hearts Card Game_
2. _Chocolate Cookies_	7. _Chocolate Pie_
3. _Popcorn and movie home_	8. _Board Game_
4. _Play Croquette_	9. _Spades Card Game_
5. _Play Badminton_	10. _Play pool with dad_

List six weekly rewards that you would really like.

1. _Golf with dad_	4. _Go to Amusement Park_
2. _Go to a movie with Friends_	5. _Go to Water Park_
3. _Go Water Skiing/Tubing_	6. _Go Rock Climbing_

If needed, copy the Daily or Weekly Rewards List from the appendices and have the student complete it.

When completed he will have a good list of things that he is truly interested in, that may motivate him to be more active and hopefully positively impact his depression. Now it's time to complete the Fun Activities Form.

Fun Activities

The purpose of this form is to help the student schedule activities that are fun, enjoyable, or rewarding in some way. Although this could be done at school it would be easiest to keep track of this at home. The goal for the student is to do at least one fun activity each day. Each day the student successfully completes an activity there will be a small reward. The parent can put an X on the day that the child is successful. A reward may be given at the end of the day, or the child may request to be given credit until he collects five successful days. At that time he can receive a larger reward. There are three things that the student must do to get ready to use the Fun Activities form. They are:

1. Choose enjoyable activities that he can participate in that will cause him to become more active on a daily basis.
2. Choose a list of daily rewards that he can pick from if he successfully completes his daily assignment.
3. Pick one weekly reward that he might want to work for if he chooses not to take the daily rewards. He must accumulate 5 daily rewards to get a weekly reward. That would suggest that if he did well all seven days he could have two daily rewards and still have the weekly reward.

Fun Activities

Name: Jarod   **Date:** 8/5

	SU	M	T	W	Th	F	SA	TOTAL
Week #1	b-ball X	Weights X	Guitar X	Weights	Swim X	Weights X	b-ball	5
Week #2	Min-Golf	Weights X	Swim X	Weights X	Guitar	Weights	b-ball X	4
Week #3	b-ball X	Weights	Guitar X	Weights	Guitar	Weights X	b-ball	3
Week #4	Min-golf X	Weights X	Swim	Weights X	Guitar X	Weights	b-ball X	5

Possible Daily Rewards

If you have completed your activity for the day you may choose one of the rewards listed below, or accumulate five for the week to get a weekly reward.

1. Card game with family
2. Chocolate cookies for me and a friend
3. Popcorn and a movie at home
4. Strawberry Cake for desert
5. Play a board game
6. Chocolate Pie
7. Play Croquette with someone

End of Week Reward

You must have refused five daily rewards in order to get the weekly reward on Saturday. The reward week starts on a Sunday and ends on Saturday.

Golf With Dad

If needed, copy the Fun Activities form from the appendices and have the parent and student complete it.

NOTE: Don't use the fun activities listed for this form as rewards for other reinforcement programs put in place for him on a daily or weekly basis.

Visualizing a Fun Activity

When the student is beginning a downward spiral and seems to be getting depressed a quick way to help him feel better is to have him visualize a time when was participating in an activity that was enjoyable or fun to him.

Visualizing a Fun Activity Strategy
Name: *Dale*   **Date:** *2/15*
Step One: Find a location where you can sit and relax for a bit. This could be the counselor's office, or any other room where you can have some time alone to use this strategy.
Step Two: Pick an activity that you would find very enjoyable, or a time when you were participating in an activity or situation when you felt very good….when you were having a lot of fun. *Mary and I were dancing at the party.*
Step Three: Do abdominal breathing for a few minutes.
Step Four: Visualize yourself doing what you have chosen in step two for about five minutes or longer if possible. Make it as real as possible. Use all of your senses if you can.

If needed, copy the Visualizing a Fun Activity Strategy from the appendices and have the student complete it.

Tool Box for Depression Reduction and Maintenance

This is a list of things that the bipolar student might consider doing to reduce depression in his life.   You may want to give him a copy so that he can make use of them if he desires.

Checklist for Children/Adolescents:

- Find outside activities that you enjoy doing with others.
- Eat three meals a day…eat right, and avoid empty carbohydrates and unnecessary fats.
- Drink plenty of water each day.
- Exercise daily. This will cause your body to release uplifting endorphins!
- Relax daily to help keep your body de-stress.

- Laugh and keep your sense of humor! Watch funny movies.
- Don't be afraid to ask for help if you are feeling overwhelmed or troubled.
- Don't hide your feelings. If you are upset talk to someone you trust.
- Set realistic goals!
- Don't use drugs or alcohol; they can increase depression, mania, and cause impaired judgment.
- Do take the medications that have been prescribed by your doctor. Don't miss one dose.
- Identify things you would like to do with friends and family and start doing them.
- Volunteer to help others (school, church, home, etc)!
- Accept compliments and praise. Try giving them also.
- Get at least eight hours of sleep a night. Go to sleep and get up at the same time each day.
- Do something that you really enjoy doing. Make it something that you can do each day if possible.
- Talk to friends daily.

Risk Signs for Suicide

Anytime a student suggests suicide, or the possibility of hurting himself, teachers, counselors, administrators and parents should take it seriously. Fawcett, Busch and Jacobs (1997) suggested that there are five indicators suggesting possible suicide. Parents and educators should be aware of these risk signs and watch to see if they are present when a student suggests that he may want to hurt himself. They are:

- The student has verbalized that suicide may be an acceptable choice for him to escape the misery that he is experiencing.
- He has discussed the means that he might use to kill himself.
- He has given away precious toys and other objects and seems to be tying up his affairs.
- The student manifests a high degree of anxiety and agitation, and at least one of the preceding factors is in evidence.
- The student becomes calm, happy, and seems at peace with himself and others after a period of mental agony and agitation. This change in mood often comes a day or two, or hours before the suicide attempt itself.

Suicide will often occur when a student is coming out of depression, not usually when he is deep in a depressive cycle. As he approaches 'normal' he actually has enough energy to commit suicide. He should be watched more closely at that point in time.

Tips for Suicidal Issues

To even think a student is suicidal is scary for anyone involved.   Life is more valuable that words can describe. It is essential that all educators keep in mind what should be done if there is even a hint that a student may be suicidal. Here are some tips that should be considered if there is any indication that the student is suicidal.

60

- Always consider any suicide threats as being real.
- If the student is at school and he has identified a way in which he would attempt suicide, remove the threat, e.g., belt, ribbon, pencil (break pencils in half), etc. You may want to remove any easy method that he could use to attempt suicide.
- Don't hesitate to get help. Call for help immediately from the office. When the student gets to the office the counselor, or other appropriate staff, should evaluate him to determine if he is indeed at risk for suicide. If the counselor believes that the student is suicidal (see 'Risk signs for Suicide' above) it is essential that the student be protected from himself. If the school has a police officer on staff, he may be able to take the student to the hospital. The parents should also be called. They may want to take their child to a specific hospital.
- If the student has had multiple suicide threats, or if there is current risk of suicide, school staff should not leave him unattended while he is at school. Escort him between classes, have someone eat with him, or have him eat in a self-contained room, have someone go with him to the bathroom to monitor for his safety, etc. It may be that a self-contained setting would be best if suicide is a possible issue.

It is important that school staff do all that they can to provide for the safety of a student who is at risk. It's a reality that the hospital may release these students even though they may still be at risk for suicide. When that is the case, it is important that the school be forewarned so that they can take the necessary precautions. Even so, if the student has historically had suicide issues and has recently been in the hospital, it may be prudent to place him on a suicide watch until his physician says he no longer needs it.

Educational Strategies for Depression

Here are a few strategies that may be utilized for students who are depressed. It is important to do what you can to bring the student out of his depressed state, or at least reduce it, so that he can function in the classroom and learn. Some of these strategies are fun and can be abused by any child, including a depressed child. Make sure that he indeed needs the strategy and is not just acting depressed to avoid work.

- The student may look to be inattentive. However, bipolar students who are in the depressive phase of their disorder will lack the energy to focus and do their work. It is important to check with the student to make sure that he understands what to do, and possibly how to get started. Don't ask if he understands. It is much to easy for the student to say, 'Yes.' Ask him to explain what he is supposed to do.
- Depressed students are similar to ADHD students in that they need redirection. When a bipolar student is not focusing, the teacher should utilize an agreed upon verbal, or non-verbal prompt that will help direct the student back to the task at hand.
- If the depression is more severe, the student may need to go to a safe place where he can talk to someone he trusts.
- If the student is so depressed that he must have constant redirection, it may be in his best interest to go to a more self-contained setting in order to get more one-on-one attention.
- A bipolar student who is depressed may need go to a more restrictive setting so that the teacher/counselor/staff can help pull him out of the depression. This

may be done by utilizing the 'Visualizing a Fun Activity Strategy', or by doing things that he has identified as being fun or enjoyable (see Fun Activities forms).

- Depression will slow the body down and make the student lethargic. If the student is lethargic, or doesn't seem to have any energy, have him take a walk with an aide. It could be around the building, or around the track. He may respond if you have him lift weights with someone monitoring him. Have him do something physically challenging. Exercise will produce endorphins that in turn will make him feel better.
- Pair the student with another student who has volunteered to help. Have the two of them play a game that the depressed student enjoys.
- Challenging computer games can help stimulate the student.
- If the school has a game system, he could play a game that calls for another student to play with him or against him in combat, fighting, etc.

ADHD
and Bipolar Disorder

Chapter Five

Attention Deficit/Hyperactivity Disorder or ADHD is one of the most prevalent disorders found in the public school system as of date. Nurse's drawers are filled with psycho-stimulants and other medications that treat the various forms of ADHD. It seems like more and more students are having difficulty with inattention, hyperactivity and impulsivity in the classroom. Teachers are dealing with multiple students with this disorder, whereas merely a few years ago there were fewer children identified. Students are having difficulties with focus, activating to task, staying on task, organization, planning, impulsivity, hyperactivity, processing speed, working memory and many more characteristics of this disorder. The interesting thing is that ADHD and Bipolar Disorder share many of the same characteristics. Actually, many students will meet the full criteria for both ADHD and Bipolar Disorder at the same time. This simply means that the student may have more than one disorder at the same time. However, there are some researchers who suggest that ADHD is a precursor to the development of full-blown Bipolar Disorder, and that the student either has one disorder or the other. Regardless, it is important to determine if a student has Bipolar Disorder or ADHD simply for the reason that different medications are used to effectively address each problem. In addition, there are additional strategies needed when the student is bipolar. The following checklist describes the symptoms of ADHD. To be determined to have ADHD, the behaviors must have persisted for at least 6 months to a degree that is maladaptive and inconsistent with the student's developmental level.

> *Many students will meet the full criteria for both ADHD and Bipolar Disorder at the same time.*

Attention Deficit/Hyperactivity Disorder Checklist

The student may have inattentive ADHD if he has six or more of the following symptoms of inattention.

Inattention	**Yes**	**No**
1. The student doesn't give close attention to details, or he makes careless mistakes in schoolwork.	___	___
2. The student has problems sustaining attention in tasks or play activities.	___	___
3. The student does not seem to listen when spoken to directly.	___	___
4. The student has trouble following through on instructions and fails to finish schoolwork.	___	___
5. The student has difficulty organizing tasks and activities.	___	___
6. The student avoids, dislikes, or is reluctant to engage in tasks that require sustained mental effort (such as schoolwork or homework).	___	___
7. The student loses things necessary for tasks or activities (e.g., school assignments, pencils, books, or tools).	___	___
8. The student is often easily distracted by extraneous stimuli.	___	___
9. The student is often forgetful in daily activities.	___	___

The student may have hyperactivity or impulsivity if he has six or more of the following symptoms of hyperactivity-impulsivity.

Hyperactivity		
1. Student fidgets with hands or feet, or squirms in seat.	___	___
2. Student leaves seat in classroom or in other situations in which remaining seated is expected.	___	___
3. Student runs about or climbs excessively in situations in which it is inappropriate (in adolescents, may be limited to subjective feelings of restlessness).	___	___
4. Student has difficulty playing or engaging in leisure activities quietly.	___	___
5. Student is often "on the go", or often acts as if "driven by a motor".	___	___
6. Student often talks excessively.	___	___

Impulsivity		
7. Student often blurts out answers before questions have been completed.	___	___
8. Student often has difficulty waiting his turn.	___	___
9. Student interrupts or intrudes on others (e.g., butts into conversations or games).	___	___

If you answer yes to some of the above symptoms the student may have ADHD. Adapted from the Diagnostic and Statistical Book of Mental Disorders IV – TR. Copyright 2000, American Psychiatric Association.

ADHD or Bipolar

Segments of this book were written to assist the professional and parent better determine whether the student has ADHD or Bipolar Disorder. Although it is best to let a professional help determine which disorder a student may have, this chapter does provide specific information that may help determine which disorder is most likely present. There are many characteristics that can be seen in both ADHD and Bipolar Disorder. However, there are also some significant differences in these two disorders. Consider the following:

ADHD and Bipolar Disorder	
ADHD	**Bipolar Disorder**
ADHD with hyperactivity exhibits ongoing over-activity (unless the student is medicated). He may get tired toward the end of the day.	With Bipolar Disorder over-activity may be episodic. However, if he is hypomanic or manic he will be overactive all day long and not tire out.
ADHD students do not seem to respond to Mood stabilizers. However, if he does respond, it suggests that he is probably bipolar.	ADHD stimulants may very well push bipolar students into increased symptoms of mania.

Characteristics of ADHD and Bipolar Disorder

Some characteristics of ADHD and Bipolar Disorder look the same, but have different motivations. Others show the same type of behavior, but it is more or less intense in some way. This is not an exhaustive list of the characteristics of ADHD or Bipolar Disorder. However, it is a good start for those trying to get a handle on which disorder seems to be most evident. These characteristics are documented in the works of Papolos & Papolos (2002), Geller (1997), Popper (1996), Miklowitz (2002), and others.

ADHD	Bipolar
An ADHD child breaks things carelessly while playing (non-angry destructiveness)	A Bipolar child breaks things as a result of anger. He has severe temper tantrums where he releases extreme amounts of physical and emotional energy. Aggression towards others and physical property damage sometimes occurs.

An ADHD child usually calms down in twenty to thirty minutes (maybe less).	A Bipolar child may continue to feel and act angry for up to four hours or more.
An ADHD child rarely regresses, e.g., displays disorganized thinking, language, and body position.	A Bipolar child regresses and often has disorganized thinking, language and body position during the episode.
An ADHD child does not lose memory of events.	A Bipolar child may iose memory of the tantrum or event.
An ADHD child is typically triggered by a lack of structure.	A Bipolar child overreacts to limit-setting, is triggered by anxiety (look for PTSD issues), or by sensory/emotional over-stimulation.
An ADHD child usually arouses quickly and attains alertness within minutes. However, they are tired and often do not get a good night sleep…especially hyperactive-impulsive students.	A Bipolar child often stays up late, and is irritable upon early morning arousal. He may have slow arousal and have irritability, fuzzy thinking, or somatic complaints when he gets up (may last for a few hours).
An ADHD child seems to wear himself out and get tired during the day (this may be a medication issue).	A Bipolar child is not usually tired during the day.
An ADHD child can see reality for what it is. He can make good judgments, but he just doesn't take the time to do so.	A Bipolar child is grandiose and believes that he can do things that he can't do (impaired judgment). Doesn't think things through…even if he does, it is often flawed thinking.
An ADHD child may destroy the bed covers, but he does not have excessive nightmares or night terrors.	A Bipolar child often has severe nightmares or night terrors. Themes of explicit gore and bodily mutilation are often reported.
An ADHD child will not have significant shifts in mood, e.g., depressed to manic.	A Bipolar child will often have mood shifts during the day, or at the least during the week.
An ADHD child's misbehavior is often accidental and usually caused by inattention, impulsivity, or over-activity.	A Bipolar child will intentionally provoke or misbehave. Some are seen as the 'bully on the playground'.
An ADHD child may sleep 5-9 hrs. However, he will often be tired because he doesn't get good REM (rapid eye movement) sleep.	A Bipolar child has a decreased need for sleep (3-6 hrs), e.g., may stay up late and get up early and not seem to have any bad effects from it.
An ADHD child's racing thoughts are fragmented; bits and pieces of hundreds of things that distract or draw his attention.	A Bipolar child often has racing thoughts. Will usually give concrete answers to describe his thoughts, e.g., "I need a stoplight up there." My thoughts broke the speed limit." Can tell you about a specific 'topic' he is racing about. His speech is usually goal directed.
An ADHD child may engage in behavior that can lead to harmful consequences without being aware of the danger.	A Bipolar child is often a risk, or sensation seeker.

An ADHD child is often immature for his age. As a result, sexuality comes along at a slower pace because of psychosocial or developmental delays.	A Bipolar child tends to have strong early sexual interest and behavior. He may be sexually inappropriate for age e.g., use explicit sexual language, sexual pictures.
An ADHD child usually does not have psychotic symptoms or reveal a loss of contact with reality.	A Bipolar child may exhibit gross distortions in perception of reality or in the interpretation of emotional events.
An ADHD child will be elated (Giggle, excited, extremely 'happy') when special events occur.	A Bipolar child will be elated for no apparent reason, e.g., giggling in the classroom when peers are not, laughing for no apparent reason, etc. At the same time he may be sensitive or easily irritated.
An ADHD child may have restless tension as seen in an inability to keep his legs, hands, etc. still. This occurs all day long.	A Bipolar child will have the same problem with restlessness, but it may cycle through the day, often getting worse at night (depends on type of bipolar).
An ADHD child can be impulsive and react to his environment, not so much his inner turmoil.	A Bipolar child will be impulsive due to a swing in moods. If hypomanic, judgment fades. If depressed he may have a need to find a way to reduce his depression or energize himself.
An ADHD child will probably be inattentive or distractible all day long, every day of the week (pending medication).	A Bipolar child may be inattentive for a time and then become attentive as he pulls out of his depression. If he goes too far into the manic side he will lose attention again. Attention is often cyclical...may be hour by hour or day by day.
An ADHD child may be self-centered, but is usually so because of a sense of frustration at being unable to focus.	A Bipolar child seems to be unable to see other's perspective in a situation. He will do whatever is necessary to justify his position. Very irritable.
ADHD children may talk of suicide as a control issue. Usually there is no intention, plan, etc. for follow through.	A Bipolar child may have a morbid fantasy about death, hurting others, etc. Suicide is the leading cause of death of people with Bipolar Disorder.
An ADHD child would rarely intentionally hurt self or others. If something were to occur it would be more of an accident due to inattention.	A Bipolar child will intentionally hurt self or others with purpose. This purpose will often seem to be malevolent or grandiose in nature, i.e., creative ways to hurt someone who has offended him.
An ADHD child will have non-directive meltdowns. They are usually short in duration.	A Bipolar child will go into a rage and direct it at a person, or some available target. It is deliberate and intentional in nature. He may attack those in authority.
An ADHD child may speak out of turn (even have a lot to say), but can be redirected to task.	When in a manic state, a bipolar child will have a verbal outpouring, speaking without stop even when someone tries to stop him.

Overlapping Symptoms of ADHD and Bipolar Disorder

There are a number of symptoms or characteristics that overlap. This is one of the reasons why it is so difficult to tell which disorder is actually present. For instance, ADHD has characteristics of hyperactivity, impulsivity, inattentiveness, lack of judgment, irritability, dangerous behaviors, and depression. Bipolar disorder also has the very same characteristics. There is a telling difference though. With ADHD the characteristics are more constant and less intense. Those who have Bipolar Disorder exhibit these behaviors with an intensity that is much greater than that found in ADHD students. Although a bipolar student may exhibit these characteristics with greater intensity, his behavior may also fluctuate depending on whether or not he is in a hypomanic or manic state. In addition, Bipolar Disorder also includes mood shifts, a decreased need for sleep, grandiosity, elation, delusions and hallucinations. The chart below gives you a brief snapshot of some of the overlapping symptoms.

Overlapping Symptoms of ADHD & Bipolar Disorder		
ADHD	**Overlapping Symptoms**	**Bipolar**
Same as overlapping symptoms accept: • More constant • Less Intense	Hyperactivity Impulsivity Inattentiveness Lack of Judgment Irritability Dangerous behaviors Depression	Mood shifts Decreased need for sleep. Grandiosity Elation Delusions & Hallucinations Behaviors are less consistent depending on whether or not the student is manic or depressive. See Manic Symptoms in Chapter Three.

Strategies for ADHD or Bipolar Disorder

Each of the characteristics or symptoms indicated above, for both the ADHD and Bipolar child, can cause significant problems for both school and home. This section will provide specific strategies for both the ADHD and Bipolar symptoms.

Destructive Tendencies

An ADHD child breaks things carelessly while playing (non-angry destructiveness).

> Primary Strategies:
> - Redirect the student into a safer situation.
> - Adjust the environment by removing breakables where possible.
> - Greater supervision when around things that could be broken.

A Bipolar child breaks things as a result of anger. He has severe temper tantrums where he releases extreme amounts of physical and emotional energy; aggression towards others and physical property damage sometimes occurs.

> Primary Strategies:
> - Teach anger control strategies.
> - Remove him to a safe location if he starts to become angry.
> - Use restraint if he is a threat to himself, others or property.

Calm Down Time

An ADHD child usually calms down in twenty to thirty minutes (maybe less).

> Primary Strategies:
> - Place the student in a time out room or in a 'cool off' place until he regains composure.
> - Provide training in anger management.

A Bipolar child may continue to feel and act angry for up to four hours or more.

> Primary Strategies:
> - Place the student in a more restrictive setting where he can be monitored. It may take much of the day for him to calm.
> - Document and notify parents concerning anger episode.
> - As he seems to regain some degree of control, review calming or anger reduction strategies. Do them with the student if necessary to help him calm down.
> - Teach stress management techniques.

Regression and Behavior

An ADHD child rarely regresses, e.g., displays disorganized thinking, language, and body position.

> Primary Strategies:
> None Necessary.

A Bipolar child regresses and often has disorganized thinking, language and body position during the episode.

Primary Strategies:
- Place student in a more restrictive setting until he can regain control.
- Document and notify parents concerning episode.
- Assure that the student is physically protected. He may not be able to take care of himself.

Loss of Memory Regarding an Event

An ADHD child does not lose memory of events.

Primary Strategies:
None Necessary.

A Bipolar child may lose memory of the tantrum or event.

Primary Strategies:
- If the student cannot remember the event or his behavior during the event, do not press him. He may very well be telling you the truth.
- If the student is emotionally distraught allow him to stay in a safe place until he feels better, or has better control of his emotions.
- Document and notify parents. If he honestly can't remember, he has been in a manic rage state and may need to see his physician.

Typical Triggers of Behavior

An ADHD child is typically triggered by a lack of structure. Poor social skills also play a role in appropriate responses.

Primary Strategies:
- If the student is stressed due to the amount of work, social pressure, etc. remove the cause and give him time to calm down.
- Placement in a more restrictive setting until he has calmed may be necessary.
- Teach social skills.
- Consider placing this student with more structured teachers.

A Bipolar child overreacts to limit-setting or is triggered (look for PTSD issues).

Primary Strategies:
- Consider a more restrictive setting, do not remove limits. He must be responsible for his behavior.
- Identify if there are emotional triggers (specifically PTSD issues) that may be causing him to overreact to limits.
- Prepare him for change and set rules in advance.
- Stress reduction may need to be considered.
- Evaluate any sensory issues and remove sensory overload. It may be a result of something he sees, hears, smells, etc.

Early Morning Arousal & Alertness

An ADHD child usually arouses quickly and seems to do much better in school in the morning.

> Primary Strategies:
> - More difficult core classes should be scheduled for the morning if possible.

A Bipolar child often stays up late and is irritable upon early morning arousal. He may have slow arousal and have irritability, fuzzy thinking, or somatic complaints when he gets up (may last for a few hours).

> Primary Strategies:
> - If a student is not sleeping enough hours it is probably a result of a manic or hypomanic state.
> - Medication may need to be reviewed.
> - Get to bed early and at a consistent time. Wake time should also be consistent.
> - Bipolar students may need to have less difficult classes in the morning.

Running Out of Gas Factor

An ADHD child seems to wear himself out and get tired during the day.

> Primary Strategies:
> - Medication may need to be adjusted.
> - Evaluate how well the student is actually sleeping. Is he still exhausted in the morning? If so, he may not be getting enough REM sleep.

A Bipolar child is not usually tired during the day.
> Primary Strategies:
> - Medication may need to be adjusted, especially if he is in a manic or hypomanic state.
> - Have parents evaluate if the student is sleeping well. If not, the sleep/wake cycle may need to be adjusted.

Grandiosity and Judgment

An ADHD child can see reality for what it is. He can make good judgments, but he just doesn't take the time to do so.

> Primary Strategies:
> - Student may need to work on impulsivity issues.

A Bipolar child is grandiose (inflated self-esteem or self-worth, usually manifested with thinking or talk that suggests he believes that he is the greatest, or has special attributes or abilities) and believes that he can do things that he can't do (impaired judgment). This student doesn't think things through ...even if he does, it is often flawed thinking.

> Primary Strategies:
> - When a student is grandiose his medication is probably off. Notify parents so they can have their physician evaluate if there needs to be a change.
> - Student may need to be placed in a more restrictive setting for safety.
> - Relaxation strategies may be beneficial to help him calm.

Nightmares or Night Terrors

An ADHD child may destroy the bed covers, but he does not have excessive nightmares or night terrors.

> Primary Strategies:
> None Necessary.

A Bipolar child often has severe nightmares or night terrors. Themes of explicit gore and bodily mutilation are often reported.

> Primary Strategies:
> - Student may be overcome by negative thoughts during the day. Use cognitive strategies to remove negative thoughts.
> - Do not let the student view shows that are morbid or bloody. He needs to avoid all types of morbid, violent, or bloody visual input regardless of where it comes from.

Shifts in Mood

An ADHD child will not have significant shifts in mood, e.g., depressed to manic.

> Primary Strategies:
> None Necessary.

A Bipolar child will often have mood shifts during the day or at the least during the week.

> Primary Strategies:
> - When student is in a manic or depressive state he may need to be in a more structured, supportive environment.
> - If in a hypomanic or manic state he will need lots of structure and will need to have assistance in reducing stress if he is to have any chance of controlling his hypomanic behaviors.
> - If he is in a depressive state he will need to have individual assistance in working through his depressive issues. He may need to exercise or utilize a variety of strategies that might help him reduce his depression.

Misbehavior is Usually Caused by

An ADHD child's misbehavior is often accidental and usually caused by inattention or over-activity.

Primary Strategies:

- When possible structure his environment to reduce the possibility of accidents.
- Dc not allow unstructured play unless it can be controlled to a point that you can ensure some degree of safety for all.
- Organized games or activities that are less apt to provide opportunity for accidents would be best suited for the ADHD student.

A Bipolar child will intentionally provoke or misbehave. Some are seen as the bully on the playground.

Primary Strategies:
- If the student provokes others or intentionally misbehaves, place him in a more restrictive setting.
- Do not allow this student to be alone with other children when in a manic or hypomanic state.

Sleep

An ADHD child usually sleeps about 5-9 hours, even if he is a bit fitful (lack of REM sleep).

Primary Strategies:
- None necessary unless the student is too fitful to get a good night sleep. If so, sleep aids may need to be considered (medication, relaxing tea, etc.).

A Bipolar child has a decreased need for sleep (3-6 hrs and sometimes less), e.g., may stay up late and get up early and not seem to have any bad effects from it.

Primary Strategies:
- Student needs to be evaluated by a psychiatrist or specialist. Medication is probably needed.

Racing Thoughts

An ADHD child's racing thoughts are fragmented; bits and pieces of hundreds of things that distract or draw his attention.

Primary Strategies:
- Redirect the student and get him to focus on a self-selected task that is interesting to him.

- Reduce sensory input.

A Bipolar child often has racing thoughts. Will usually give concrete answers to describe his thoughts, e.g., "I need a stoplight up there." My thoughts broke the speed limit." The student can tell you about a specific 'topic' he is racing about.

Primary Strategies:
- Redirection is often difficult when a student is at this stage, but it should be attempted.
- If the problem is too distracting for the student to learn and it appears that he may be spiraling into a pure manic state take him to a safe location where he can attempt some 'relaxation' techniques.

> *When a child is Inattentive due to a seretonin imbalance, the brain is in slow gear. The student may be trying to focus or respond, but information comes to him slowly. The racing brain has so much going on that the student has to work through information to find what he needs to give feedback to.*

Danger and Sensation Seeking

An ADHD child may engage in behavior that can lead to harmful consequences without being aware of the danger.

Primary Strategies:
- None necessary unless the child is extremely hyperactive and impulsive. If unattended he may accidentally hurt himself or another. There is probably no intent to harm.

A Bipolar child is often a risk or sensation seeker.

Primary Strategies:
- When in a hypomanic or manic state the student may take unnecessary risks. He must be monitored at all times.

Sexual Maturity

An ADHD child is often immature for his age. As a result, sexuality comes along at a slower pace because of psychosocial or developmental delays.

Primary Strategies:
- Not an issue as far as sexual misconduct is concerned.

A Bipolar child tends to have strong early sexual interest and behavior. He may be sexually inappropriate for age e.g., use explicit sexual language, sexual pictures.

> Primary Strategies:
> - Monitor this student when he is in a hypomanic or manic state. This is when his sexual interest peaks.
> - Notify his parents about the specific sexual language, acts, drawings that are being produced so that they can communicate it to the child's doctor.
> - Discussion about what is appropriate and not appropriate needs to be done by the counselor and/or parent.

Psychotic Symptoms

An ADHD child usually does not have psychotic symptoms or reveal a loss of contact with reality.

> Primary Strategies:
> - None necessary.

A Bipolar child may exhibit gross distortions in perception of reality, or in the interpretation of emotional events.

> Primary Strategies:
> - Child is probably in a manic state along with experiencing a psychotic episode. Do not confront or say he is not hearing or seeing what he is reporting.
> - Report the event to his parents immediately.
> - Place the child in a more structured setting where he won't disrupt other students and where someone can spend time with him.
> - Try to get him to focus on specific aspects of reality without telling him to stop hearing or seeing things. For instance, counselor picks up a football in her room and says, "Johnny, do you have a football like this?" Discuss reality that can be seen and felt at the moment.
> - Have him identify items in your room and what they are used for. Engage him in communication that is as normal as is possible. Get him to focus on 'reality'.

Elation or Excitement

An ADHD child will be elated (Giggle, excited, extremely 'happy') when special events occur.

> Primary Strategies:
> - Redirect and get the student back on task.

A Bipolar child will be elated for no apparent reason, e.g., giggling in the classroom when peers are not, laughing for no apparent reason, etc. At the same time he may be sensitive or easily irritated.

Primary Strategies:
- When a bipolar child becomes elated he is going into, or is in a manic phase. Find a safe, more structured location for the child.
- If he is able, have him practice some stress reduction exercises to help calm him.
- Consider doing other hypomanic reduction strategies if the student is able.

Restless Tension

An ADHD child may have restless tension as seen in an inability to keep his legs, hands, etc. still. This occurs all day long, pending medication.

Primary Strategies:
- Contact parents and report the behaviors. This may be a medication issue.
- Keep this child busy doing constructive things. If he does not have something to do, he will find something to do. Usually, it will not be what a teacher would choose.
- Use redirection to preferred activities or academic alternatives.
- Consider using some form of exercise to help this student reduce some of his restlessness, e.g., walking, running, or doing some other form of exercise.

A Bipolar child will have the same problem with restlessness, but it may cycle through the day, often getting worse at night (or he may have days of restlessness and days where he is down or lethargic).

Primary Strategies:
- Contact parents and report the behaviors. His medication may need to be adjusted.
- Consider using some form of exercise to help this student reduce some of his restless ness just as suggested above.
- If he is depressed he may need to have someone work with him to do some depression reduction strategies.
- If he is becoming manic he may need to practice some hypomania or mania reduction strategies.

Impulsivity

An ADHD child can be impulsive and react to his environment, not so much his inner turmoil.

Primary Strategies:
- Look for patterns of impulsiveness and alter antecedants.
- Teach strategies to help the student learn to control impulsiveness.
- Teach planning skills. This helps with some forms of impulsiveness.

A Bipolar child will be impulsive due to a swing in moods. If hypomanic, judgment fades and he does things without thinking. If depressed, he may have a need to find a way to reduce his depression or energize himself.

Primary Strategies:
- Medication may be need to be adjusted.
- The more manic the greater the need for a more restrictive setting.
- Allow time to do a relaxation strategy in a safe environment.
- Teach strategies to help the student learn to control impulsiveness just as you would do an ADHD student.

Inattention & Distractibility

An ADHD child will be inattentive or distractible all day long (pending medication).

Primary Strategies:
- Redirection to task.
- Preferential seating....preferably close to the teacher.
- Proximity control is often helpful with inattentive or distractible students.

A Bipolar child may be inattentive for a time and then become attentive as he pulls out of his depression. If he goes too far into the manic side he will lose attention again. Attention is often cyclical.

Primary Strategies:
- When depressed provide student with encouragement and redirection.
- When manic consider a more restrictive setting where redirection will have a better chance of being successful.

Self-Centered

An ADHD child may be self-centered, but is usually so because of a sense of frustration at being unable to focus.

Primary Strategies:
- Look for sensory distractions (visual, auditory, etc.) and remove them.
- Determine if there are academic frustrations that could be remedied.

A Bipolar child seems to be unable to see other's perspective in a situation. He will do whatever is necessary to justify his position. Very irritable.

Primary Strategies:
- Set strong limits and consequences for self-centered behavior.
- Consider a more restrictive setting to think through self-centeredness with help. Student must be taught during 'normal' periods of time that he must not exhibit self-centered behavior.

Suicide

ADHD children may talk of suicide as a control issue. Usually there is not intention, plan, etc. for follow through.

Primary Strategies:
- Document and notify administration and parents.
- Place the student in a self-contained setting so that he can think about the consequences of threatening suicide.

A Bipolar child may have a morbid fantasy about death, hurting others, etc. Suicide is the leading cause of death of people with Bipolar disorder.

Primary Strategies:
- If he states that he is thinking about/planning suicide, document and notify administration and parents.
- Place the student in a self-contained setting and place him on a suicide watch.
- Have the counselor or some other staff member help him work through the suicidal issues.
- Escort to all locations including bathroom until 'crisis' no longer exists.

Harm to Self or Others

An ADHD child would rarely intentionally hurt self or others. If something were to occur it would be more of an accident due to inattention.

Primary Strategies:
- Look for patterns. Determine where 'accidents' most often occur and reduce them by changing antecedants.

A Bipolar child may intentionally hurt self or others with purpose. This purpose will often seem to be malevolent or grandiose in nature, i.e., creative ways to hurt someone who has offended him.

Primary Strategies:
- Provide consequences including a more restrictive placement.
- Place the student in a time out room or in a 'cool off' place for a designated period of time.
- If you perceive that he is becoming hypomanic or manic, place him in a more restrictive setting so that he will be less apt to hurt himself or others.

Meltdowns or Trantrums

An ADHD child will have non-directive meltdowns. This is driven by a feeling of being overwhelmed, overstressed, and out of control. Usually is short in duration.

Primary Strategies:
- Look for antecedants and reduce them.
- Use anxiety or stress reduction techniques.
- Place the student in a time out room or in a 'cool off' place until he regains composure.

A Bipolar child will go into a rage and direct it at a person, or some available target. It is deliberate and intentional in nature. He may attack those in authority.

Primary Strategies:
- Assure for the protection of self, student and others as well as property.
- Place the student in a time out room or in a 'cool off' place until he regains composure. This may take a greater portion of the day if it was a result of his mania. If it is 'normal' anger he may not need as long to cool off.
- Help him use anger or stress management strategies.

Speaking Out of Turn

An ADHD child may speak out of turn (even have a lot to say), but can be redirected to task.

Primary Strategies:
- Use redirection to task.
- Place another task in front of the student and ask him to begin it.

When in a manic state a Bipolar child will have an outpouring of verbage, continually shifting topics speaking without stop even when someone tries to stop him.

Primary Strategies:
- Attempt to redirect student...if it fails and it probably will direct him to a more restrictive setting where he can speak without disturbing other students. Periodically attempt to redirect to appropriate task.
- When possible do a stress reduction strategy to help the student get a handle of the hypomania.

Modifications for ADHD/Bipolar Disorder

There are hundreds of modifications and strategies that can be used to assist a student who is exhibiting problems with ADHD or Bipolar Disorder. These are just a few that can be implemented in the classroom.

Provide the Student with a Low-Distraction Work Area
- In order to reduce distractions, computers and other equipment with audio functions used by others should be used with earphones to eliminate the sound being broadcast into the classroom or work area.
- Always seat this student in a low-distraction work area in the classroom, e.g., away from doorway.

Prepare the Student for Transitions

- Prepare the student in advance for upcoming changes to routine, e.g., field trips, transitions from one activity to another, etc.
- Plan supervision during transitions, e.g., between subjects, classes, recess, lunchroom, assemblies, etc.

Adaptations for a Student with Hyperactivity

- Allow the student to move around. Provide opportunities for physical action, e.g., let him pace in the rear of the classroom, run an errand, wash the blackboard, get a drink of water, go to the bathroom, etc.
- Make sure the student is provided with opportunity for physical exertion if his over-activity seems to be getting the best of him, e.g., walking, running, etc.
- Consider using a stationary bike with a book stand.
- Have the student highlight key terms on notes given to him in class.

Alter Presentation of Lessons or Accommodations for Assignments

- Provide this student with a note-taker to record classroom discussions and lectures.
- Allow time to complete an activity before introducing the next one.
- Provide student with a weekly syllabus, in advance, of upcoming week's assignments and lessons.

Shorten Assignments

- Break instructions into short, sequential steps so the student can better understand what is expected.
- Hand out longer assignments in short segments
- Schedule shorter work periods with built in reinforcers.

Support the Student's Participation in the Classroom

- Allow extra time for student to answer questions or time to form a thoughtful answer.
- Identify the student's strengths, alter the format of a presentation to take full advantage of his strengths (teach to his strengths).

Classroom and Homework Assignment Adaptations

- Modify classroom and homework assignments, e.g., student does fewer problems per concept.
- Allow this student to keep a back-up set of textbooks at home.

Alter Testing and Evaluation Procedures

- Provide the student with other opportunities, methods or test formats to demonstrate what he knows.
- Allow the student to take tests or quizzes in a quiet place in order to reduce distractions.

Alter the Design of Materials

- Whenever possible the instructions should be next to the questions to which they relate, and test questions should visually stand-out from the test answers (on multiple choice, matching, etc.).
- Reduce visual clutter on tests and make type larger where possible.

Skills Training
- Provide the student with a regular program in study skills, test taking skills, organizational skills, and time management skills.
- Provide daily assistance/guidance to the student in how to use a planner on a daily basis and for long-term assignments; help the student break larger assignments into smaller, more manageable tasks.

Create a Safe Environment for Learning
- Praise in public.
- Reprimand in private.
- Determine effective motivational techniques for the student. These must be changed often to assure that they continue to work.

Parental Involvement
- Use the student's planner for daily communication with the parent.
- Do e-mails or phone calls to assure that ongoing communication is maintained with parents.
- Involve parents in selection of the student's teachers.

Most of the above listed modifications would be beneficial for both ADHD and Bipolar Disorder students, as well as a number of other co-existing conditions.

Anxiety
and Bipolar Disorder
Chapter Six

Most Bipolar students also experience significant anxiety. Untreated, anxiety can debilitate the student as much as the bipolar condition does...only in a different way. Various studies have suggested the following:

- 20.8% of people with Bipolar Disorder experienced panic disorder at some time in their lives compared to 10.0% of people with unipolar depression and 0.8% of people without mood disorders.
- People with Bipolar Disorder were 19 times more likely than people with no mood disorder to develop a panic disorder, and were almost two times more likely to develop panic disorder than people with unipolar depression.
- Studies show that family members of people with Bipolar Disorder have a higher rate of anxiety disorders, and of personality traits such as compulsive personality associated with anxiety disorders.
- Another study suggests that social phobia is more likely to occur during a depressive episode, while panic and OCD (Obsessive-Compulsive Disorder) may occur at any time.

All forms of stress or anxiety, whether it is general anxiety, obsessive-compulsive disorder, social anxiety, post traumatic stress disorder, etc., can trigger the bipolar child into a mood state. Because of this, all anxiety issues must be addressed in order to assist the bipolar student as he attempts to control his mood switches.

Stress & Anxiety

Stress is a killer. It damages the physical and emotional self. Studies have shown that stress actually damages the brain. Obviously, this makes it very important to avoid stress, especially for the bipolar student who is already at risk. These students already have a high level of stress in their lives. It would take very little additional stress to be triggered into a depressed, hypomanic, manic, or rage state.

- Miklowitz reports that, "We are reasonably certain that stress affects the course of your illness, or increases the chances that you will have an episode of mania or depression if you already have Bipolar Disorder. Your level of stress may also affect how long it takes you to get over bipolar episode" (Miklowitz 2002).
- Stress not dealt with leads to anxiety. It also reduces the brains ability to function effectively.
- Anxiety not dealt with can lead to a disruption of normal life activities, sickness and eventually death.

> *Stress affects the course of your illness, or increases the chances*
> *that you will have an episode of mania or depression*
> *if you already have Bipolar Disorder.*

Miklowitz (2002) and others have suggested that there are particular types of stress that are more impacting than others to individuals who have Bipolar Disorder. Some of these are, 1) significant life changes, 2) the sleep wake cycle, 3) patterns of daily activity and social stimulation, and 4) conflicts with significant others. These findings were identified with adults, but seem to be issues with children and adolescents also.

- **Significant Life Changes:** Significant life changes are one area that easily produces significant stress in children, adolescents and adults. Mom and dad fighting, parents getting a divorce, death of a parent, friend or even a loved pet, car accident or medical crisis are all examples of significant life changes that can trigger a bipolar episode.

- **Sleep Wake Cycle:** The sleep wake cycle also can set off episodes. Research has suggested that even minor changes in the sleep-wake rhythms can trigger an episode (Wehr, 1987). To put it simply, if the student goes to bed at a different time, goes to sleep at a different time, or wakes up at a different time that he normally does, it can disturb the sleep-wake rhythm which in turn can trigger a bipolar episode.

- **Patterns of Daily Activity and Social Situations:** If patterns of daily activity and social situations change it can produce bipolar episodes. This may occur when the student, 1) leaves for school at a time different from usual, 2) goes to school with someone different than he usually goes to school with, 3) has unusual stops after school, 4) doesn't eat at the 'usual' time, 5) doesn't walk his dog at his normal time, or 6) if he experiences any other changes that he is not prepared for. These are all rhythms of social life that need to be maintained, or it can produce bipolar episodes (Malkoff-Schwartz, 1998).

- **Conflicts with Significant Others:** Conflicts with significant others can be very problematic. Any significant conflict with a friend, sibling, parent, teacher, or administrator can trigger bipolar episodes.

Types of Stress that Significantly Impacts Bipolar Episodes

1) Significant life changes.

2) The sleep wake cycle.

3) Patterns of daily activity and social stimulation.

4) Conflicts with significant others.

Basic Signs of General Stress

There are a number of signs of stress that can lead to anxiety and numerous body symptoms. Here are a few.

1. Feeling scared, jumpy
2. Headaches, twitchy eyes, face blushes or feeling hot
3. Neck or shoulder tightness
4. Cold hands, fingers are tight
5. Gassiness, burping, cramping sensation, acid stomach, stomach ache
6. Shallow, rapid breathing, racing feelings in your chest, shortness of breath
7. Fidgety, restless feelings, can't sit still
8. Jaw clenching, tight lips, teeth grinding
9. Sweaty hands, hands that shake

The student's level of stress may also affect how long it takes to get over a bipolar episode.

Benefits of Practicing Stress Reduction Strategies

The great thing about stress reduction strategies is that they really do work. Students who are experiencing ongoing anxiety or stress can actually reduce their overall level of stress by simply practicing stress management techniques on a day to day basis. Benson (1984) stated that there are a number of benefits that can occur when a person practices daily for several weeks.   Some of the benefits are:

- Reduced anxiety
- Less insomnia
- Fewer headaches
- Lower blood pressure
- Lower overall stress
- Control over panic attacks and other anxiety inducing situations
- Less hyper-ventalization

Preparing to Use a Stress Reduction Technique

According to Benson, for a stress reduction technique to work it is important that at least four elements be present (1984). Regardless of the relaxation technique that is used, it is important to prepare with the following in mind.

- The student must go to an alternate location where it is quiet. There can be no (or minimal) distractions and he must be assured that he will not be interrupted.
- The student should use a mental device that can be repeated silently (in the mind or in a low tone). Some people have chosen to use a visual image that keeps their mind from wandering.
- The student needs to maintain a passive attitude. He should not force his response to the relaxation technique. Tell the student to avoid fighting with any distracting thought. Instead, he should simply return to the thought, image or vocalization that was being used (See Relaxation and Intrusive Thoughts in this Chapter).
- The student should get as comfortable as possible. His head, arms, legs and body should be completely relaxed. He may want to take off his shoes, loosen the belt, and make everything as comfortable as it can possibly be before he begins to relax.

De-stress the Environment

One of the first things an educator can do to reduce stress for a bipolar student is to alter the environment. This alone can have a tremendous impact on the student. Even before If you start to see signs of stress in a bipolar student it is important that you do what you can to reduce stress provoking situations as much as is possible in order to avoid a rage state or a manic episode. Here are some things that can be done to reduce stress in the classroom environment.

- **Reduce Visual Distractions:** Keep large bulletin boards and hanging objects to the back of the room. The less clutter there is in the front of the room the easier it will be for all students to focus in on what is important in the classroom.

- **Full Spectrum or Natural Light vs Fluorescent Light:** Students and teachers will relax, have fewer headaches, be less agitated, and more focused if regular lights are used instead of fluorescent lights. Most people have no idea how much a simple change in light can positively impact students.

- **White Noise:** Use a sound machine, or air filter to mask unwanted noises. Small noises, that most students cannot hear, can irritate bipolar students who are already sensitive. Mask some of the unwanted sound with white noise. In doing so the student may be less agitated and will often be able to focus better while in class.

- **Soothing music:** Music can also have a profound effect on some students. It can do many things that are positive or constructive. Two evident benefits are that it, 1) helps calm the student, and 2) helps reduce unwanted noise that can irritate the student (much like white noise mentioned above).

WARNING: Scientists have only recently discovered how stress negatively affects brain function. Stress hormones have been shown in animals to be directly toxic to memory centers. Brain cells can die with prolonged stress. Managing stress effectively is essential to good brain function.

Quick Stress Busters

Some students simply need some simple stress reduction strategies that can be used while they are in the classroom. When that is the case, any of the following strategies can be used to reduce mild stress. Teach the bipolar student these quick stress busters so that he can immediately start to relax when he begins to feel uptight or stressed. It is important that bipolar students start to relax as soon as possible when they begin to feel tensed up. This helps control rage states and manic tendencies. Teach these to the student.

- **Head Rolls:** Teach the student to roll his head around his shoulders stretching the neck muscles in every direction as he moves.
- **Push Downs:** Have him push down on his chair.
- **Eye Time Out:** Have him turn away from teacher…look at clock, window, down at desk and close his eyes for a moment. He should take a deep breath, do a body check, relax and open his eyes again.
- **Side to Side:** Have him lean over and try to touch the floor on each side of his desk stretching his side as he does.
- **Iron Man:** Have him tense his whole body from the tips of his toes to the top of his head for 2-3 seconds and then let it go. Do this two or three times as often as needed.
- **Vacation:** Have him find a place during lunch or between classes where he can close his eyes for just a minute and visualize himself relaxing at a favorite vacation spot.
- **Deep Breathing:** Have him go to a safe, quiet place and seat himself comfortably. He should close his eyes and do deep breathing. Tell him to let his breath in for a count of 3-4 seconds and breath out for a count of 3-4

seconds. He should take ten of these deep breaths whenever he needs to relax.

- **Refocus:** If something is irritating him and it seems to be causing him to stress, have him refocus on what he should be doing. He should say to himself, "I'm going to focus on the teacher.", or "I'm going to listen to what she is saying."

Although these quick strategies can help a student when he has mild stress, it may take additional strategies to help him get a handle on more significant stress. The following strategies are extremely beneficial to bipolar students who need to, 1) reduce overall stress in their lives, and 2) reduce situational stress as it occurs.

Benefits of Abdominal Breathing

Abdominal breathing has been taught for years to those who have wanted to learn to relax and reduce stress. There's a good reason for this....it works. There are a number of benefits that are obtained when a student does abdominal breathing.

- First, there is an increased oxygen supply to the brain and musculature. The increased oxygen supply can improve concentration. When the mind is racing it becomes increasingly difficult to focus attention. Abdominal breathing will help quiet the mind and energize it for learning at the same time.
- Second, abdominal breathing can stimulate the parasympathetic nervous system. This part of the autonomic nervous system promotes a state of calmness.
- Third, when the body relaxes it can more efficiently rid itself of bodily toxins. Many toxic substances in the body are excreted through the lungs.

Basic Abdominal Breathing

Basic abdominal breathing is the foundation for most stress management techniques. It is important that the student learn how to properly breathe in order for him to utilize the strategies recommended in this book. There are three basic steps to basic abdominal breathing. They are:

- The student must first find a quiet place to sit or lie down.
- Once comfortable he must breathe deeply and slowly through his nose (take 3-4 seconds to breathe in and 3-4 seconds to breathe out).
- Have him use abdominal breathing; not his chest when he breathes. If he is lying down he should be able to see his stomach rising and falling as he breathes, not his chest. It should appear as if he is breathing with his stomach.

Warning about Improper Breathing

When a student is suffering from anger, agitation, hypomania, phobias, panic, or other anxiety disorders it is easy if not natural to breathe improperly. The student must learn to consciously breathe properly if he is to avoid improper breathing when stressed.

- The student may breathe shallowly or too high up in his chest. Breathing that is too shallow will not provide the benefits that abdominal breathing will provide.
- In addition, if the student breathes shallowly he may hyper-ventilate. Shallow breathing, when rapid, can lead to hyper-ventilation which in turn, can cause physical symptoms very similar to those associated with panic attacks. These physical symptoms produce more anxiety and makes the student feel worse.

When improper breathing is used, bipolar students may very well become more anxious which can possibly trigger an episode. The student must be taught to breathe right so that he can help himself control episodes. Once he learns proper breathing he will be ready to learn relaxation techniques that can be used along with proper breathing.

Relaxation and Intrusive Thoughts

Not only must the student learn to breathe properly, but he must also learn how to focus his mind in a way that will produce benefits. Many a student has attempted to relax, only to have an intrusive thought overwhelm him and actually produce stress. It is important that the student be taught how to avoid intrusive thoughts while he is using meditation or any other relaxation technique that calls for a mental exercise, e.g., visualization, words, etc. He must understand that to successfully relax he must learn how to get rid of intrusive thoughts. The key is this. If a thought comes to his mind he must simply refocus on his word, phrase, feeling, or image. Under no circumstances is he to try to tell it to go away, try to force it out, or acknowledge the thought in any way. This will give the intrusive thought power and make it more difficult to get rid of. With this in mind, it is important that the student learn one or more stress reduction techniques. Here are some examples of stress reduction techniques that can be used to help the bipolar student reduce general and acute stress.

Meditation for Relaxation and Health

Mediation has been used by numerous cultures for years as a means of relaxing and achieving inner peace. Here is an example of how this can be used to help a bipolar student reduce stress and relax. Explain the following steps:

- The first step calls for the student to use deep breathing for a few minutes in order to calm his mind and body. When he is relatively relaxed he should go to step two.
- The second step requires that he select a word or phrase to focus on. In Benson's book entitled, Beyond the Relaxation Response, he describes how a word or phrase of special personal significance (such as, "I am at peace," "Let go, let God") deepens the effects of meditation.
- Explain how on each exhalation he should repeat this chosen word or phrase. This can be done silently if desired. Encourage him to continue to use abdominal breathing while meditating.

Teach the student to use this strategy for a minimum of 12 minutes. Based on Benson's research at about twelve minutes the physiological benefits begin. Have him set a goal to increase his minutes to a minimum of 30 minutes a day. This will help control or minimize his manic or rage states by reducing his overall level of stress and by helping him maintain an ongoing state of calm.

Quick Relaxation Technique

This is an easy and fun way to relax. There are times that a bipolar student needs to relax quickly....needs to calm down when he is starting to feel stressed or manic. This is a self-management technique that can be taught to the student so that he can use it when he needs to reduce his stress very quickly.

- Step One: Teach the student to recognize that worry, anxiety, or tension may very well be triggering him. As he learns to sense these destructive feelings have him go to step two.
- Step two: When he senses stress and needs to relax, he should do a body scan. He should start with the top of his head. He should relax his eyes, open his mouth a little, relax his shoulders, arms, back, and stomach. He should also relax his hips, legs, feet and toes. Everything should be relaxed.
- Step Three: Now it's time to do something odd, but very effective. Have the student breathe through his feet. He should feel the air as it rises up his legs and centers in his stomach. If he can't sense it, have him try to visualize the movement up his legs and into his lower abdomen.
- Step Four: He should exhale slowly and feel the air as it goes back down his legs and out the bottom of his feet. He should focus on how the air feels as it goes down his legs and out the bottom of his feet.
- Step Five: The student should repeat this process a minimum of three and four times, or until he feels more relaxed and calm. If he wants, he can do this for five, ten, or even thirty minutes to relax.

Progressive Muscle Relaxation Technique

If the student wants to use the Progressive Muscle Relaxation Technique the following process should be taught. This can be taught by the counselor, teacher, or parent. Have the student sit in a comfortable chair, bean bag, or lie on the floor to do this relaxation technique. This stress-reduction method calls for the student to tense his body and relax it. It works best when he tenses up groups of major muscle groups one at a time for about ten seconds, before he suddenly relaxes them. When the student gets the 'feel' for how to use this method have him do the technique all by himself. Here are the muscle groups you want the student to tense.

Step One: Have him squeeze his eyes shut tight, his lips together, and tighten his face muscles. Relax after a few seconds.
Step Two: Next he should tighten his neck and shoulder muscles. Relax after a few seconds.
Step Three: Have him make a fist with each of his hands and squeeze his fingers together as tight as he can as he tightens his biceps and shoulders. Relax after a few seconds.
Step Four: Have him tighten his stomach and his derriere (your behind, the place you sit on, etc.) Relax after a few seconds.

Step Five: Last, have him squeeze his toes, calves and thigh muscles as tight as he can. Relax after a few seconds.

- Now that he knows what to do, have him do all five steps by himself, holding each muscle group for about ten seconds before he completely relaxes. Tell him to let all of his muscles go completely limp. He should let himself be like a rag doll. Ask him to notice the contrast in how his muscles feel. He should notice the sense of warmth and calmness spreading through his body.
- It is important that he focus on the tension and then the calmness of his body…he shouldn't let his mind wander.
- When stress he should do this sequence two or three times, or until you feels more relaxed.

This technique is good for some students and actually can trigger stress in others. It should be taught so that the student can determine if the technique is helpful. If it is helpful, it is a very good way of breaking down body tension and reducing both external and internal stress that can trigger manic or rage states.

Positive Imagery and Relaxation

Maxwell Maltz in his book titled, Psychocybernetics highly recommended this technique. He believed that it could be used for stress, anxiety, depression, and many other issues. To use this technique to relax, or reduce anxiety, the student must first identify a special place that he can visualize that is peaceful and calm. It may be a place on a beach, a cabin on a mountain top, a garden, or anything else that he finds to be totally relaxing. The following process should be taught to the student.

To begin with it would be helpful if the student could either draw, or find a picture that shows the scene that is most relaxing for him. The goal is for him to be able to put the picture clearly in his mind. If he doesn't have a picture, or can't draw one, he may want to write down exactly what he would want his scene to look like. The more his scene is like real life, the more powerful it can be. If it is on a beach, he should feel the sand beneath him, the sound of the waves against the shore, the birds, the wind whistling through the palm trees, and the smell of fresh salt water. He should use as many of his senses as he can. When he knows what the scene is suppose to look like he should begin to build it in his mind. When he is finished and can call up the image he is ready to use it as a relaxation strategy.

> **Step One:** Have him get into a comfortable position and begin to use abdominal breathing to settle down.
> **Step Two:** When he starts to feel relaxed, have him visualize the spot he created.
> **Step Three:** Have him stay at his selected scene for as long as he needs to in order for him to totally relax (try for a minimum of 12 minutes).

Deflating Anxiety

Sometimes the student may continue to have problems with stress, anxiety, and panic even after he has used a stress reduction strategy. The following exercises, or suggestions will help him deal with stress that is acute or seems to resist stress reduction strategies.

- First of all, tell the student hat he should not focus on his feelings, especially the physical sensations. The uncomfortable feelings will probably get worse if he does.
- If he is panicking he may be breathing too much oxygen. He needs to reduce his oxygen intake. He should breathe into a bag for a short while until he calms down.
- If he is experiencing a panic attack have him keep saying, "I am ok."
- Have him read something interesting or calming to take his mind off of the anxiety.
- He could count things that are boring, e.g., tiles on the floor, on the ceiling, etc.
- He could play a game that requires his complete attention.
- Have the student repeat memorized information, capitols, states, etc.
- He could go for a walk. Exercise helps reduce panic attacks.

Stress Monitoring

Bipolar children need to monitor their stress, or it can cause tremendous problems for them. In order to reduce stress the student has to be able to identify when he is experiencing stress. Once he is capable of identifying a specific stressor, he must be willing to utilize a stress management technique. The following Stress Monitor form will help the student monitor his stress.

Stress Monitor		
Name: Jarad	**Date:** 1/20	
Rating Scale: 1 = No Stress 2 = Mild Stress 3 = Moderate Stress 4 = Major Stress		
Event	**Level of Stress**	**Method for De-stressing**
Noise and congestion in hallway	3	Sat at desk and did deep breathing
Mark poked me and called me a name	4	Went to safe spot and did 'Positive imagery'
Kids talking in class bothering me	1	Took a breath and refocused on teacher

If needed, copy the Stress Monitor form from the appendices
and have the student complete it as needed.

Anger and Stress

Anger is an extremely devastating and harmful emotion. It can cause untold emotional distress and can also produce physical problems for the individual. Anger untreated in a bipolar student can trigger manic or depressive episodes. As a result, it is imperative that parents, teachers, counselors, etc. identify ways in which anger can be reduced. In his book entitled, *Anger control: The Development and Evaluation of an Experimental Treatment*, Raymond Novaco (1975) extended Stress Inoculation Training to treatment of anger. Novaco states in his book that, "Anger is fomented, maintained, and influenced by the self statements that are made in provocative situations." The underlying assumption is that anger is triggered by the thoughts of the individual.

Anger is exhibited when painful, stressful situations are triggered by our own thoughts. The bipolar child is much more apt to be sensitive when painful, or stressful situations occur. It becomes easy for him to blame others for his pain, to get upset when others do not abide by the rules of society, e.g., class rules and expectations, school rules, law, etc. As a result, it is important to help the student develop tools or strategies that will address anger.

Stress Inoculation Training for Anger

This is an adaptation of Novaco's work. There are five steps to using stress inoculation training to reduce anger. They are:

1. First, the student must learn and master some relaxation techniques.
2. Second, he must identify specific anger issues and rate them in order of significance.
3. Third, he must identify positive thoughts or counters that can help him cope with each area of anger that is problematic.
4. Fourth, he must apply the positive thought or counter using visualization.
5. Last, he needs to practice the counter in real life.

Step One: Master Relaxation Techniques

There are a number of techniques described in this chapter that the student can choose from as he seeks to develop skills to overcome stress. He needs to pick at least two strategies and learn them well. In addition, there are a few short de-stressing techniques that can be used for less stressful situations (see 'Quick Stress Busters'). Below is a list of the stress reduction strategies taught in this chapter.

- Basic Abdominal Breathing
- Mediation for Relaxation and Health
- Quick Relaxation
- Progressive Muscle Relaxation
- Positive Imagery and Relaxation

Step Two: Hierarchy for Anger and Counters

Once the student has chosen two stress management strategies and has learned how to use them, its time for him to identify what makes him angry.

- Using the Anger Reduction Form have the student write down fifteen or more ongoing situations that cause him to experience anger.
- When he is finished, he should rank each anger issue from most angry (1) to least angry (20).
- Identify at least one counter for each anger issue.
- Rate each anger issue on a scale from 1 = no anger to 10 = significant anger.

Possible Counters for Anger

- **Count to Ten:** Before the student acts, he should simply close his eyes (if it is safe to do so) and slowly count to ten.
- **Time Out:** Cooling off is critical to handling anger. The student might want to find a safe place where he can be alone and calm down.
- **Visualize a STOP SIGN:** When he is about to become angry, he might replace his angry thoughts with a large blinking stop sign.
- **Exercise (if you have the opportunity**): He might consider some physical activity, e.g., walking, running, cycling, weightlifting, etc.
- **Deep Breathing:** Anger can be reduced by simply taking a few minutes to do deep breathing.
- **Laugh:** It's hard to be angry and laugh at the same time. Think of something funny, e.g., a joke.
- **Walk Away:** Sometimes it is simply best to walk away and deal with the anger at a later time.
- **Refocus:** In school the student can refocus on something that he should be doing instead of his anger.
- If you have other methods that help you diffuse anger try them out.

Step Three: Use the Counter

After the student has identified his anger issues and the counters that can be used to overcome them, it's time to utilize the whole technique.

- A. Have the student pick one of the relaxation strategies that works best for him. Have him take a few minutes to relax.
- B. While he is in the relaxed state have him visualize the first anger issue he wants to address. He needs to make it as real in him mind as he can. He should see the scene, feel his feelings, hear what the person is saying. When he starts to really feel the anger he should go to the next step.
- C. Block out the image, thoughts, etc and relax again. When he is relaxed he should visualize the situation again. However, this time he should see himself successfully using the counter or coping strategy for that anger situation. He should play the scene over and over using the successful counter for at least a minute. He should feel his anger being reduced as he effectively uses the counter.

D. When he is finished successfully using the counter in his mind he should rate his anger again. 1= no anger up to 10= extremely angry. Hopefully he has reduced his anger compared to the rating he had when he first started. If not, he may need to visualize being successful for additional periods of time until he can reduce the anger to a level that is acceptable. When his anger has been reduced to a 1, 2, or 3 go to the next step. He can come back and work on another anger issue after he has learned to effectively control this particular anger issue.

Step Four: Practice your counter or coping statement in real life

At this step the student should attempt to utilize his coping strategy in real life. If his anger comes back at a level that is overwhelming, he should return to step three and work on the specific anger issue again and again until it no longer produces significant problems in real life.

Anger Reduction				
Name: Jack			**Date:** 2/29	

Instructions:
   1) Write down situations where you experience anger.
   2) Rank the anger experiences from most angry to least angry.
   3) Rate your level of anger on a scale from 1-10 (1= No anger 10 = Rage).
   4) Identify a counter for each anger issue.
   5) Combine a relaxation technique with the counter and use them (chapter 6).
   6) Rate your level of anger using the above scale after you complete step 5.				

Rank	Anger Situations	Initial Anger Rating	Counter	Post Anger Rating
1	When kids push me in the hallway.	7	Time out	3
2	When kids talk loud in class and I can't concentrate.	5	Count to Ten and refocus	2
3	When others call me a name.	8	Walk away and Deep Breathing.	4

If needed, copy the Anger Reduction form from the appendices and have the student complete it.

Social Anxiety and Bipolar Disorder

Social Anxiety Disorder is also known as Social Phobia. Bipolar students often experience social anxiety secondary to their primary issues. Social anxiety disorder is characterized by fear and anxiety in social situations, extreme shyness, and timidity and concerns about being embarrassed in front of others. Studies have found that social anxiety disorder affects up to 5% of children, and is the third most common psychiatric disorder in childhood.

Symptoms of Social Anxiety

There are numerous symptoms that are indicative of this disorder.   Some of the more common symptoms are:

- Avoiding eye contact
- Speaking softly
- Trembling
- Fidgetiness
- Nervousness
- Refusing to speak in front of the class
- Miss school due to headaches, stomachaches or fears

Student Strategies for Social Anxiety

If the student is experiencing social anxiety there are a number of strategies that can be implemented to help handle it on an ongoing basis. Some strategies that the student can use to help with this disorder are:

- He could watch how others are successful in social situations. As he observes others he should write down how they handle various situations. He should also think about how he might attempt some of those things in his life.
- It is important to begin with proactive exercises such as relaxation techniques, deep breathing, meditation, etc. that will help reduce overall stress. This in turn will help him deal with social anxiety.
- He should record times that he is speaking. Using a tape recorder the student can hear what he needs to do to improve his speaking voice and volume. He should periodically review recordings to see how he is improving.
- Use imagery techniques to play out a scenario of the social situation he will be facing. He should see himself being successful.
- When he is going to be in a position where he will have to speak, he should take time to rehearse what he wants to say. He may want to try speaking in front of family or friends for practice.
- When he is practicing his speech, he should take time to practice smiling and making eye contact. These are important skills when he is in social situations.
- Finally, he should focus on his strong points and praise himself when he does things well. He should avoid putting himself down.

Obsessive-Compulsive Disorder and Bipolar Disorder

Another condition that often co-exists with Bipolar Disorder is Obsessive-compulsive disorder. This is also an anxiety based disorder that can trigger manic and depressive cycles when not controlled to some degree. Obsessive-compulsive disorder, or OCD, includes anxious thoughts or rituals that the student believes he can't control. Students who have OCD are often plagued by persistent, unwelcome thoughts or images, or by the urgent need to engage in certain rituals.

For instance, the student may be obsessed with germs or dirt, so he will wash his hands over and over. He may be filled with doubt and feel the need to check things repeatedly. Obsessive-Compulsive students will often spend long periods of time touching things or counting. In addition, they may also become pre-occupied by order or symmetry. Regardless, of the obsessive or compulsive issue, it causes stress and anxiety for the student. Bipolar students do not handle added stressors well. As previously stated, stress can trigger depressive, manic and rage states in bipolar students. As a result, it is imperative that teachers, counselors, parents, etc. do all they can to reduce any OCD issues in a student who has Bipolar Disorder. The following checklist will help you determine if the student has OCD symptoms.

Obsessive-Compulsive Disorder Checklist   Yes   No

Obsessions

1. The student has recurrent and persistent thoughts, impulses, or   ____ ____
images that are intrusive and inappropriate and that cause marked anxiety.
2. The student has thoughts, impulses, or images that are not   ____ ____
simply excessive worries about real-life problems.
3. The student unsuccessfully attempts to ignore or suppress such   ____ ____
thoughts, impulses, or images.
4. The student recognizes that the obsessional thoughts, impulses,   ____ ____
or images are a product of his own mind.

or   Compulsions

1. The student has repetitive behaviors (e.g., hand washing,   ____ ____
ordering, checking) or mental acts (e.g., praying, counting, repeating words silently) that he feels driven to perform in response to an obsession, or according to rules that must be applied rigidly.
2. The student's behaviors or mental acts are aimed at preventing   ____ ____
or reducing distress or preventing some dreaded event or situation; however, these behaviors or mental acts either are not connected in a realistic way with what they are designed to neutralize or prevent, or are clearly excessive.
3. The student has recognized that the obsessions or compulsions   ____ ____
are excessive or unreasonable. **Note:** This does not apply to children.

4. The student realizes that the obsessions or compulsions cause   ____ ____
marked distress, are time consuming (take more than 1 hour a day), or significantly interfere with his normal routine, or academic functioning, or usual social activities or relationships.

If you answer yes to some of the above symptoms the student may have Obsessive-Compulsive Disorder. Adapted from the Diagnostic and Statistical Book of Mental Disorders IV – TR. Copyright 2000, American Psychiatric Association.

Agreement to Heal

If the student does in fact have Obsessive-compulsive disorder issues it is important for him to want to get better. He must also be willing to do what ever it takes to reduce the obsessive or compulsive issues that are stressing his life. The following is a list of things that the student should keep in mind as he seeks to address his OCD issues. You may want to share these guidelines with the student (see appendices for a copy you can give student).

- You must commit to doing what it takes to overcome OCD issues. That means you must be willing to be uncomfortable to get better. When you practice exposure and ritual prevention exercises it will be easy to say, "That's too hard." "I can't do that." It will be uncomfortable! It will be difficult! However, if you continue to press forward and use the techniques you will gradually reduce your obsessive and compulsive tendencies. Commit to doing what it takes to get better.
- Don't be afraid to get angry at the specific OCD issue. Give it a name....specifically, give it a funny name that is as powerless as you can make it, e.g., Dumbo, Dizzy, Toto, Diddles, or Bugger. When the specific OCD issue starts to cause a problem for you call it by name...tell it you are angry with it and don't want to play.
- When confronted with a compulsion, make a distinction between behaviors that, 1) are probably not harmful or dangerous to you, or 2) are probably harmful or dangerous to you. Touching a doorknob and not washing your hands is probably not a harmful or dangerous activity. However, counting signposts while you drive (ride a bike) could be potentially dangerous. You need to get a handle on these potentially dangerous compulsions first.
- Don't go into an avoidant mode. Any avoidance you use to deal with your OCD will simply make it worse. Utilize ERP (Exposure, and Ritual Prevention) techniques as part of your day to address OCD issues.

Obsessive-Compulsive Disorder in School

The following characteristics can often be found in students who are exhibiting Obsessive-Compulsive disorder in the school setting.

- The student may have fatigue and drowsiness due to lack of sleep. He may be exhausted from completing rituals that he must go through every night. NOTE: If the student is Bipolar and in a manic state he will not be fatigued or drowsy.
- The student may develop odd behaviors or rituals. For example he may counting tiles on the ceiling or floor, walking in specific patterns through doorways, touch or tap certain things in a certain order, or sit and stand repeatedly. The student will have more distress and frustration than normal when things are disorganized.

- The student appears to develop an uncharacteristic sloppiness or carelessness in completing his homework and classroom assignments, e.g., lots of erasures, mark overs, etc.
- The student may use tissues, books, elbows to open doors or lockers. He will avoid any physical contact that is not 'protected'. He may refuse to shake hands or share materials as a result of contamination fears. If he does touch anyone or anything he may be compelled to go wash his hands as soon as possible.
- The student counts or focuses on lucky and unlucky numbers.
- The student may appear to be perfectionistic. He sets extremely high standards that are often impossible to meet.
- The student is extremely focused on making sure that his things are neat and tidy. Everything must be in the right place or he will have to 'fix' it. Even so, he may repeatedly rearrange his environment to make sure it is in 'proper order'.
- The student appears overly distressed when there is a change in routine or when seemingly minor activities are interrupted.
- The student has a sudden avoidance of familiar things. He may develop significant fear of harm, death or contamination.
- He may also try to convince peers that they should also avoid situations, things, etc. that are not always rationally connected to his fears.
- The student may become very slow, deliberate or perfectionisic in his work. As a result, he may have many incomplete assignments.
- The student appears to have an inability to activate to or complete tasks. What may be normally and clearly within the students area of ability are not completed due to repetitive rituals such as re-reading, counting or checking.
- The student frequently checks his day timer, book bag, pockets, under his desk or chair to make sure he has his things.

If a student is exhibiting a number of these symptoms or characteristics it is highly suggestive that he may indeed have obsessive-compulsive disorder.

Obsessive-Compulsive Traits that Parents Can Look For

Parents also need watch to see if their child is exhibiting traits or characteristics of OCD. Once identified, treatment and modifications can be implemented both at home and school. Here are some common symptoms that may be found at home if a child has OCD.

- Being overly concerned about germs and dirt
- Raw, chapped hands from constant washing
- Unusually high rate of soap or paper towel usage
- A sudden drop in test grades
- Unproductive hours spent doing homework
- Holes erased through test papers and homework
- Needs phrases to be repeated
- Answers a question multiple times
- A persistent fear of illness
- Insistence on having things in certain order or symmetry
- A dramatic increase in laundry
- Exceptionally long amount of time spent getting ready for bed (rituals)

- Continual fears that something terrible will happen to someone
- Constant checks of the health of family members
- Reluctance to leave the house at the same time as other family members
- Rituals that are repeated over and over (touching things a certain amount of times, having a certain place to sit, getting out of a chair a certain way, etc.)

> *It cannot be determined that a student has this disorder simply because he exhibits a few traits or characteristics. Check with a doctor or mental health professional if you are concerned that the student may be experiencing obsessive-compulsive disorder.*

Breaking Free of Pure Obsessions

If in fact the student does have obsessive-compulsive disorder, there are numerous techniques that can be used to help him effectively cope. However, before you can help him address any specific obsessions, he must be able to identify the obsessive thoughts. Have the student write down his obsessive thoughts on the Identifying Obsessive Thoughts form. Below is an example of how the form might be used. Each thought should be rated based on its severity: Have him rate each thought on a 1- 5 scale based on how problematic it is on a daily basis. 1 = Minor Irritant 5 = Dangerous Thought/Possible Serious Problems.

Identifying Obsessive Thoughts					
Name: *Mary* **Date:** *1/20*					
Rating Scale: 1 = Minor Irritant 2 = Periodically Causes Problems 3 = Causes Moderate Problems 4 = Causes Significant Problems 5 = Dangerous Thought/Possible Serious Problems					
1. *Saw a sign post while driving and was compelled to count them.*	1	2	3	4	**5**
2. *I must keep various personal items in certain order.*	1	**2**	3	4	5
3. *I must wash my hands each time I open a door with my hand.*	1	2	**3**	4	5
4. *I find myself counting tiles on the ceiling when I am upset.*	1	**2**	3	4	5

If needed, copy the Identifying Obsessive Thoughts form from the appendices and have the student complete it.

Identifying Obsessive Thoughts

Once the student has identified the obsessive thoughts that are causing difficulties for him he is ready to evaluate how each obsession might cause him to exhibit compulsive behaviors. The following technique is both straightforward and practical. There are four steps to this technique. They are:

1. Evaluate each obsessive thought.
2. Thought vs Action: Is this obsessive thought something you would act on?
3. Accept the thought.
4. Utilize an exposure exercise.

Obsessive Thoughts

Name: *Jesse*   **Date:** *1/20*

Step One: Evaluate Obsessive Thought
Identify the specific thought. Was there an antecedent? List the coping strategies that you use to avoid thinking about this specific thought.

Obsessive thought	Antecedent	Coping Strategy
Need to count sign posts. This is dangerous	*Saw a sign post while driving and was compelled to count them.*	*Self-Talk Strategy*

Step Two: Thought vs Action
Rate how much you believe that you would actually act on this particular obsessive thought. 1 = would not act on it   5 = would act on it almost every time.

1	2	3	4	5̶

Step Three: Accept the thought knowing that you usually won't act on it.
If this obsession is one that would cause you to exhibit a compulsive act and it is troublesome to you go to step four (anything rated a 4 or 5). If it is merely a thought that rarely produces problems for you (anything rated 1 or 2), pick another obsessive thought and evaluate it. If you rated the obsession a three you have to decide if it is problematic enough to go to step four.

Step Four: Confront the thought and do exposure exercises to habituate to the thought.

The goal of exposure exercises is meant to help you accept the thought in your mind without it causing discomfort or triggering you to a compulsive action. Chances are you will not get rid of the unwanted thought. However, you can learn to control it. Here are a few Exposure Exercises that may be helpful.

1. Imaging, Exposure and Response Prevention Technique
2. Verbal Exposure and Response Prevention Technique
3. Taped Exposure and Response Prevention Technique
4. Written Exposure and Response Prevention Technique

*If needed, copy the Obsessive Thoughts form from the appendices
and have the student complete it.*

Step one calls for the student to evaluate each obsessive thought that is troubling him. Once he decides which though he wants to focus on he should, 1) write down the obsessive thought to be addressed, 2) attempt to identify the antecedent (something that happened just prior to the thought), and 3) list a coping strategy that could be used to control that particular obsessive thought (see 'Quick Strategies for OCD'), or utilize another coping strategy that would help deal with the obsession.

Step two calls for the student to determine if this thought is something that he would be compelled to act on. If it is, the remainder of the form should be completed. If not, the student may want to select another thought that is more problematic.

Step three calls for the student to evaluate the thought. If it is merely a thought that rarely produces problems or compulsive behaviors (anything rated 1 or 2), he should pick another obsessive thought and evaluate it. If he rated the obsession a three, he would have to decide if it is problematic enough to go to step four. If this obsession is one that would cause him to exhibit a compulsive act and it is troublesome or dangerous for him, he should go to step four (anything rated a 4 or 5).

In step four the student must confront the thought and do exposure exercises so that he can habituate to the thought. The goal of exposure exercises is to help him accept the thought in his mind without it causing discomfort, or triggering him to a compulsive action. Chances are he will not get rid of the unwanted thought. However, he may learn to better control the thought and ultimately the compulsive behavior.

Exposure and Response Prevention Techniques (ERP)

Exposure and Ritual Prevention is one of the more powerful methods used to effectively deal with obsessive-compulsive issues. It can be used in a variety of ways. Usually this method consists of the following:

1) Exposure to feared stimuli (as identified by the student's obsessive thoughts) which increases anxiety and provokes the compulsion, and;
2) Response prevention which focuses on prevention of the compulsive response.

- Step One: The student is deliberately and voluntarily exposed to the feared object or idea, either directly or by imagination.
- Step Two: The student is discouraged or prevented from carrying out the usual compulsive response, e.g. a compulsive hand washer may be urged to touch an object believed to be contaminated, and then may be denied the opportunity to wash for several hours. Another option is to ask the child to delay the compulsive response for a short period of time. The time is increased as he is successful.

If you are focusing on pure obsessions you may only do step one in this process. Here are a few Exposure Exercises that may be helpful.

- Written Exposure and Response Prevention Technique
- Image Exposure and Response Prevention Technique
- Taped Exposure and Response Prevention Technique

Written Exposure and Response Prevention Technique

Some people journal to deal with feelings, pain, problems, etc. This can also be used for dealing with obsessive issues. Have the student follow the following simple steps to address specific obsessive thoughts.

- Step One: Have the student identify a specific obsessive-compulsive ritual or behavior from the list he has compiled (see Identifying Obsessive Thoughts form in appendix).

- Step Two: Have the student write about a five minute narrative in the first person describing the event and the feelings it produces.

- Step Three: When he is finished writing about the event, have him describe the fears and/or anxiety he is experiencing as he battles with the obsessive thought. If he does not have any fears or anxiety as he is writing, this technique will not work.

- Step Four: Have the student write the event a few times each day until the obsessive thought is no longer overwhelming to him.

Image Exposure and Response Prevention Technique

Imaging is one of the most powerful tools that can be used to reduce or change behavior. It can be effectively utilized with the Exposure & Ritual Prevention technique. This is a great homework exercise, especially for students that are very image based. This imaging exercise must be used on a daily basis to be effective.

- Step One: Have the student identify a specific obsessive-compulsive ritual or behavior from the list he has compiled (see Identifying Obsessive Thoughts Form in appendix).

- Step Two: Help the student write about a five minute narrative in the first person describing what would happen if he did not check, or exhibit the behavior or ritual.

- Step Three: Have the student visualize the event just as he wrote it, as if it were actually happening. It must be as real as possible. The first time the student visualizes the scene have him describe it in detail as he builds the pictures in his mind. When he has it, the images should produce some significant fear and anxiety as he battles with the obsessive thought. If not, this technique will not work.

- Step Four: Have the student visualize the situation at least twice a day—run through the visualization at least three or four times in each session if you are working with him one- on-one.

Taped Exposure and Response Prevention Technique

This is an adaptation of the Exposure & Response Prevention technique mentioned above. It is used with students who are more auditory in nature. It is used in the same way with only minor modifications.

- Step One: Have the student identify a specific obsessive-compulsive ritual or behavior from the list he has compiled (see Identifying Obsessive Thoughts Form in appendix).

- Step Two: Have the student write about a five minute narrative in the first person describing the event and the feelings it produces.

- Step Three: Have him record this narrative onto an audio tape or digital recorder. He may want to say it over and over until he has at least fifteen minutes of tape.

- Step Four: Have the student listen the event, as if it were actually happening. It must be as real as possible. The first time the student listens have him describe the fears and/or anxiety he is experiencing as he battles with the obsessive thought. If he does not have any fears or anxiety, this technique will not work.

- Step Five: Have the student listen to the recording at least twice a day—run through the recording at least three or four times in each session if you are working with him one- on-one.

> *The goal is to cause the student's mind to habituate to the situation to the point that it no longer evokes excessive discomfort. The more fear provoking the visualization can be, the greater the ultimate success.*

PANDIS: Pediatric Autoimmune Neuro-psychiatric Disorder Associated with Streptococci

A word of warning! In at least one case obsessive-compulsive disorder can be avoided or gotten rid of. Some children develop obsessive-compulsive disorder as a result of, or in association with streptococci infections. The following information is important in dealing with this form of obsessive-compulsive disorder (Swedo, 1998).

- Recent research suggests that some children with OCD may develop this condition after experiencing one type of streptococcal infection.

- This condition is referred to by the acronym PANDAS, which stands for Pediatric Autoimmune Neuropsychiatric Disorders Associated with Streptococcal infections.
- Its hallmark is a sudden and abrupt exacerbation of OCD symptoms after a strep infection. This form of OCD occurs when the immune system generates antibodies to the streptococcal bacteria, and the antibodies cross-react with the basal ganglia of a susceptible child, provoking OCD (Garvey, 1998).
- In other words, the cause of this form of OCD appears to be antibodies directed against the infection mistakenly attacking a region of the brain and setting off an inflammatory reaction.

It is very important to get medical treatment if there is a sudden onset, or worsening of OCD symptoms after a student has had (or is having) an upper respiratory problem (strep infection). This disorder can be treated if caught in time.

Quick Strategies for OCD

There are many quick strategies that can help control OCD tendencies. The following are just a few simple methods that the student may want to try as he attempts to control his OCD either at home or at school. These are strategies for the student to use.

- **Self-Talk Strategy:** When an obsessive thought enters your mind immediately yell, 'Stop' to yourself. Find a positive statement that counters the thought. For instance, Instead of, "I need to check to see if I locked the door again." Positive Response: Say "I know checked the door!", over and over as you walk away.

- **Visualization Technique:** Identify a behavior that you feel compelled to check over and over. Let's look at locking the door again. When you leave your home and as you lock the door say to yourself, "I am locking the door." After you lock the door, pause for a moment to do the visualization technique. In your mind see yourself locking the door, putting the key in the lock, turning it, pulling it out and checking that it is locked. When you are finished with the visualization check the door again and say to yourself, "I have checked it and the door is locked." You can use this technique with many OCD issues.

- **Exaggerated Humor Technique:** Deliberately increase the frequency or intensity of the obsessive thought. Visualize it in an exaggerated and humorous way.

- **What If Thinking Strategy:** If you are afraid of something happening simply ask yourself, "What is the worst thing that can happen if I don't check this?"

OCD Strategies for Home

This book is not intended to be a complete work on OCD or any other disorder other than Bipolar disorder and how it negatively influences a student's ability to learn. However, there are some simple strategies that should be considered by parents that can help these children with academics.

- Schedule your child's homework. There should be a time set aside each evening to do homework. Even if he doesn't have homework, have him work on something educational for a short period of time (it doesn't have to be a long period of time). Building consistency is important.
- Don't let your child get involved with something else that cannot be finished before it is time for homework. The bipolar child will often want to finish what he starts, especially if he also has OCD.
- The OCD student should have a special location where he does his homework. It should have good lighting, materials needed for homework, etc. If he cannot work in the same area, have supplies in a box that can be carried to the alternate location.
- Model learning for your child when he is doing homework. Turn off the TV and read a book, or work with other children using educational games.
- Structure and routine are important for the OCD child. When structure or routines are changed or not followed, OCD behaviors can become more severe.
- Try to schedule his days so that they are similar. Wake up time, dinner time, homework time, and bedtime should be at the same time each day. You may want to put a visual schedule on a board or refrigerator that shows when things are supposed to happen during the day.
- If there are changes in routine or schedule, let the child know in advance how it is changing. Preferably make a visual schedule for that day showing the differences. Do this at least a day in advance where possible and remind him on multiple occasions that the day will be different. The reason for this is that the bipolar and OCD child does not handle change well. When change occurs is causes stress. Any child who has co-existing conditions of Bipolar Disorder and OCD need to have stress minimized as much as possible.
- Set specific family rules, i.e., "Homework before play." "Room cleaned before TV."
- If inappropriate behavior is not a result of the disability the child must be disciplined. If he isn't, he will learn how to manipulate the home and school.
- Even if the behavior is OCD related, there will be times that he can control it. Identify a signal that you can use to let your child know he is being a bit compulsive. It won't always work, but it will help him learn to work on the behavior.

Classroom Strategies for OCD

Here is a list of proactive methods that might be used in the school that could help the obsessive-compulsive student cope more efficiently.

- Educate the student's peers about OCD.
- Be attentive to changes in the student's behavior.
- Develop an understanding of the purpose or function of the student's behaviors.
- Try to redirect the student's behavior. This works better than using "negative consequences."
- Utilization of the counselor to work on some aspects of his OCD that are specifically related to education would be beneficial.

- Use a visual schedule to help the student sense structure. This is extremely important for an OCD student.
- Don't change the schedule unless you communicate it to the OCD student in advance.
- Use a stress management strategy daily to reduce the general level of overall stress. This may need to be done in the counselor's office, or another safe place.

Modifications

- Allow the student to do assignments such as "oral reports" in place of writing...may also consider using computers for written work.
- Allow the student to turn in late work for full credit.
- Allow the student to redo assignments to improve scores or final grades.
- Post a daily schedule in a highly visible place so the students will know what to expect on a daily basis.

Post Traumatic Stress Disorder and Bipolar Disorder

Post Traumatic Stress Disorder occurs when a student experiences a trauma that is so significant that it fails to be resolved. As a result, it persists to trigger reactions for at least 6 months after the event. These events can be as simple as mom and dad yelling at each other at a critical time, a car accident, gunfire, watching television and seeing a plane explode or the results of a plane crash, and any other traumatic event that happens on a daily or weekly basis.

PTSD flashbacks are memories of past events that intrude into the current state of mind in a way that is nearly as real as the initial event. These events may be played back in detail, or may be vague and difficult to identify. Usually flashbacks cannot be predicted. Obviously, these PTSD flashbacks are especially traumatic for bipolar students.

It is important to identify the PTSD issues so that the counselor (school or private) can work on desensitizing him to each PTSD that he may have. These issues are not effectively dealt with in the classroom. They usually require one-on-one help. If not dealt with, the PTSD issues can continue to exacerbate the bipolar issues. It is important that school counselors and staff be aware of potential PTSD issues with children. Studies have provided much insight regarding PTSD. Results of some of these studies are listed below.

- According to studies, 15 to 43% of girls and 14 to 43% of boys have experienced at least one traumatic event in their lifetime. Of those who have experienced a trauma, 3 to 15% of girls and 1 to 6% of boys could be diagnosed with PTSD.
- Post-Traumatic Stress Disorder, PTSD, is an anxiety disorder that can develop after exposure to a terrifying event or ordeal in which grave physical harm occurred or was threatened.
- The triggering of a PTSD may also trigger a mood state in bipolar students.
- Children and adolescents may experience PTSD as a result of natural disasters, man made disasters, motor vehicle accidents, plane crashes, severe burns, violent crimes such as kidnapping, rape or murder of a parent, sniper fire and

school shootings, exposure to community violence, peer suicide, and sexual and physical assault.

- Children have a tendency to act out their flashbacks rather than verbally communicate what happened.
- Children will also communicate what happened to them by doing the same thing to others.

The following is a list of some of the symptoms or characteristics of PTSD. If the student has experienced some of these symptoms or characteristics during a two week period of time you may want to complete this quick checklist to see if he meets any of the criteria for PTSD.

> *Children have a tendency to act out their flashbacks rather than verbally communicate what happened.*

Post Traumatic Stress Disorder Checklist   Yes   No

1. The student has experienced, witnessed, or was confronted with an event or events that involved actual or threatened death or serious injury, or a threat to the physical integrity of self or others.   ____ ____

2. The student's response to the event involved intense fear, helplessness, or horror. **Note:** In children, this may be expressed as disorganized or agitated behavior.   ____ ____

3. The student has recurrent and intrusive distressing recollections of the event, including images, thoughts, or perceptions. **Note:** In young children, repetitive play may occur in which themes or aspects of the trauma are expressed.   ____ ____

4. The student has recurrent distressing dreams of the event. **Note:** In children, there may be frightening dreams without recognizable content.   ____ ____

5. The student acts or feels as if the traumatic event were recurring (includes a sense of reliving the experience, illusions, hallucinations, and dissociative flashback, including those that occur on awakening or when intoxicated). **Note:** In young children, trauma-specific reenactment may occur.   ____ ____

6. The student exhibits intense psychological distress when exposed to internal or external cues that symbolize or resemble an aspect of the traumatic event.   ____ ____

7. The student has a physical reaction when exposed to internal or external cues that symbolize or resemble an aspect of the traumatic event.   ____ ____

8. The student attempts to avoid thoughts, feelings, conversations, activities, places or people associated with the trauma.   ____ ____

9. The student may not be able to recall an important aspect of the   ____ ____
    trauma.
10. The student feels detached or estranged from others.   ____ ____
11. The student has a restricted range of affect, e.g., unable to have   ____ ____
    loving feelings.
12. The student has a sense of a foreshortened future, e.g., does not   ____ ____
    expect to have a career, marriage, children, or a normal life span.
13. The student has persistent symptoms of increased arousal (not   ____ ____
    present before the trauma), e.g., difficulty falling or staying asleep,
    irritability or outbursts or anger, difficulty concentrating, hyper-
    vigilance or exaggerated startle response.

If you answer yes to some of the above symptoms the student may have Post Traumatic Stress Syndrome. Adapted from the Diagnostic and Statistical Book of Mental Disorders IV – TR. Copyright 2000, American Psychiatric Association.

Factors that Trigger PTSD

Williams and Poijula (2002), have identified three types of factors that can trigger or influence PTSD. For more detailed descriptions of each type of factor see Williams and Poijula's work. There are three factors that impact PTSD. They are:

- Pre-event Factors
- Event Factors
- Post Event Factors

Pre-event Factors

There are factors that happen prior to the traumatic event that makes a person more susceptible to developing PSTD. Even so, there are times that the traumatic event is so significant that pre-events may not play much of a role. Here are some pre-events that may make a student more apt to develop PTSD.

- Previous exposure to severe adverse life events or trauma
- Earlier depression, or anxiety that impacts brain chemistry
- Ineffective coping skills
- Multiple early losses of people, possessions, home, etc.

Event Factors

Event factors specifically relate to the student at the time of the trauma. If he is at the center of the event, close to the event or involved with the event in some way, he would have a greater possibility of developing PTSD. So, if the event happens at school, happens to him, involves someone he knows or is associated with, or if the event impacts a group of people he is associated with, it may have a significant impact on him. Some event factors for PTSD may be:

- Geographic nearness to the event
- Level of exposure to the event
- Duration of trauma

Post Event Factors

Post even factors occur after the event and can contribute to ongoing issues with PTSD. If the student does not get the support he needs, is not able to do anything about the event or help those involved, or if he simply lets things happen around him without taking any action it may make it more difficult for him to deal with, or resolve any PTSD issues that may have been internalized. Some post event factors for PTSD may be:

- The absence of good social support
- Not being able to do something about what happened
- Being passive rather than active, e.g., he lets things happen to him

In addition to Williams and Poijula's book, information may be found in Meichenbaum's book, A Clinical Handbook/Practical Therapist Manual (1994), that discusses these various factors in greater detail.

Psycho-education and PTSD

One of the methods used to treat PTSD issues is psycho-education. This calls for the student to be able to accurately remember the event so that he can safely deposit it in his past where it can no longer cause difficulties. A bipolar student is already sensitive. If he is experiencing PTSD, it is very easy for him to be triggered into depression, mania or a rage state. Many of the techniques already discussed in this chapter can help control the stress brought on by PTSD, or place it in the past where it belongs. Relaxation exercises, can help reduce the overall stress resulting from traumatic events, while Exposure and Response Prevention Techniques (often used for OCD issues) can help the student process the memories in order to put them in perspective, and keep them from triggering traumatic anxiety responses. The following strategies can help a student deal with issues resulting from PTSD. The student could:

- Use relaxation exercises to reduce overall stress and the stress produced from PTSD issues.
- Use Exposure and Response Prevention Techniques to reduce the effect of PTSD.
- Use Journaling to address PTSD Issues. Have him write about what happened without trying to put things in order or make sense. Tell him to just let the words flow and see what comes out. Pennebaker (1977) stated that journaling about experiences that are upsetting can in fact help reduce or rid the person of PTSD issues.
- Use specific strategies that help stop flashbacks (Williams & Poijula, 2002). Not all will work for everyone. The student should try various strategies until he finds a few that works well for him. Here are some examples:

- Repeatedly blink your eyes hard.
- Use deep breathing…focus on the air as it goes in and out of your body.
- Clap your hands or stamp your feet on the floor.
- Wash your face with cold water.
- Say positive statements about yourself.

If the student can force his mind to focus on something else, he will have a chance of stopping the flashbacks from occurring or causing problems.

PTSD and Elementary Aged Children

Clinical reports suggest that children may not experience visual flashbacks, or amnesia regarding many aspects of the trauma. Studies do suggest that elementary aged children experience:

- **Time Skew:** Some children may have difficulty properly sequencing trauma related events when attempting to recall what happed from memory.

- **Omen Formation**: An omen is a belief that warning signs occur prior to the trauma that actually predicts that it may occur. Because of this, the child who has PTSD will often believe that if he is alert enough, he will recognize warning signs. As a result, he may be able to avoid future traumas.

- **Post Traumatic Play:** Elementary children also have a tendency to exhibit posttraumatic play of the trauma utilizing play, drawings, or verbalizations. Posttraumatic play is a literal representation of the trauma. It actually involves the need to compulsively repeat some aspect of the trauma over and over and does not seem to provide a relief from anxiety.

PTSD and Adolescents

Adolescents respond to PTSD much like adults. Some of the most predominant characteristics found in adolescents are as follows:

- Adolescents are more likely to engage in traumatic reenactment, in which they incorporate aspects of the trauma into their daily lives.
- Adolescents are more likely than younger children or adults to exhibit impulsive and aggressive behaviors as a result of the PTSD.

Coping with PTSD

When a child experiences trauma, whether it produces post traumatic stress issues or not, it is important that he know how to deal with it. Trauma not addressed can cause ongoing anxiety. Here are some things that a student can do to help deal with trauma as it occurs.

- Sleep at least 8 hours a night
- Stick to his daily routine
- Eat healthy and exercise daily
- Take time to relax and do something that is calming and peaceful
- Cut back on unnecessary tasks
- Reduce overall stress
- Time with family and friends who are supportive
- Talk to someone trustworthy about feelings and fears
- Work through the feelings…don't hold them inside
- Get support and help from church, friends, or community resources

Attempting all the above is not necessary. However, it is essential that the student do some things that will help him deal with trauma. If the trauma turned into a PTSD these strategies will help the student reduce overall stress which in turn will help him get a handle on the symptoms of PTSD.

Treating PTSD in Children and Adolescents

Although some children show a natural remission in PTSD symptoms over a period of a few months, a significant number of children continue to exhibit symptoms for years if untreated. The following points suggest what needs to be done to help these children.

- Even though research is scant, it appears that Cognitive-Behavioral Therapy (CBT) is the most effective approach when working with children and adolescents.
- CBT for children will often include having the child discuss the traumatic event. For children or adolescents this is best when coupled with relaxation exercises in order to help keep them calm.
- For children who are not able to deal with the trauma directly you may want to consider utilizing play therapy.
- Stress/Anxiety management techniques have been proven to be helpful.
- Psycho-education about PTSD symptoms and their effects is also beneficial and should be taught with both the child and the parents present.
- Research shows that the better parents cope with the trauma, and the more they support their children, the better their children will function.
- Use Exposure and Response Prevention Techniques to help minimize or get rid of PTSD issues.
- Utilize the strategies for flashbacks to help deal with immediate issues produced by PTSD.

Additional Co-existing Disorders & Bipolar Disorder

Chapter Seven

As previously stated, having a co-existing condition simply means that the student may have more than one disorder occurring at the same time. If the student has Bipolar Disorder he may very well have other disorders. He may have ADHD, various anxiety disorders as discussed in the previous chapters, or any of the disorders listed in this chapter. Each of these conditions can complicate Bipolar Disorder. Studies have actually found that the severity of psychiatric disorders, specifically bipolar disorder, is strongly related to comorbidity or co-existing conditions (Kessler, 2005).

It would be extremely difficult to include all of the possible co-existing disorders and identify strategies to deal with each. However, in addition to ADHD and Anxiety issues there are some additional co-existing conditions that often cause problems in a school environment. The specific co-existing conditions that are addressed in this chapter are:

- Conduct Disorder
- Oppositional Defiant Disorder
- Psychosis or Delusional Thinking
- Substance Abuse

Bipolar disorder is a condition that is biological in nature. Actually, recent studies have identified a gene that may play a role in the disorder. Regardless, it is biologically based. Conduct Disorder and Oppositional Defiant Disorder, on the other hand, is a result of choice. There are two specific characteristics that distinguish Conduct Disorder and Oppositional Defiant Disorder from Bipolar Disorder.

Comparing ODD/CD and Bipolar Disorder

It is important to be able to identify if a student has co-existing Oppositional Defiant Disorder (ODD) or Conduct Disorder (CD) in addition to Bipolar Disorder. Individuals with ODD or CD have a problem with being socially maladjusted. Basically, what this means is that they do not appear to be bound by social rules, regulations, etc. They do what they want to obtain what they desire, and don't particularly like it when someone gets in their way. They choose to behave inappropriately. They choose to be oppositional or hurt people if they can't get what they want. When combined with Bipolar Disorder, this condition can be very dangerous. A bipolar student who is manic and has no controls could easily hurt others even if he is not in a rage state. The chart listed below shows some basic differences between ODD/CD and Bipolar Disorder.

Comparing ODD/CD and Bipolar Disorder	
Conduct Disorder (CD) or Oppositional Defiant (ODD)	**Bipolar Disorder**
When CD or ODD students do something wrong, they do so with no guilt...no remorse.	Bipolar students will feel guilt and remorse for no apparent reason. They may not be able to communicate it when they are in a hypomanic or manic state, but in most cases the guilty feelings are there.
CD or ODD students are sometimes paranoid for good reason....they have said/done something wrong and don't want to get caught.	Bipolar students feel paranoia at times. However, it is not a result of being 'guilty' as much as it is a distortion of perception.

Currently, the research shows that in many respects, conduct disorder is a more severe form of oppositional defiant disorder. Severe oppositional defiant disorder can lead to conduct disorder. Milder oppositional defiant disorder usually does not. The common thread that separates conduct disorder and oppositional defiant disorder is safety. If a child has conduct disorder there are safety concerns. Sometimes it is the personal safety of others in the school, family, or community. Sometimes it is the safety of the possessions of other people in the school, family or community. Often the safety of the child with conduct disorder is a great concern.

> *The common thread that separates CD and ODD is safety. If a child has CD there are safety concerns.*

114

Oppositional Defiant Disorder

Oppositional defiant disorder occurs when the student loses his temper, argues with adults, actively defies or refuses to comply with adult's requests or rules and basically exhibits non-compliant behavior. To be diagnosed, the student must exhibit a pattern of negativistic, hostile, and defiant behavior lasting at least 6 months.

Oppositional Defiant Disorder Checklist

		Yes	No
1.	The student often loses his temper.	___	___
2.	The student often argues with adults.	___	___
3.	The student often actively defies or refuses to comply with adult's requests or rules.	___	___
4.	The student often deliberately annoys people.	___	___
5.	The student often blames others for his mistakes or misbehavior.	___	___
6.	The student is often touchy or easily annoyed by others.	___	___
7.	The student is often angry and resentful.	___	___
8.	The student is often spiteful or vindictive	___	___

If you checked yes to some of the above symptoms the student may have Oppositional Defiant Disorder. Adapted from the Diagnostic and Statistical Book of Mental Disorders IV – TR. Copyright 2000, American Psychiatric Association.

Educational Strategies for Oppositional Defiant Disorder

It is extremely difficult to deal with ODD and CD in an educational environment. These students have a tendency to find and push buttons on everyone, including teachers, counselors, and administration. They will often require specific strategies and lots of structure, if educators are to successfully handle them. The strategies listed below may be helpful for an ODD student:

- Use subtle reinforcements. Put a positive note in a returned test, paper, etc. Be inventive about where you could put it.
- An ODD student needs structure. When the structure is not appropriate an ODD student will become symptomatic.
- Avoid sharply worded verbal directives, e.g., "Johnny, turn around a pay attention!" It will embarrass him and he will have to save face by getting back at you.
- Avoid Gestures, facial grimaces, or body language that suggests disapproval. The ODD student may take the gestures wrong and react to them.
- Use a visual cue, e.g., a picture card that denotes a particular activity that tells the student what needs to be done next. Structured teaching works well for children with ODD, particularly those at the preschool and primary level because

it moves them through work tasks without requiring the teacher to give a verbal directive. Verbal directives given in front of peers is a common antecedent for noncompliance.

- A student with ODD will have difficulty with change. When an ODD student is suddenly (at least from his perspective) told to stop a task, he may not cope well with the unanticipated request. He needs a cue that will prepare him for any transition he may be facing.
- Let the student know that there will be a consequence for each violation. The consequence does not have to be major or last a long time. If he breaks a rule there is a consequence.
- No Second Chances. If a rule has been broken a consequence must be given. No discussion!
- Speak softly when you pass the student. He should be the only one who can hear what you say.
- Consider independent work if he has less difficulties when working alone.
- Clearly communicate the rules, procedures, daily schedule, and how activities are structured.
- Decide if the defiance is momentary. Many ODD students will comply after an initial outburst if given a moment's time. Regardless, if this student needs to learn to control his temper and express himself more appropriately.
- If the student has offended or negatively affected others he should be required to make a fair restitution. Once he has, the issue should be closed and not discussed again. Just an apology is not enough, although it should be part of the restitution.
- Communication with an ODD student must not be emotional when you are correcting him.
- Do not try to change the student's behavior by rationally explaining what is appropriate. Your communication must be strategy based. This was your behavior...this is the consequence.
- When you give a directive, the student should be given a choice between two acceptable alternatives whenever possible.
- The more energy you put into a consequence the less effective it becomes. Your energy must be seen when the student is exhibiting appropriate behavior...not inappropriate.

Conduct Disorder

As previously stated, Conduct Disorder may be seen as a more severe form of oppositional defiant disorder. Conduct Disorder occurs when the student goes beyond verbal abuse, yelling, screaming, threatening, etc. and begins to actually hit, kick, or hurt other people, animals, or destroy property. The following research gives additional information regarding Bipolar Disorder and Conduct Disorder.

- Conduct Disorder occurs in approximately 22% of bipolar children (Geller, 1995).
- Conduct Disorder occurs in approximately 18% of bipolar adolescents (Geller, 1995).
- In a study of bipolar youths Kovacs (1995) found that 69% had co-existing problems with Conduct Disorder at some time in their life.

116

- Conduct Disorder may be an initial manifestation of prepubertal-onset Bipolar Disorder according to Geller (1997).
- Co-existing Conduct Disorders appear related to poor judgment and grandiosity. As an example, a 10 year-old child stole a dirt bike that was worth several hundred dollars. He did not appear to be concerned at all when the police appeared and tried to explain the possible consequences.
- During adolescence conduct disorder can be exhibited by running away and having sexual flirtations, stealing money, jewelry, or other expensive items, and driving under the influence. All the above can and do place these students in legal jeopardy.

> *In a study of Bipolar youths Kovacs found that 69% had co-existing problems with Conduct Disorder at some time in their life.*

Conduct disorder may be defined as a repetitive and persistent pattern of behavior where the basic rights of others are violated. At least three or more of the criteria listed below must have been evidenced over the past 12 months, with at least one criteria present in the past 6 months. Check yes if the symptom occurred within the last year.

Conduct Disorder Checklist

		Yes	No

Aggression to People and Animals

1. The student often bullies, threatens, or intimidates others. ____ ____

2. The student often initiates physical fights. ____ ____

3. The student has used a weapon that can cause serious physical ____ ____
   harm to others (e.g., a bat, brick, broken bottle, knife, gun).
4. The student has been physically cruel to people. ____ ____

5. The student has been physically cruel to animals. ____ ____

6. The student has stolen while confronting a victim (e.g., mugging, ____ ____
   purse snatching, extortion, armed robbery).
7. The student has forced someone into sexual activity. ____ ____

Destruction of Property

8. The student has deliberately engaged in fire setting with the ____ ____
   intention of causing serious damage.
9. The student has deliberately destroyed others' property (other ____ ____
   than by fire setting).

Deceitfulness or Theft

10. The student has broken into someone else's house, building, or car.   ____ ____
11. The student often lies to obtain goods or favors or to avoid obligations (i.e., "cons" others).   ____ ____
12. The student has stolen items of nontrivial value without confronting a victim (e.g., shoplifting, but without breaking and entering; forgery).   ____ ____

Serious Violations of Rules

13. The student often stays out at night despite parental prohibitions, beginning before age 13 years.   ____ ____
14. The student has run away from home overnight at least twice while living in parental or parental surrogate home (or once without returning for a lengthy period).   ____ ____
15. The student has often been truant from school, beginning before age 13 years.   ____ ____

If you checked yes to some of the above symptoms the student may be experiencing Conduct Disorder. Adapted from the Diagnostic and Statistical Book of Mental Disorders IV – TR. Copyright 2000, American Psychiatric Association.

Educational Strategies for Conduct Disorder

In addition to the strategies suggested for Oppositional Defiant Disorder the following strategies should be considered for Conduct Disorder (CD) students.

- Provide extensive structure for a CD student. A self-contained setting may be necessary if he continues to hurt others or break things.
- He needs to be monitored during transition times, or not be allowed to transition with other students.
- Consider escorting this student when he is transitioning in the hallways.
- Restraint should be used if he hurts self, others, or if he is causing significant property damage.
- Utilize the police on campus if the student hurts others, breaks property, etc. Don't hesitate to get the police involved. Conduct Disorder students need strong consequences in order to realize that they cannot get away with causing damage or hurting others.

Psychosis, Delusional Thinking and Bipolar Disorder

Psychotic symptoms are often a common occurrence in children and adolescence who have Bipolar Disorder. As a result, these children are often misdiagnosed as having schizophrenia. The following information can be helpful in determining if the student has Bipolar Disorder or schizophrenia.

- Some severe episodes of mania or depression include symptoms of psychosis or delusions.
- Common psychotic symptoms are :
  - Delusions: With delusions the student holds false, unusual or odd beliefs that are not usually accepted by others. For instance:
    - Paranoid Delusions (student believes that others are plotting against him)
    - Grandiose Delusions (student has exaggerated ideas of his importance or identity)
    - Somatic Delusions (Student, who is a physically healthy person, believes that he has a terminal illness)
  - Hallucinations: With hallucinations the student has a sensory perception that has no outside stimulus. For instance:
    - Student hears others speak that no one else can hear
    - Student sees things that no one else can see
    - Student feels or smells things that no one else can feel or smell
- According to DSM–IV-TR criteria you have Bipolar Disorder instead of schizophrenia if:
  - You experience severe swings of emotion and energy or activity levels.
  - Your hallucinations or delusions do not appear until before/after the onset of your mood swings (if they occur before or after your mood swings you would most likely be diagnosed as being schizophrenic).

Strategies for Dealing with Psychotic Episodes

The following strategies may be used with bipolar students who are also experiencing psychotic episodes.

- Provide distance…do not invade the student's space. Remember, closeness is probably not comforting…it is something to be feared.
- If there are disturbances in basic trust, it is important to do what is necessary to rebuild or build a trust based relationship. Students who have a problem with trust often have difficulties with separation issues, become clingy, and don't believe that others can be trusted. They have a significant fear of abandonment.
- If the student seems to be overwhelmed with feelings and is going through an episode, you need to attempt to help the student stop thinking about what is happening inside his head.
  - Do not ask the student to tell you more about his feelings….this will only exacerbate the situation.
  - Use calming interventions instead. With a calm but firm voice say, "I know you are upset. Let's relax first and then we can talk. Take a deep breath and let it out slowly." You may need to have the student take multiple deep breathes before he is calm enough to speak.
  - If he is still stressed, use another stress management technique until he feels better.
- After the student is somewhat calmed, ask questions that will help identify what has triggered the situation. Tell the student that you are going to ask specific questions that will help him communicate what happened. Take your time and

help him start from the beginning. For instance you may ask, "How did it begin?" "What were you doing at the time?" "What happened next?" Do not let the student talk about his feelings! Make sure that he focuses on data. Lead him through the event in a sequential manner.

- If the student is hearing or seeing things and asks if you "hear" or "see" what he is experiencing, be honest and say, "no."
- If it is possible, do things that are normal to help him refocus on reality. Take a walk, talk about what you see, what you can hear, smell, etc. Avoid feelings and don't talk about his delusions or hallucinations.
- Check to see if the student has taken his medication. If he has not, you will need to contact the parent to see if the medication can be brought to school. A single missed dose can cause a psychotic episode where the student hears or sees things that others cannot see or hear.
- If the student has taken his medication, keep him safe, but call the parent to determine what needs to be done. The parent may choose to take the student to the doctor. If the parent refuses to pick up the student he will need to be placed in a safe, self-contained environment where he can be watched. If he becomes harmful to self or others, call the police and have him taken to the hospital.

Substance Abuse and Bipolar Disorder

Substance abuse has been one of the greatest problems of our society for generations. Treatment centers abound. Therapists who address substance abuse and alcohol problems can be found in abundance. However, no matter how much treatment is available, it appears that substance abuse is continuing to be a major problem for thousands upon thousands of people. It's not surprising that those who have Bipolar Disorder are drawn to alcohol or substance abuse due to their instability and desire to be 'normal'. The sad thing is that all those who have been drawn to drugs and alcohol have severe complications with their Bipolar Disorder. There are numerous studies that speak to the dangers of substance abuse or alcohol abuse as it relates to Bipolar Disorder. Results from some of the studies are listed below:

- One specific study suggests that substance use is associated with the development of bipolar disorder for some individuals (Strakowski, 1998).
- Another study has found that substance abuse can uncover an affective disorder in genetically vulnerable individuals. In other words, substance abuse might trigger a person to exhibit Bipolar Disorder (Markou, 1998).
- Substance use has a negative impact on clinical outcomes in patients with bipolar disorder (Tohen, 1998).
- The percentage of alcoholic bipolar patients who attempt suicide is almost twice that of nonalcoholic bipolar patients (Morrison, 1974; Feinman, 1996).
- Substance abuse is found more often with mixed manic-depressive episodes (Himmelhoch, 1976).
- Those who are currently abusing substances have an increased frequency of mood swings, and more hospitalizations than those bipolar patients who are not using substances (Sonne, 1994).
- Co-existing substance abuse is associated with shorter time to relapse into mania (Tohen, 1990).

- Studies also suggest that it takes a longer time to recover from a mood episode when substance abuse is current (Tohen, 1996).
- Bipolar patients with who have co-existing substance abuse issues have lower recovery status, poorer role functioning, and lower quality of life than bipolar patients who do not use illegal substances (Weiss, 2005).

It is important to note that the effects of drugs and alcohol can mimic behaviors that are symptomatic of Bipolar Disorder. As a result, it is essential that drug or alcohol issues be addressed before Bipolar Disorder is diagnosed. It may very well be that the substance abuse is actually what is causing the mood switches.

> *Treatment for co-existring substance abuse is an important part of the students overall treatment plan. Actually, until the substance abuse issues have been resolved it is extremely difficult to address any other condition effectively.*

- If the student has characteristics of any type of Bipolar Disorder and uses drugs or drinks alcohol, he may have drug/alcohol induced behavior. In other words, it may not be Bipolar Disorder that is causing the behavior. Consider these:
    - If the student's symptoms occur only after he uses a street drug it is probably not Bipolar Disorder.
    - If his symptoms occurred after he drank large quantities of alcohol over a period of days or weeks, it is probably not Bipolar Disorder.
    - If his bipolar symptoms were reduced, or went away shortly after he stopped taking drugs or when he stopped drinking alcohol, it is probably not Bipolar Disorder.
- Manic behavior can be a result of a person using cocaine, LSD, amphetamines or heroin. States of drug induced psychosis can also be seen as a result of these drugs.
- Alcohol abuse can lead to depression.
- Impulsivity is a prominent characteristic of both Bipolar Disorder (Swann, 2004) and substance abuse disorder (Moeller and Dougherty, 2002).
- Bipolar Disorder with substance abuse is a well-documented pattern of psychiatric presentation (Krishnan, 2005)
- Akiskal noted that 50% of his bipolar patients engaged in polysubstance abuse (multiple drugs). He stated that this was due to the desire to self-medicate (Akiskal, 1996).

If a bipolar student is on illegal drugs or drinking alcohol he is endangering his life and making his bipolar symptoms worse. It is important that the student get off drugs and/or alcohol if he is to have any chance at controlling his bipolar symptoms and normalizing his life to any degree. It's sad to note that many children are tempted to use drugs and alcohol for a variety of reasons. It is up to parents, and school staff to a point, to identify how to minimize the temptations. Here are some reasons some students may use drugs:

- The desire to fit in with the crowd
- Poor self-esteem
- Observations at home or elsewhere that suggest such behavior is acceptable
- To appear more grown up
- To block out painful thoughts, feelings, etc.
- Self-medication to control behavior and feelings

> *Approximately 50 percent of people with Bipolar Disorder have drug and/or alcohol abuse or dependence problems—the highest rate across all patients with major psychiatric illnesses.*

Warning signs of Alcohol or Drug Abuse

There are a number of warning signs that may be observed when a student is using alcohol or drugs. Some of the more obvious signs are:

General Changes

- Delinquent behavior
- A drop in grades or performance at school
- A change of friends
- Family relationships begin to deteriorate

Physical Changes

- Change in eating habits
- Change in sleeping habits
- Red eyes
- Persistent cough
- Blackouts

Self-Medication

For years students have self-medicated for a variety of reasons. Some students were ADHD, bipolar, anxious or depressed. Students who had such disorders that were untreated would often find illegal ways of addressing the turmoil within. Bipolar students (and adults) who aren't on proper medication find the need to self-medicate even more necessary due to the constant frustration and mood switches that often occur. Some of the favorite drugs of choice that are used for specific aspects of Bipolar Disorder are:

- Manic State: Alcohol, Heroin (downers). These help calm or bring down the student.
- Depressed State: Cocaine, Meth., Uppers. These give the student energy.
- Agitated State: Marijuana. This helps the student overcome agitation.

> *The use of illegal drugs or alcohol has a negative impact on judgment, ability and brain function.*

Strategies for Dealing with Substance Abuse Issues

Drug or alcohol addiction must be dealt with before you can treat any other disorder including bipolar. The use of illegal drugs or alcohol can cause major problems for a bipolar student who is on medication. The effect of legal drugs may be minimized, or can be enhanced producing a danger to the student.

- First and foremost, a student who has Bipolar Disorder who is also abusing illegal drugs must get help for his substance abuse. At school this student may need to be protected from himself.
- This student may need to be in a self-contained classroom, or be escorted from class to class to assure that he does not have access to drugs.
- Counseling regarding drug use in general and its dangers are essential. More specifically, it is important that he realize that combining illegal substances with drugs used for Bipolar Disorder can either cause the bipolar medication to not work, or possibly produce death.

Educational Strategies for Students with Bipolar Disorder

Chapter Eight

There are numerous issues that must be considered when a student has Bipolar Disorder. Each of these issues may cause significant problems for the student if they are not appropriately addressed in the educational setting. There are thirty-two different issues related to Bipolar Disorder identified in this chapter. Suggested educational strategies/modifications are listed for each issue. This does not suggest that there aren't other strategies that might be considered. Here are the thirty two issues related to Bipolar Disorder that are addressed.

- Medication Issues
- Inability to Awaken
- Overheated and Dehydrated from Physical Exertion
- Embarrassed When Participating in Team Sports
- Fluctuations in Energy and Motivation
- Difficulty Concentrating and Remembering Assignments
- Difficulty Reading and Comprehending
- Difficulty Understanding Complex, Multi-Step Directions
- Difficulty Answering Written Questions within a Designated Time Frame

- Difficulty Understanding Complex or Muiti-Part Questions on a Written Test
- Difficulty Writing
- Embarrassed When Speaking in Front of Others
- Sensation or Risk Seeking Episodes
- Psychotic Symptoms or Distortions of Perception
- Inappropriate Elated Mood & Behavior
- Episodes of Inattention & Distractibility
- Episodes of Restless Attention & Agitation
- Episodes of Overwhelming Emotion
- Episodes of Impulsivity & Impaired Judgment
- Manic Episodes of Grandiosity

- Self-Centeredness & Combative Behaviors
- Episodes of Hyper-sexuality
- Poor Social Skills or Relationships With Peers
- Fluctuation in Energy & Emotion
- Episodes of Tearfulness and Crying at School
- Episodes of Frustration and/or Rages At School
- Too Overwhelmed By Anxiety or Emotional Status To Attend School
- Experiences Loss of Control that Endangers Self, Others or Property
- Suicidal Thinking & Morbid Thoughts
- Constant Talking

Medication Issues

Strategies

- Make sure that medication is taken privately, not in front of other students or staff.
- Provide teachers/staff with the necessary information about how stomach pain, vomiting, and dehydration can be serious side effects for a student taking lithium, valproate medications, and some of the other medications used in the treatment of Bipolar Disorder.
- Allow this student to have unlimited access to water.*
- Allow this student to have unlimited access to a restroom.*

* Monitor these! If the student abuses strategies they will have to be adjusted.

Inability to Awaken

Strategies

- If possible, schedule core academics later in the day. In many cases Bipolar kids function better later in the day.
- If possible, delay the students starting time, or give the student a study hall first period.
- If possible, allow the student to take less mentally stressful classes at the first of the day, e.g., art, P.E., band, choir, etc.

Overheated and Dehydrated from Physical Exertion

Strategies

- Because of medication issues you should allow this student to excuse himself from gym class on hot days if it becomes a problem for him.
- If heat and dehydration become a problem you may want to replace gym class with individual workouts, another healthful activity, or study hall.
- Allow for individualized workouts, weight lifting, aerobic exercises, etc. in a cooler area so the student can exercise at a pace that does not cause problems for him.

Embarrassed When Participating in Team Sports

Strategies

- Excuse the student from participating in team sports until the anxiety is treated.
- Provide the student with one-on-one coaching in sports rules and techniques.
- Permit the student to substitute individual physical activities, such as aerobic workouts or swimming laps that do not involve competing in groups.
- Offer the student counseling at school to address his concerns about team sports.

Fluctuations in Energy and Motivation

Strategies

- This student needs a location where he can feel safe if he is in a depressed mood.
- He will need a similar place when he goes into a manic state.
- The student may have periods of the day where he functions well. He should be in regular classes when this occurs.
- When this student becomes more depressed and his energy is low, academic demands should be reduced.
- When this student becomes hypomanic and his energy is high, increase opportunities for achievement (unless he gets out of control).
- Provide strategies that will help him come out of his depressed mood, e.g., engage in conversation, show personal interest in his hobby, pair him with an adult mentor that he can access with a special pass..
- Provide strategies that will help him come out of his hypomanic state.

Difficulty Concentrating and Remembering Assignments

Strategies

- Give a task option that requires the use of fine motor skills, e.g., working with a craft, putting a project together.
- Provide a second set of text books for the student to use at home.
- Develop an individualized organizational system.
- Have the student record his assignments daily in an individualized organizational system.
- Teacher should check the system as often as needed to assure success.
- Have teachers and parents sign the organizational system daily so that the student's progress can be carefully monitored.
- As part of this organization system there should be a reminder at the end of the school day that tells the student which materials he needs to take home.
- With the student's input develop a subtle visual/verbal cue for redirection in the classroom.
- Modify classroom and homework assignments according to the student's fluctuations in energy and concentration.

- Provide teacher notes or the equivalent to the student.
- Allow the student to send himself an emailo or voice mail message abouit homework.
- Put a checklist of things to do, to remember, etc. (wipe off board) inside his locker.

Difficulty Reading and Comprehending

Strategies

- Use colored overlays (of their choice) over reading material. NOTE: The student may have Irlen syndrome if he has reading problems. Check to see which color overlay helps him read the best as well as reduces glare and eye strain.
- Read tests to the student.
- Provide the student with recorded books.
- Break the assigned reading into manageable segments.
- Monitor the student's progress. Periodically checking for comprehension.
- Have the student read out loud to himself (can be a whisper).
- Check for learning problems, e.g., dyslexia, Irlen Syndrome.
- Ask questions that guide the student to form a 'movie' in their mind about the reading material. This will help with retention of material.

Difficulty Understanding Complex, Multi-Step Directions

Strategies

- Make sure the student has written down the directions.
- You may need to give the student a visual copy of the directions.
- Break assignments into manageable steps. Have the student tackle these steps one at a time.
- Ask the student to tell you what he is supposed to do....assure understanding.

Difficulty Answering Written Questions within a Designated Time Frame

Strategies

- Allow the student to finish testing after school or at other appropriate times.
- Provide for extended time on tests.
- Allow for oral responses.
- Allow word processing for written assignments.
- Accept short answer responses.

Difficulty Understanding Complex or Multi-Part Questions on a Written Test

Strategies

- Use multiple choice, matching type of tests.
- Allow the student to take tests in a safe, more restrictive setting.
- Allow for test administration by a teacher or aide who can help clarify questions for the student.

Difficulty Writing

Strategies

- Allow the use of a word processor for writing assignments, but encourage the development of written skills.
- Provide a calculator for math.
- Allow the use of graph paper to help keep columns straight for math.
- Allow the use of colored paper.
- Use full spectrum or natural light (you may want to seat the student next to a window if it provides natural light).
- Give the student additional time to complete written work.

Embarrassed When Speaking in Front of Others

Strategies

- Excuse the student from speaking in front of the class until the anxiety is treated.
- Provide the student with one-on-one coaching to reduce performance anxiety.
- Give the student advance notice about speaking and make sure he knows what to say. Start with small statements to assure greater possibility of success. Small success can help overcome the embarrassment.
- Allow the student opportunities to speak informally in class to build confidence (point out success to student in private).

Sensation or Risk Seeking Episodes

Strategies

- If the student exhibits risk taking behavior, or is sensation seeking at school, it is important to identify where he exhibits such behavior and provide him with a shadow that can monitor him.
- Escorts should be used if he is a danger to himself.
- If he risk seeks because of audiences, remove the audience or change the time so the audience will not be there.

- Remove the privilege of going to certain places, if risk seeking behavior has occurred at that location.
- Never lecture, argue or over correct.

Psychotic Symptoms or Distortions of Perception

Strategies

- Do not argue of challenge the students perspective.
- Attempt to refocus the student's attention with non-stressful questions.
- Protect him from other students. Don't let them encourage him.
- If the student is becoming emotionally agitated, either remove the student or remove the other students.
- Document the episode and notify the parents and your LSSP/psychologist (medication may need to be adjusted).
- Don't attempt to discuss or rationalize the episode...he is not in a rational state.
- Try to get him to sit and focus on stress relievers or mental blocking techniques (pacing tends to escalate behavior).
- Have him focus on specific items around him. Discuss what is real in the environment.

Inappropriate Elated Mood & Behavior

Strategies

- If possible, channel behavior into an activity with movement, e.g., have the student go on an errand with an assistant.
- Redirect and give the student time to comply.
- If behavior continues to escalate, provide a safe, calming place to go to until the student calms down.
- Encourage the student to sit and relax (stress reduction and mind blocking techniques should be employed).
- Heavily reinforce others who are not encouraging the behavior.
- Give a task that requires fine motor coordination, e.g., making a card house.

Episodes of Inattention & Distractibility

Strategies

- Frequent, purposeful breaks. Over time, teach this student to increase the time between breaks.
- Allow the use of a fidget.
- Redirect and give time to comply.
- Reward on task activities.
- Verify that assigned task is age and level appropriate.
- Reduce distracters whenever possible (identify triggers).

Episodes of Restless Attention & Agitation

Strategies

- Provide a safe place to regroup, chill, or do stress reduction exercises.
- Reward the student when he independently seeks out his safe place, or when he returns to task.
- Provide a purposeful activity that reduces anxiety.
- Engage the student in random conversations that are non-threatening.
- Frequent change of activity.
- Verify task is age and level appropriate.
- Send student on a pre-arranged errand (note to counselor, library, etc.).
- "Make a Deal": If the student completes the required task, then he can......
- Work physical activity into their day, e.g., last ten minutes of lunch he can shoot baskets with adult mentor, walk around the track or building.

Episodes of Overwhelming Emotion

Strategies

- Provide a more restrictive, safe setting where the student can go for privacy until he regains self-control.
- Set behavioral goals each week with the student, and reward the student for meeting those goals.
- As part of the organizational system include daily communication between parents and school regarding any behaviors or other incidents that are interfering with the student's ability to function in school.
- Identify and reduce the antecedents (triggers) that precede the student's loss of control.
- Work on stress or anxiety reduction methods that the student can use to help self-manage.

Episodes of Impulsivity & Impaired Judgment

Strategies

- Provide structure and consistent expectations. This should also include consequences that will help teach appropriate response/action.
- Redirect in a neutral manner.
- Allow for natural consequences so learning can occur...discuss afterwards.
- Encourage stress relieving breathing if anxiety or stress occurs.
- Identify triggers and responses. Remove/reduce triggers and teach appropriate replacement behaviors.
- Reward stopping behavior when triggered by a warning sequence that provides visual and verbal cues. Greater rewards should be given if the student independently stops the behavior before it becomes a problem.

Manic Episodes of Grandiosity

Strategies

- Provide a safe place to regroup or chill.
- Don't try to rationally stop the behavior, wait it out.
- Document, notify the parent and school psychologist or LSSP (there is probably a medication issue that needs to be addressed).
- Focus on reality or objects in the environment when you talk with him.
- Attempt stress reduction strategies.

Self-Centeredness & Combative Behaviors

Strategies

- Teach replacement behaviors frequently.
- Use a safe more restrictive setting to give the student time to calm down.
- Provide a replacement Social Skills behavior such as 'Showing Sensitivity to others'.
- Place him in situations where he will have to use the replacement behavior.
- Use a behavior monitoring form and mark it each time you catch him exhibiting the behavior. Rewards based on reduction of inappropriate behaviors.
- Don't argue or lecture.
- Reinforce compliance heavily.

Episodes of Hyper-sexuality

Strategies

- Document and let both parent and school psychologist/LSSP know about any sexual behavior (there may be a physical reason for some hyper-sexual behavior).
- Teach a replacement behavior.
- Direct the student to keep his hands on top of desk.
- Redirect to task and keep the student busy.
- Remove student to a more restrictive setting (if necessary) during episode.

Poor Social Skills or Relationships with Peers

Strategies

- Specific skills should be identified that need to be worked on in the classroom and/or in any special setting.
- Group work to develop social skills would be beneficial.
- Place the student in a safety zone. Put him around other students who would be less apt to have conflict with him.
- Put students who seem to trigger him across the room and behind him.

- Have zero tolerance for bullying. This applies to this student or those who may bully him.
- Allow an opportunity for him to excel in front of a peer utilizing a peer buddy system, etc.)

Fluctuation in Energy & Emotion

Strategies

- Don't make a big deal about the fluctuations of behavior. Just "Ride the Wave". Distract the student by engaging him in a random conversation.
- Change activity or environment to counterbalance mood state.
- Allow student time to regroup.
- Stress relieving exercises if manic (will also help with depression).
- Movement exercises if depressed or down.
- Engage the student in meaningful activity.

Episodes of Tearfulness and Crying at School

Strategies

- Give the student advance permission to leave the classroom and go to a more restrictive setting when he feels depressed or believes he is about to cry.
- Arrange a private signal when leaving the regular classroom becomes necessary. This will reduce anxiety and allows the student to maintain self-control while avoiding public humiliation and further distress.
- Give him time with counselor or other safe person to help work through feelings.

Episodes of Frustration and/or Rage at School

Strategies

- Provide the student with individual work that is less difficult.
- Provide optional accelerated individual work in all academic areas.
- Keep the student busy. When he is finished reward him if it is appropriate. There should be no down time.
- Drops in blood sugar levels can trigger loss of control in some children. See that he has access to protein snacks as needed.
- When he is frustrated or angry you may need to reduce the academic demands to a manageable level.
- Provide a safe place to go chill, or work on his own.
- Stay calm and do not react to frustration or anger. Consider facial expressions, body posture, tone, etc.
- Provide the student with a safe location.
- Teach the student to identify the early stages of their anger or anxiety, e.g., tension in jaw, tightness in shoulders, face, grinding teeth.

To Overwhelmed By Anxiety or Other Emotions to Attend School

Strategies

- If the student will not come to school, start by bringing him to the school entrance. He may not get out of the car....let him gradually get closer to getting to his first classroom.
- Place the student in a smaller setting where he feels safe. It may be in the counselor's office, or any other place where the student is willing to go.
- When he is comfortable have him begin to attend one regular education class that he is interested in.
- You may have to briefly shorten the day just to get him started attending school again.
- Have adult mentor do a home visit or call to show concern.

Experiences Loss of Control that Endangers Self, Others or Property

Strategies

- If at all possible, use a team intervention when restraint is necessary.
- Use Physical restraint only as a last resort and only as long as is necessary.
- Make sure that procedures/strategies described in the student's Behavior Intervention Plan (if he is in special education) have been implemented.
- If the student is not in special ed. consider local guidelines for restraint.
- Use the least of amount of physical force that is necessary to protect any student involved or to reduce significant property damage.
- Place the student in a self-contained setting, or in a restrictive time out room until he calms.
- Remove other students if the student will not leave his classroom (classroom clear).
- Document and notify parents, administrators and Psychologist/LSSP/Behavior Specialist when a restraint occurs.

Suicidal Thinking or Morbid Thoughts

Strategies

- Have a Functional Behavior Assessment (FBA) administered to the student by a school psychologist, or other expert trained to make such an assessment. An FBA can help identify the triggers that precede the student's suicidal tendencies. This information can then be used to develop a written Behavior Intervention Plan (BIP). The BIP provides a framework from which to teach the student new ways to avoid, or cope with the stressors that provoke his dark thoughts.
- Physical restraint should be used only as a last resort, and only after procedures described in the student's BIP have been implemented. In addition, restraint should be used only after parents have signed release forms, and should only be administered by trained staff.

- Place the student on a suicide watch both at home and at school. This would mean that the student should not be alone at any time. If he needs to go to the bathroom a teacher would need to either go into the room, or be outside the doorway and check on him if he stays more than a minute or two.
- The student should be in a self-contained classroom if he has threatened suicide. Such a placement would allow for the staff to protect him much more efficiently.

Constant Talking

Strategies

- When a student is in a manic state and seems to be unable to stop talking, he may need to be placed in a more restrictive setting.
- Communicate to the student that he is going into a manic state, and that he needs to use one of his thought stopping, or calming techniques.
- Let the parents know about the episode so they can call the physician to see if medication changes may be needed.
- Reduce the stress in the student's environment. If possible, use stress reducing strategies.
- Consider using calming music.
- Consider using aroma therapy for relaxation to help the student calm down.

General Strategies for Bipolar Disorder

In addition to the specific strategies listed in this chapter there are a number of general strategies that can be used with bipolar students. Here are some strategies you may want to consider:

- Arrange small classes with a good teacher/aide/student ratio.
- Provide teachers and staff with training on how to teach students with Bipolar Disorder and other neurological brain disorders.
- Place the student with Bipolar Disorder with other emotionally vulnerable and fragile students, not with students whose behavior is the result of criminal or gang activities.
- Group the student with other intelligent, creative students when applicable.
- Where possible include art therapy and music therapy classes as part of the student's curriculum.
- Make social skill development an integral part of the core curriculum.
- Give the student weekly contact with the school's social worker, psychologist, and any other professionals that the student's Individual Educational Plan (IEP) designates should work with the student.
- If the student needs to be restrained, make sure the school's staff has obtained parental releases before any restraint is implemented. Only qualified individuals trained in restraint should be allowed to restrain the student. Before restraint is considered, teachers and staff should first try to de-escalate the student's behavior as outlined in the student's Behavioral Plan.

Teaching the Elements of Self-Monitoring

Chapter Nine

It is not until a student can self-monitor that he is truly on the road to recovery. The bipolar student needs to be self-assured that he can deal with his problems. To do this he needs to learn how to identify various symptoms that may be indicative of a mood swing in process. If he can catch the mood swing before it gets too severe, he can utilize learned strategies that will help him overcome or compensate for the bipolar symptoms. Teaching self-monitoring is like teaching a social skill. There are specific elements that must be included and practiced in order for it to be an effective tool in reducing mood switches. Here are the basic elements that must be present if self-monitoring is to be successful.

- **Establish Motivation:** The student must have either intrinsic (preferred), or extrinsic motivation to reduce inappropriate thoughts/behaviors. He must also want to develop replacement thoughts/behaviors that are positive in nature.

- **Teach the Appropriate Language of Self-Monitoring.** Teach the student that he must focus on specific behaviors. He must be able to accurately and specifically identify the behaviors that are being monitored.

- **Teach the Concept of Honesty.** The student must learn that if he is going to be able to change behaviors that are causing problems for him or others, he must first be honest with himself. He must acknowledge that the behavior is problematic and that he needs to get rid of, or reduce it. If the student cannot be honest with the Self-Monitoring, it will not be effective.

- **You Must Teach the Student to Listen to His Conscience.** Inside all of us is a little voice that speaks when we do something wrong...or there should be. If that little voice is not there the student has more problems than just experiencing Bipolar Disorder. Most people have some values inside of them that calls out

137

when they do something wrong. It's important that teachers and parents teach the student that it is important to listen to that voice. Start with helping him identify what that voice sounds like. Have him think about things he could do that is wrong, and then have him listen to what the inner voice that tells him. It should be saying something like, "You know that's the wrong thing to do. Don't do it." If the student can listen to this inner voice he will be able to honestly, and effectively monitor his behavior.

- **When Self-Monitoring is Used the Student's Teachers Should Praise Accurate Self-Reporting.** In the beginning, don't focus on behavior as much as you do the student's accuracy of self-reporting. The student must learn that accurate self-reporting is the most important aspect to self-monitoring. When a student begins to accurately self-report, it is important that you praise him for being honest and responsible. Also, consider providing rewards until the student realizes how important it is to accurately self-monitor.

Self Monitoring Devices

There are a multitude of self-monitoring devices that can be utilized by students to help them keep tract of their condition, and current emotional/behavioral status. The following self-monitoring forms or tools are explained in this chapter.

- Personal Warning Signs for Mood Shifts
- Daily Mood Diary
- Warning Signs for Depression
- Warning Signs for Mania
- Self-Monitoring Form for Multiple Behaviors by Period
- Self-Monitoring Form for Multiple behaviors by Day
- Monitoring Communication
- Personal Time Outs

Self-Monitoring

1. Establish Motivation.
2. Teach the Appropriate Language of Self-Monitoring.
3. Teach the Concept of Honesty.
4. Teach Him to Listen to His Conscience.
5. Praise Accurate Self-Reporting.

Identifying Your Warning Signs

Before a student can self-monitor he must be able to identify the specific signs that suggest he is going into a manic or depressive state. To do this the student may need help from those around him who have watched him as he begins to exhibit specific early warning signs. One important point that must be kept in mind is that even when the student only exhibits mild manic tendencies it is important that he seek help, relax, take a time out, etc. If it is not done, he can easily be triggered into an unhealthy mood state. Have the student sit down with his parents or other caretakers that understand him well, and fill out the Personal Warning Signs for Mood Shifts form. See the sample to see how it is filled out and used. This form will help the student identify the specific warning signs that may suggest he is going into a manic or depressive state. Once the student has this list, he can monitor himself for those specific warning signs.

Personal Warning Signs for Mood Shifts Self-Monitoring							
Name: _Johnny_		**Date:** _1/15_					
Instructions: 1) With help from parents, teachers and friends identify the early warning signs that suggest you may be in the early states of a mood switch. 2) List early warning signs for depression, and hypomania or mania. 3) Once you have this list it may become a very individualized self-monitoring device for you mood switches. Check daily to see if you are exhibiting any of the early warning signs.							
Early Warning Signs	**Sun**	**Mon**	**Tues**	**Wed**	**Thurs**	**Fri**	**Sat**
Hypomanic/Manic							
Argumentative		/				/	
Failure to Take Medications	/						
Sexually High Energy		//	//	//	//	/	///
Depressive							
Extremely Fatigued	/	//		///	.	//	
Hard Time getting out of bed							
Sleep Disturbance	/	////	///	//	///	//	

If needed, copy the Personal Early Warning Signs for Mood Shifts form from the appendices and have the student complete it.

Daily Mood Diary

A Mood Diary is extremely important for anyone who has Bipolar Disorder. Daily checks to determine if the student is beginning to experience either mania or depression, is essential in order to avoid setbacks. There are multiple methods to keep a mood diary. The following method is straightforward and easy. You may want the student to keep the diary in a binder. He should rate how well he is doing each day of the week. Adults should monitor whether or not the student is completing the diary, as well as if there are any mood shifts that could suggest potential problems. Here is how the student might utilize the Daily Mood Diary.

Daily Mood Diary					
Student's Name: *Johnny*			**Date:** *1-5 to 1-11*		
Instructions: Using a 1-5 scale, mark the number that describes your mood for the day. 1 = sad, depressed 3 = average feeling alright 5 = very happy, manic like					
Sunday	1	2	3̶	4	5
Specific comments about how you were either low (1) or high (5)					
Monday	1	2	3	4	5̶
Specific comments about how you were either low (1) or high (5) *Really agitated today…had kids irritate me and I almost exploded.*					
Tuesday	1	2	3̶	4	5
Specific comments about how you were either low (1) or high (5)					
Wednesday	1	2̶	3	4	5
Specific comments about how you were either low (1) or high (5) *Not much energy today…felt a bit lethargic.*					

If needed, copy the Daily Mood Diary form from the appendices and have the student complete it.

If you notice that the student is swinging into a depressive state based on his diary, you may want to begin to work on exercises identified in chapter four that help deal with mild to moderate depression. It is important to begin as soon as possible when you see the student starting to go into a depressed state. The same thing applies if the student begins to shift into a manic state. If he is beginning to show hypomanic characteristics you may want to implement one of the stress management techniques shown in chapter six, or one of the other strategies that deals with mania that can be found in other chapters in this book. If repeated use of the strategies don't work, and either the depression or hypomania gets worse, the student will probably need to visit his doctor.

Warning Signs for Depression: Self-Monitoring

If a student wants to specifically self-monitor for possible depression he may use the Warning Signs for Depression Self-Monitoring form. This form is a bit more specific regarding aspects of depression that can slip in unnoticed. Have the student check these characteristics for a week. He should put a check next to the characteristic and under the date if that particular warning sign occurs during the day. If not, it should remain blank. Space is provided for the student to add a specific aspect of depression that isn't listed on the form.   Once he gets a baseline for the week, he can check himself daily to see if he is experiencing any changes. Here is an example of how this self-monitoring form may be used.

Warning Signs for Depression
Self-Monitoring

Name: *Johnny* 　　　　　　**Date:** *1/5*

Instructions:
1) Put a checkmark under the date each time one of the warning signs occurs on a day by day basis.
2) If you have a depressive behavior that is not listed you may want to write it into one of the spaces provided so that you can monitor it also.

Depression Warning Signs	Sun	Mon	Tues	Wed	Thurs	Fri	Sat
Extremely Fatigued		//	//	/	/	///	
Hard Time getting out of bed		/	/	/		/	
Sleep Disturbance							
Avoiding Crowds							
Insecurity							
Negative Attitude	/	///	////	//	//	////	/
Difficulty Concentrating		///	//	////	//	///	
Difficulty Experiencing Pleasure							
Feeling Down about Self			/				
Change in Appetite							
Procrastination							
Poor Judgment							
Extreme Difficulty Concentrating							
Poor Self-Confidence							
Thoughts of Suicide or Self Harm							

If needed, copy the Warning Signs for Depression: Self-Monitoring form from the appendices and have the student complete it.

Warning Signs for Mania: Self-Monitoring

Just as with depression, the bipolar student will want to self-monitor for possible hypomania or mania. An easy way to do this is to use the Warning Signs for Mania Self-Monitoring form. This form will help the student catch hypomanic behavior before it becomes extreme. Have the student check to see if any of these characteristics are causing problems for a week. He should put a check next to the characteristic and under the date if that particular warning sign occurs during the day. If not, it should remain blank. Space is provided for the student to add a specific aspect of mania that isn't listed on the form. Once he gets a baseline for the week, he can check himself daily to see if he is experiencing any changes. Here is an example of how this self-monitoring form may be used.

Warning Signs for Mania
Self-Monitoring

Name: Sherry   **Date:** 1/25

Instructions:
1) Put a checkmark each time one of the warning signs occurs on a day by day basis.
2) If you have a manic like behavior that is not listed you may want to write it into one of the spaces provided so that you can monitor it also.

Manic Warning Signs	Sun	Mon	Tues	Wed	Thurs	Fri	Sat
Argumentative	///				/		//
Insomnia		/				/	
Failure to Take Medications							
Sexually High Energy							
Overactive		//	//	////	//	///	
Controlling							
Unnecessary Risk Taking							
Change in Appetite							
All-Knowing							
Self-Medicating							
Poor Judgment							
Very Talkative	/	////	///	//	///	//	
Thrill Seeking							
Drug/Alcohol Use							
Racing Thoughts							
Sleeping Less		/				/	

If needed, copy the Warning Signs for Mania: Self-Monitoring form from the appendices and have the student complete it.

Self-Monitoring for Multiple Behaviors

This self-monitoring form is meant to be used when the student has multiple behaviors that need to be addressed. For instance, if a bipolar student is not organized, not on task, and is easily distracted it can cause anxiety which in turn may lead to difficulties with his bipolar condition. The fewer the tallies for each behavior, the greater the reward should be. With the student's assistance identify a number of rewards and determine which ones should be used for various levels of tallies made on a daily basis for each behavior identified (see chapter 12). Work with the parent to assure that the rewards are something that the student would be willing to work for. The more you can reduce the frustration that is produced by such behaviors the less the student may have mood switches or rage states. The teacher must be able to verify that the student has monitored his behavior accurately.

Self-Monitoring
Multiple Behaviors by Period

Name: Susan **Date:** 1/29

Instructions:
1. Identify one to three behaviors that need to be monitored. List them across the top of this form. The student is to put a check in each box each time he exhibits that behavior during each period.
2. Add the number of tallies that you have from behavior one, two and three to get the total number for the day. Quality and quantity of rewards are dependent on the number of overall tallies for the day. The fewer tallies the greater the reward.

Period	Behavior #1 Not staying on task	Behavior #2 Disorganized	Behavior #3 Distractible
1	///	/	/
2	//		
3	//		/
4	//	/	
5	//	/	
6	///		/
7	/		
8	///	/	/
9	/////	/	//
Number of Tallies	23	5	6

If needed, copy the Self-Monitoring: Multiple Behaviors by Period from the appendices and have the student complete it.

Self-Monitoring for Multiple Behaviors

This is another self-monitoring form that can be used for multiple behaviors. However, instead of monitoring based on class period this form calls for the student to monitor specific behaviors for a full day. This is best used when a student has decreased unwanted behaviors to the point that classroom by classroom monitoring is no longer needed. This form should be used when specific behaviors are now being exhibited only a few times a day, not a few times each class period. As with any self-monitoring form, rewards may be set up to help motivate the student to personally improve his behavior.

<table>
<tr><td colspan="11" align="center">**Self-Monitoring**
Multiple Behaviors by Day</td></tr>
<tr><td colspan="11">**Name:** *Hank*   **Date:** *1/5*</td></tr>
<tr><td colspan="11">Instructions:
1. Identify the behaviors that need to be monitored. List them in the space provided below. Put a mark across the number each time you exhibit an appropriate behavior.
2. The fewer marks made for each behavior the greater the reward should be.</td></tr>
<tr><td colspan="11">**Behavior**</td></tr>
<tr><td>Off task</td><td>1̶</td><td>2̶</td><td>3̶</td><td>4</td><td>5̶</td><td>6̶</td><td>7̶</td><td>8̶</td><td>9</td><td>10</td></tr>
<tr><td>Talking in class</td><td>1̶</td><td>2̶</td><td>3̶</td><td>4</td><td>5</td><td>6</td><td>7</td><td>8</td><td>9</td><td>10</td></tr>
<tr><td>Did not activate to task</td><td>1̶</td><td>2̶</td><td>3̶</td><td>4</td><td>5̶</td><td>6̶</td><td>7</td><td>8</td><td>9</td><td>10</td></tr>
</table>

If needed, copy the Behavior Monitoring: Multiple Behaviors by Day from the appendices and have the student complete it.

Monitoring Communication

This self-monitoring form helps the student focus on communication issues. He is given the opportunity to monitor both positive and negative communications. Obviously, the goal is to help him increase positive communication and reduce negative communications. Any negative communication can cause others to react to him, and in turn trigger the student into a depressive, manic or rage state. Rewards can be given for a specific number of positive statements. An average between the negative score and the positive score could be taken to come up with a number. For instance if the student had 8 positive statements, but also had 8 negative statements he would have an overall score of 0. The negative number would be considered a minus number. A plus score of 3 or lower would not warrant a reward. A plus score of 4 to 7 might yield a small reward. A plus score of 8-10 would be a more significant positive reward.

Monitoring Communication											
Name: *Shirley*			**Date:** *10/5*								
I will check how many times I am negative or positive from: *Monday 8:00 A.M.* until *Monday 4:30 P.M.*											
Positive Communication	1	2	3	4	5	6	7	8	9	10	
Negative Communication	1	2	3	4	5	6	7	8	9	10	

If needed, copy the Monitoring Communication form from the appendices and have the student complete it.

Personal Time Outs

Each bipolar student must be taught to be a self-advocate. Of all people this student knows when he is getting anxious, stressed, overwhelmed, angry, starting to feel manic, etc. When he perceives this, he must be able to communicate that he needs a break. He should be taught to say, "Please excuse me." or "I need to take a break, please." Some students may need a visual aid that can be used to ask for a time out, rather than having to verbalize what they need. A card may be used, or any other item that shows that the student has the right to leave class. Regardless of what method is used, the student needs to be allowed to utilize the Personal Time Out whenever it is needed. Teachers must know that when a bipolar student makes this request, it is important that he be allowed to take the break or time out. When a bipolar student realizes that he needs a break it is important that he take initiative to time himself out and de-stress in a safe location. Sometimes he may simply need a short break after which he can go back to class and continue to work. Here are some examples of how he may choose to take his personal time out.

- Getting a drink
- Going to the bathroom
- Taking a short walk
- Going to the counselor or another safe person
- Go to a more restrictive setting where he can chill

There are multiple self-monitoring techniques as well as other behavior management forms in this chapter and in other parts of this book that are intended to help the bipolar student maintain a healthier, more consistent life style. Obviously, a student could not utilize all of these forms. It would be impossible to do so. It is important that he and those who work with him identify the forms or strategies that would be most beneficial for him.

The hall pass is but one method that can be used for a personal time out. It is best to individualize the pass so that it brings no unwanted attention to the student.

Hall Pass

Additional Personal Time Out Cards can be found in the appendices, or you can make one of your own that the student can use.

Medication
and Bipolar Students
Chapter Ten

An interesting, yet frustrating observation is that no doctor can assure you that he knows how a child will respond to any medication. Each child's body and brain is unique and medications will react uniquely to each child. The good news is that each medication has a particular function....sometimes more than one in treating various disorders or conditions. Assuming that a proper diagnosis is made, the medication that is chosen should be beneficial. Students with Bipolar Disorder must have medication to control their condition. Without it they will often fall into either a debilitating depression, or will become so manic that they may need hospitalization. Either state is unacceptable. Those who have Bipolar Disorder must be ready to take medication for the rest of their lives if they want to live a relatively sane, safe life.

> *Students with Bipolar Disorder must have medication to control their condition. Without it they will often fall into either a debilitating depression or will become so manic that they may need hospitalization.*

Numerous studies have been and are being done regarding what medications work best with children who have Bipolar Disorder. In addition, it is only a matter of time before new medications will be developed that will provide additional relief for bipolar students. Here are some of findings regarding medication and bipolar disorder:

- A 1998 study of lithium showed a 60 percent response rate after six weeks.
- A 2000 study comparing lithium, Tegretol, and Depakote showed respective positive response rates of 42, 34, and 46 percent.
- A 2003 Topamax study that was stopped after adult trials failed, but which showed a trend toward efficacy in kids.
- Two small 1999 retrospective studies using Risperdal as an add-on showed 82 percent improvement in manic and aggressive symptoms, a 69 percent in psychosis, and an eight percent improvement in ADHD.
- A small 2003 study of Risperdal showed a 70 percent improvement in mania.
- A small 2001 study of Zyprexa showed a 62 percent improvement in mania.
- A small 2002 double blind study using Seroquel as an add-on to Depakote found the combination more effective in treating mania than Depakote alone.
- Lithium and Depakote can result in hair loss, weight gain, and acne which are huge issues for kids. Many Depakote users also had polycystic ovary syndrome to contend with.
- Kids in one Risperdal study gained 4.4 pounds, and in the Zyprexa study 12 pounds in just 28 days.
- Studies suggest that most bipolar children need combination treatment. In addition to one or more mood stabilizers or ant-psychotics, 34 percent need stimulants and six percent require an antidepressant.
- Antidepressants, however, pose a high risk for triggering students into mania, and thus should be used cautiously.

Matching Drug and Condition

It is important to match proper drug with condition when addressing bipolar issues. When an individual has Bipolar Disorder he is at risk of switching into hypomania or mania, or possibly developing a rapid cycling condition during treatment with antidepressant medication. As a result, it is important to use mood-stabilizing medications alone or in combination with antidepressants in order to minimize this tendency to switch.

- Lithium and valproate are the most commonly used mood-stabilizing drugs today. However, research studies continue to evaluate the potential mood-stabilizing effects of newer medications.
- Atypical antipsychotic medications, including clozapine (Clozaril), olanzapine (Zyprexa), risperidone (Risperdal), quetiapine (Seroquel), and ziprasidone (Geodon), are being studied as possible treatments for Bipolar Disorder. Evidence suggests clozapine may be helpful as a mood stabilizer for people who do not respond to lithium or anticonvulsants. Other research has supported the efficacy of olanzapine for acute mania, an indication that has recently received FDA approval. Olanzapine may also help relieve psychotic depression.
- If insomnia is a problem, a high-potency benzodiazepine medication such as clonazepam (Klonopin) or lorazepam (Ativan) may be helpful to promote better sleep. However, since these medications may be habit-forming, they are best prescribed on a short-term basis. Other types of sedative medications, such as zolpidem (Ambien), are sometimes used instead.

Medications for Bipolar Disorder

There are numerous medications that have been used to deal with Bipolar Disorder. The following is a list of the medications often used and some of the more common side effects. Some of these have not been approved for people under the age of 18. Regardless, the medications are still given to help with depression, mania or psychotic episodes. *Before you allow your child to take any of these medications it would be prudent for you to be aware of the more serious side effects before your child begins treatment.* If he exhibits any of the more serious side effects you should immediately talk to your doctor. The different types of medications often used are:

- Anti-Depressants
- Mood Stabilizers
- Anti-Psychotics
- Sleep Aids

Important

Before you allow your child to take any of these medications it would be prudent to look up the more serious side effects, so that you can be aware of them before your child begins treatment.

Anti-Depressants

Anti-depressants are placed into three basic classes. There are selective serotonin reuptake inhibitors commonly referred to as SSRI's, atypical antidepressants, and tricyclic antidepressants.

Selective Serotonin Reuptake Inhibitors

SSRIs are one of the most popular antidepressants on the market today. They affect the chemicals or neurotransmitters that nerves in the brain use to send messages to one another. These neurotransmitters are released by one nerve and taken up by other nerves. Neurotransmitters that are not taken up by the other nerves are 'reabsorbed' by the same nerves that released them. This process is called reuptake. Selective Serotonin Reuptake Inhibitors work by inhibiting the reuptake of serotonin, an action which allows more serotonin to be available to be taken up by other nerves.

- Citalopram: Commonly known as Celexa.
- Escitalopram Oxalate: Commonly known as Lexapro
- Fluoxetine: Commonly known as Prozac
- Lluvoxamine: Commonly known as Luvox
- Paroxetine: Commonly known as Paxil
- Sertralline: Commonly known as Zoloft

149

Common side effects of SSRI's may include headaches, nausea, dry mouth, insomnia, nervousness, sexual dysfunction, diarrhea, tiredness, and agitation.

Atypical Antidepressants

These antidepressants are medications that do not fit well into any of the other medication categories. Atypical antidepressants help balance certain neurotransmitters or brain chemicals. When these brain chemicals are balanced, the symptoms of depression are relieved. Here are some of the more common atypical antidepressants:

- Bupropion hydrochloride: Commonly known as Wellbutrin
    o Side Effects: Avoid if there is an eating disorder or history of seizures. May produce anxiety, heart palpitations (rare) allergic reactions (uncommon), confusion and weight loss.

- Duloxetine hydrochloride: Commonly known as Cymbalta
    o Side Effects: May produce Dry mouth, Constipation, Decreased appetite, Fatigue, Sleepiness, Increased sweating and blood pressure problems.

- Mirtazaine: Commonly known as Remeron
    o Side Effects: May have side affects often seen with SSRI's. May also increase appetite causing weight gain.

- Nefazodon: Commonly known as Serzone
    o Side Effects: Blurred vision or other changes in vision, clumsiness or unsteadiness, lightheadedness or fainting, ringing in the ears, skin rash or itching.

- Trazodone: Commonly known as Desyrel
    o Side Effects: Low blood pressure, irregular heartbeat, skin disorders, abnormal white blood cell count, liver toxicity, and seizures (rare).

- Venlafaxine hydrochloride: Commonly known as Effexor
    o Side Effects: May have constipation, cholesterol increase, and uncommonly, allergic reaction, blurred vision, seizures, and heart palpitations (rare).

Never use an Atypical Antidepressant with a monoamine oxidase inhibitor (MAOI). It can potentially cause serious or life-threatening reactions. There should be at least a two week wait after going off an atypical antidepressant before you start an MAOI.

Tricyclic Antidepressants

Tricyclic antidepressants are the oldest class of antidepressants. They work by increasing levels of the chemicals serotonin and norepinephrine in the brain. These drugs also increase the risk of mania or rapid cycling. As a result, they are not always recommended for bipolar disorder. They are not currently used as much due to the often unpleasant potential side affects.

- Amitriptyline: Commonly know as Elavil
- Imipramine: Commonly known as Tofranil
- Nortriptyline: Commonly known as Pamelor

Common side effects of tricyclic antidepressants may include dry mouth, dizziness, blurred vision, skin rash, drowsiness, weight gain, urinary retention, constipation, confusion or trouble thinking or concentrating, profuse sweating, muscular twitches, tiredness, nausea, increased heart rate, and irregular heart rhythm (uncommon).

Mood Stabilizers

These medications are thought to be the most effective and beneficial medications for treating Bipolar Disorder. Mood stabilization is one of the greatest needs for those with Bipolar Disorder and these medications do the job better than anything else. It takes on average about 4-6 weeks for these mediations to have an effect. The four medications that are being utilized most often as mood stabilizers are:

- Lithium carbonate: Commonly known as Lithobid, Eskalith, and Lithonate
  - Common Side Effects: Tremors, weakness or muscles, diarrhea or upset stomach, frequent urination, increased thirst, difficulty when trying to concentrate, weight gain, thyroid problems kidney problems, and changes in complexion (acne).

- Valproic acid or sodium valproate: Commonly known as Depakote
  - Common Side Effects: Sleepiness, dizziness, diarrhea or upset stomach, tremors, weight gain, thinning hair, and minor fluctuates in liver functioning tests.

- Carbamazeine: Commonly known as Tegretol
  - Common Side Effects: Sleepiness, upset stomach, fuzzy vision, dizziness, headaches, minor fluctuations in liver functioning tests, and low white-blood-cell counts.

- Oxcarbazepine: Commonly known as Trileptal
  - Common Side Effects: Headaches, dizziness, sleepiness, stomach aches, vomiting, rash, and double vision.

Of the four mentioned above only lithium has been approved by the Food and Drug Administration for use by children. However, Tegretol and Depakote have been approved by the FDA to be used for mood stabilization for adults. They have also been approved for use by children as antiseizure or antiepileptic medications.

Depakote and Tegretol have been found to be effective in treating manic symptoms as well as rapid-cycling Bipolar Disorder in children. According to current research children who have rapid cycling bipolar or mixed mood states seem to respond best to Depakote.

Trileptal is the newest of the top four mood stabilizing drugs. It is a variant of Tegretol that has become a favored medication in the treatment of early–onset Bipolar Disorder in children.

*Blood testing is essential when taking a mood stabilizer.
Testing is necessary in order to monitor any anomalies, including
toxic levels of medication in the system
that could cause damage to internal organs.*

Anti-Psychotics (also called atypical neuroleptics)

The most important benefit of antipsychotic medications are that they provide prompt relief from bipolar symptoms. Aggressive tendencies, anger outbursts, destructiveness, anxiety, unable to think clearly, etc. are often seen when a child is in the middle of a bipolar experience. When such behaviors become evident, it is important to get a handle on them as quickly as possible....these drugs can assist in doing this. Not only do they control anger, aggression, etc., but they also have mood stabilization properties and help control psychotic symptoms. The following atypical anti-psychotic medications have been used in treating both children and adolescents who have Bipolar Disorder:

- Aripiprazole: Commonly known as Abilify
- Clozapine: Commonly know as Clozaril
- Olanzaine: Commonly know as Zyprexa
- Quetiaine: Commonly known as Seroquel
- Risperidone: Commonly known as Risperdal
- Ziprasidone: Commonly known as Geodon

Common side effects of Anti-psychotics are grogginess, constipation, dry mouth, dizziness, weight gain, upset stomach, headaches, and difficulty sleeping. There are some more serious side effects that can potentially occur. They include uncontrollable chewing movements, tightness of muscles in the face, neck or back, tremors in hands and fingers, tightness of muscles, and smacking of lips.

> *Although widely prescribed, none of the atypical antipsychotic medications have been approved by the FDA for use by children. As a result, they should be carefully and cautious monitored when your child takes them.*

Sleep Aids

A lack of sleep is one of the characteristics of Bipolar Disorder. Untreated these children may only sleep two to four hours a night. If sleep is a problem for your child after you have medicated him with the previously discussed medications, you may want to consider adding a short-term sedating medication to help him get the rest he needs. Three of the most widely used sleep aids are as follows:

- **Benzodiazepines**—a class of minor tranquilizers.
  Benzodiazepines include Ativan, Valium, Librium, Xanax
    - Possible Side Effects: Dizziness, headaches, upset stomach, vomiting, clumsiness, bowel difficulties, muscle aches and pains, depressed mood, excitability, nightmares, and hallucinations.
    - Intended for short term use…usually not more than ten days.
    - These medications are very addictive, dangerous in high doses and are often sold as a street drug on the black market.

- **Zolpidem:** Commonly known as Ambien
    - Possible Side Effects: Dizziness, headaches, upset stomach, vomiting, clumsiness, slurred speech, bowel difficulties, muscle aches and pains, depressed mood, excitability and nightmares. Other more serious side effects are rare.
    - FDA has not approved its use for children under eighteen.
    - Intended for short term use…usually not more than ten days.

- **Zalaplon:** Commonly known as Sonata
    - Possible Side Effects: Dizziness, headaches, abdominal pain, eye pain, menstrual pain, memory loss, nausea, tingling sensations, weakness, anxiety and confusion, dry mouth, back or chest pain, depression, constipation, ear pain, itchiness, hallucinations, rash, nosebleeds, and swelling of feet or hands. An overdose can cause death.
    - FDA has not approved its use for children under eighteen.
    - Intended for short term use…usually not more than ten days.

Specific Information and Uses of Medication

- **Drugs which have been shown to treat depression, mania, and cycling**
    - Lithium

- **Drugs which have been shown to treat mania and cycling**
  - Risperidal
  - Zyprexa
  - Seroquel
  - Tegretol

- **Drugs which have been shown to treat Bipolar Depression**
  - Lamictal
  - Lithium

Cautions and Warnings

There are a few things that should be kept in mind when certain medications are taken.

- Valproate: According to a study conduced by Vainionpaa (1999), in patients with epilepsy, valproate may increase testosterone levels in teenage girls and produce polycystic ovary syndrome in women who began taking the medication before age 20. Increased testosterone can lead to polycystic ovary syndrome with irregular or absent menses, obesity, and abnormal growth of hair. With these findings in mind, it is important that young female patients taking valproate be monitored carefully by a physician.
- Using antidepressant medication to treat depression in a person who has Bipolar Disorder may induce manic symptoms, if it is taken without a mood stabilizer.
- In addition, using stimulant medications to treat ADHD or ADHD-like symptoms in a child with Bipolar Disorder may worsen manic symptoms.
- If manic symptoms develop or markedly worsen during antidepressant or stimulant use (usually for ADHD), a physician should be consulted immediately, and diagnosis and treatment for Bipolar Disorder should be considered.

Dealing with Side Effects

Part of the tradeoff for taking medications that help deal with various illnesses and disorders is the fact that most medications have side effects. Two of the most common side effects that cause children and adolescents difficulties are weight gain and sleeping problems.

Weight Gain

If this child is gaining weight there are a number of things that may be done to help. Here are some suggestions:

- Walk or run daily at home. If you can do this as a family it is even better. It promotes family life, which is extremely important for the bipolar child.
- Parents should encourage the school to put their child in a program that promotes weight maintenance.
- Send lunches with student to school. Although this won't assure that he gets a healthier meal, it at least gives him a greater opportunity to eat better.
- Home meals and snacks should be healthy.

Sleep Loss

If this child is having difficulty sleeping the following things could be done to help:

- Drink Chamomile tea.
- Avoid caffeine before bedtime (cokes, coffee, sport drinks, etc.).
- Take a hot bath or shower to relax the muscles.
- Exercise daily, but not just before you go to bed.
- Put lavender on the pillowcase, or use lavender oils (aroma therapy) to help with relaxation.
- Some people sleep well when they have a glass of warm milk before bed time.

Information for Parents of Bipolar Children

Chapter Eleven

Although much of this book is meant for educators, there is valuable information and many strategies in most of the chapters that can be utilized at home. However, this chapter is specifically for parents. As a parent, you need to have an awareness of the strategies that can be implemented in the school that will help your child. The greater portion of this book identifies multiple strategies for mania, depression, rage states, as well as co-existing conditions that can negatively impact your child. It is up to you, as the parent, to identify the strategies found within this work that would be most beneficial for your child and communicate to the school how you believe these strategies may be helpful in the school environment. In addition, there are specific strategies included that you can use at home to help your child as he struggles with Bipolar Disorder.

This chapter identifies nine areas that are important when working with a bipolar child. First, it is extremely important that you provide your child with emotional safety. Bipolar children are more emotionally fragile than 'normal' kids. As a result, it is imperative that you provide an emotionally safe place that is free from arguments, anger, and any other emotional turmoil. Second, it is extremely important that you provide your child with physical safety. The home must be set up in a way so that your child can be safe from himself. With this in mind, it is essential that you remove any possible weapons, or objects that could possibly be used to cause harm. Third, medication must be properly managed. This may very well be the most critical element in treating bipolar disorder. Without proper medication, the bipolar child will have ongoing social, behavioral and emotional problems. Forth, parents can also help make sure that their child has proper social support. Positive personal relationships are one of the most powerful tools for reducing depression and stabilize mood. Fifth, your child must have regular routines. If your child does not have a regular routine he may very easily be triggered into a bipolar mood state. Sixth, it is extremely important that the child maintain a consistent sleep wake cycle. In other words, the child should consistently go to bed at a certain time each night, and get up at the same time. Seventh, it is extremely important that your child avoid using illegal drugs or alcohol. Illegal drugs, alcohol, and over the counter medications can have a negative impact on any child who has Bipolar Disorder. When any of these are combined with bipolar medications the effect can be problematic to disastrous. Eight, diet can play a major role in the health and well being of the bipolar child. There are foods that can cause the bipolar child problems and should be avoided. Last, exercise plays a very important role in keeping the bipolar child stable. Towards the end of this chapter the child's legal rights are also discussed, specifically as they related to the school setting. The basic areas covered in this chapter are:

- Emotional Safety in the Home
- Physical Safety in the Home
- Medication Management
- Social Support
- Regular Routines
- Sleep Wake Cycles
- Illegal Drugs, Alcohol and Over the Counter Medications
- Diet and Bipolar Disorder
- Exercise and Bipolar Disorder
- Your Child's Legal Rights
- Things to Consider

As a parent you must learn as much as possible about how to live with your child's Bipolar Disorder. Join a parent group, read books, attend lectures, and talk to health professionals if things get serious. It is essential that you do everything that you can to maximize your child's periods of wellness and reduce the periods where his illness is causing difficulty for him. The information in this chapter is intended to help you accomplish this.

Emotional Safety in the Home

For emotional safety to occur, you must reduce inappropriate, inciting input at home. There are a number of things that should be considered if you are going to reduce stressors in the home for your bipolar child. Actually, most of these recommendations would be beneficial for any child. Consider the following:

1. As parents, you should monitor the type of input your child is exposed to. All children are impressionable. However, a bipolar child is especially vulnerable to inappropriate exposure, because when he is in the middle of a manic attack, or bipolar rage, he may very well reenact what he has seen or heard. As a result, the following should be regulated if you want to reduce serious behaviors when your child is in a manic state, or when he is in a bipolar rage.
    a. Music that has violent phrases or stories
    b. Music that is sexual in nature
    c. Videos, television, or video games that are either violent, or sexual in nature
    d. Wrestling shows
    e. Horror shows
    f. Certain chat sites (you select the ones you will let your child get on)

g. Anything that has content that your child could mimic that would be harmful, inappropriate, or tasteless

2. You may want to evaluate if you need to have sexually explicit adult magazines, DVDs, videos, etc. in the home. If it is important for someone in the family to keep such things in the house, it would be in your child's best interest if they could be locked away.

Emotional safety is important for a number of reasons. The most important reason is that when your child internalizes unhealthy information, he will have a tendency to replay them in his mind over and over. The more these auditory or visual images are played in his mind, the greater the likelihood they will be behavioralized, or exhibited by your child when he is experiencing either a manic attack or bipolar rage.

Physical Safety in the Home

It's sad to say, but true that bipolar children can have some dangerously erratic behaviors. When children are first born, parents will often go out of their way to put safety locks on cabinets, plug electrical sockets for safety, and put safety doors up in order to protect their children. Once parents realize their child indeed has Bipolar Disorder the same thing must occur again. The danger this child poses to himself, as well as any one else in his family including the pets, can be significant. As a result, it is important to do what you can to protect everyone concerned by taking certain precautions. This preventative measure can pay dividends for the family if done properly and consistently. Consider the following:

- Studies show that bipolar children are the most apt to commit suicide. Some may intentionally or unintentionally hurt others. As a result parents should:
  o Keep all medications, prescription and otherwise, under lock and key
  o Keep household cleaners and sprays locked up
  o Keep tools locked up (hammers, screwdrivers, etc.)
  o Keep weapons, e.g., hunting knives, arrows, darts, etc. locked up
  o Keep all guns locked up
  o Be aware of lamps and other items that can be picked up and used to hurt others
- Once you have set up your home for safety it is essential that you consistently check your home to make sure that the above objects are still locked up, or secured.
- You should also do daily checks of your child's room to look for any of the above items. Don't be afraid to go through your child's dresser drawers, bathroom (check the tank), closet, and any other hiding places you may be aware of.
- Bipolar children are also more apt to participate in using illegal drugs more than most children. As a result, don't be afraid to check the child's cell phone, monitor his calls at home and his e-mails.
- Don't be afraid to be picky about your child's friends.
  o Know his friends names....first and last
  o Know where he goes with his friends
  o Know his friend's parents and have their phone numbers
  o Always check on where he is going

159

Medication Management

Under no circumstances should this child miss a medication dose. Even one dose of medication missed can provoke a manic, depressive, or rage state. It is extremely important that your child not only take his medication daily, but that he also take it at a consistent time each day. Bipolar children need consistency. When change occurs it can cause stress and stress can produce anxiety that leads to mood instability. It is essential that you determine a specific time of the morning and evening when your child will take his medication.

> *Even one dose of medication missed can provoke a manic, depressive or rage state.*

There are weekly and monthly medication boxes that you can purchase at the drug store. They allow you to see whether or not medication has been taken on a daily basis over a period of time. In addition, you may want to chart when the medications are taken as part of your child's daily routine. The following is an example of a Monthly Medication Management form that could be used to manage medication usage. Either the parent or child could check the form each time the medication is taken.

Monthly Medication Management

Name: Jeri   **Date:** 5/23

Month:	List of Medications to be Taken											
	Lithium		Risperdal		Ambien							
Week One:	AM	PM	AM	PM	AM	PM	AM	PM	AM	PM	AM	PM
Sunday	X		X			X						
Monday	X		X			X						
Tuesday	X		X			X						
Wednesday	X		X			X						
Thursday	X		X			X						
Friday	X		X			X						
Saturday	X		X			X						

If needed, copy the Monthly Medication Management form from the appendices and have the student complete it.

See the appendices for daily and weekly charts that can help you monitor the side affects that medications may be having on your child.

Social Supports

Positive personal relationships are extremely important in reducing depression and to help in stabilizing mood. When a child gets depressed he will have a tendency to stick to himself, and stay away from people both at school and when he is at home. At school he may isolate and not speak with others unless spoken to, and even then it may be only the briefest of statements. When at home he may go to his room and not want to socialize with friends, go play outside, play a video game, talk with parents, etc. Social activities both at school and home are usually out of the question. This is exactly the opposite of what your child needs to do. If your child is depressed, it is essential that he find hobbies, activities, and/or social groups that he can become involved with so that he can be around and relate with others. It is through these activities and relationships that the depressive mood can be addressed. In chapter four, entitled Depression and Bipolar Disorder, there are multiple strategies that can help your child reduce depression. It is important to help him become more involved with others, and find enjoyable activities that he can participate in on a daily, or at the very least, weekly basis.

Regular Routines

Maintaining a daily routine is also essential for a bipolar child. This is one of the things that your child can control to some extent. Uncontrolled, it can produce significant negative effects. There are multiple charts that are discussed in chapter nine that can assist your child so that he can keep track of things that happen in his day. These charts allow your child to identify his mood state, when he may need to rest, relax, use strategies to de-stress (for depression or mania), or find ways to energize himself (depressed). It is extremely important for the child to consistently follow his schedule. Obviously, school is a major issue for bipolar students. Does he get to his first class on time, or his subsequent classes? Does he interact with people during the day? Have there been any changes in his regular routine? It is important that your child have a method by which he can list changes as they occur during the day. At the end of the day he needs to document if any of the changes have caused problems for him. It is important that your child know that it's not just negative encounters that can trigger his mood swings. Any high level of stimulation, positive or negative can alter his mood. The Daily Activity and Mood Chart shown in this chapter would be beneficial in helping your child maintain a daily regular routine.

> *Any high level of stimulation, positive or negative can alter his mood.*

Sleep Wake Cycles

If wellness is to be promoted, it is essential that your child consistently go to bed at a certain time each night, attempt go to sleep at the same time, and get up at the same time as much as is humanly possible. These sleep wake cycles must remain constant, especially for bipolar children or adolescents. However, maintaining this sleep wake cycle is difficult when other routines are disturbed, when your child is stressed, or when he is not tired. There are a number of things that can be done to help maintain consistent sleep-wake cycles. Here are a few suggestions that might help:

1. Have your child avoid doing anything just before he goes to bed that may stress him. Watching the news can be agitating. He can read the paper tomorrow if he is interested.
2. Avoid exercising just before bedtime. Although it can cause your child to be pleasantly exhausted, it will have a tendency to 'wake up' his system. Have him work out at least three hours before he goes to bed. When he works out in advance, it exhausts his body and gives it a chance to calm down. Sleep will come much more quickly under those conditions.
3. If he is keyed up before bedtime, help him find ways to relax and gear down. He may want to read a book for a bit.
4. If he is struggling with getting to sleep he shouldn't try to go to sleep. Sounds funny doesn't it? If he tries to sleep his mind is at work. When his mind is at work, it causes him to maintain an alertness which counters sleep. If he finds himself trying to go to sleep, have him try a thought stopping technique, or do a relaxation technique that causes him to gear down (refer to the relaxation strategies found in chapter six). If that doesn't work he may want to focus on the act of sleeping. For instance, what does the bed feel like? Is it cozy, warm, and comfortable? If so, he could concentrate on how comfortable the bed feels.
5. Have him drink warm milk before he goes to bed, or he could drink chamomile tea to help him sleep. Consider using aromatherapy. Certain scents can cause relaxation and produce sleepiness. If your child continues to have trouble sleeping, or if he is sleeping too much, you may need to tell his doctor about it.
6. He should not have any caffeine or over the counter drugs that might stimulate him.

Basic Things the Child Can Do To Help Himself Sleep Better.

- Avoid stress just before you go to bed
- No exercise just before you go to bed
- Read, listen to calming music, etc. to calm down
- Don't try to go to sleep....relax
- Drink warm milk, chamomile tea, or use aromatherapy
- No caffeine or other legal over the counter drugs that might upset body chemistry

Daily Activity and Mood Chart

Name: _Tisha_   **Date:** _3/25_

Early Morning Rate Your Mood	-3 -2 -1 0 1 2 3 Very Depressed normal Very Elated		
	Time	Identify any routine changes or events.	Did you relate with anyone socially at this time? If so, who?
Time you are out of bed	6:30	None	
Morning Breakfast	7:15	None	
On time for 1st period	8:20	None	Spoke to Mary about class work.
On time for 2nd period	9:05	None	
On time for 3rd period	10:00	John pushed me in hallway before class.	
On time for 4th period	10:55	None	
Lunch	11:50	List what you ate: Hot dog and fries and water Who did you eat with? Visited with Mary, no problems.	
Mid Day Rate Your Mood	-3 -2 -1 0 1 2 3 Very Depressed normal Very Elated		
	Time		
On time for 5th period	12:25	Late for class	
On time for 6th period	1:20	None	
On time for 7th period	2:15	None	
Schools out	3:10	None	Talked with John about homework.
Dinner time	6:00	List what you ate Pork chops, green beans and salad with some ice tea.	
Homework	7:00	Did math...no other homework Exercised for thirty minutes after homework.	
Time to bed	9:30	None	
End of Day Rate Your Mood	-3 -2 -1 0 1 2 3 Very Depressed normal Very Elated		
Have there been any changes that have caused you a problem? If so, write it down in the space provided.	John made me mad and I thought I was going to lose control...used a stress management technique and calmed down.		

If needed, copy the Daily Activity and Mood Chart from the appendices and have the student complete it.

Have your child use the Daily Activity and Mood Chart to help monitor mood, sleep cycles, socialization, eating habits, and his daily routine.

Illegal Drugs, Alcohol and Over the Counter Medications

A child with Bipolar Disorder may be tempted to use illegal substances or alcohol when his symptoms begin to cause difficulty for him. The sad thing is that whether he has been diagnosed or not, if he has Bipolar Disorder he will have a tendency to self-medicate to control his symptoms. Parents must do everything that is possible to assure that their child does not use any illegal substance or alcohol. Any use can compromise the prescribed medication and trigger manic, depressive, or rage state behaviors. If your child has a problem with substances, ask your doctor for help, consider taking him to a self-help group such as AA or Marijuana Anonymous, or admit your child to a treatment center, or residential program. It may save his life if you do. Some over-the-counter medications for colds, allergies, or pain can interfere with sleep, mood, or alter the effectiveness of his bipolar medicines. Check with your physician before giving your child over the counter medications.

Illegal Substances and Alcohol

- Do not allow your child to drink alcohol…even small amounts can alter bipolar drug effectiveness.
- Do not allow your child to use any illegal drugs…they can alter prescription drug effectiveness.
- Don't be afraid to check your child's room for drugs or alcohol.
- If you have alcohol in your home, lock it up and periodically check it to make sure that your child is not using it.

With this in mind, if your child starts to exhibit any of the following you should call your doctor:

- Changes in sleep, or energy
- Changes in medication side effects
- Significant mood shifts either to the manic or depressive side
- Suicidal or violent feelings

Diet and Bipolar Disorder

In addition to medications or alcohol, there are specific food items that can contribute to bipolar issues. For instance, it has been documented that sugar and caffeine can contribute to depressive affect, and as a result can make a child more susceptible to bipolar mania and rage. Instead of drinking soft drinks, coffee, etc. have your child drink

164

at least eight glasses of water a day. Research shows that water helps detoxify the body. Toxins have been linked to depression and dysphoric mood.

> *Research shows that water helps detoxify the body.*
> *Toxins have been linked to depression*
> *and dysphoric mood.*

There is growing evidence that nutrition plays a role in psychiatric disorders, including Bipolar Disorder. Kathryn Connor, MD, of Duke University Medical Center, Durham, North Carolina suggested that there is growing interest in the hypothesis that nutritional deprivation may contribute to psychiatric disorders. In addition, there appears to be an implication that enhanced nutrition may have a positive impact on mental health. This hypothesis was the topic of discussion at the American Psychiatric Association 2004 Annual Meeting in New York, NY, with experts reviewing the potential uses of omega-3 fatty acids in the treatment of bipolar disorder.

Stroll and colleagues did a study on the use of Omega-3 fatty acids to determine if they would be helpful in the treatment of bipolar disorder. Patients who received the omega-3 fatty acids:

1) Stayed well significantly longer
2) Showed a significant decrease in depressive symptoms
3) Demonstrated significant clinical improvement
4) Displayed significant improvement in global functioning compared with patients who had received a placebo

Jonathan Alpert, MD, PhD, of Massachusetts General Hospital and Harvard Medical School in Boston, Massachusetts completed a study on Folate. They found that folate had a positive impact depression. Several studies have found that depression could be decreased for those who resisted medical treatment only, simply by adding folate to their treatment regimen (Coppen and Bailey, 2000; Alpert, 2002). Although these studies were completed with adults, children and adolescents may very well respond the same way, if they have lower levels of folate in their system.

Davidson conduced a double-blind placebo-controlled trial of chromium picolinate in 15 patients with atypical depression. His study found that 70% of those patients in the chromium group had a drop in depressive symptoms, compared with 0 out of 5 (0%) patients in the placebo group. Overeating and fatigue also improved among a subset of patients in the chromium group (Davidson, 2004). This was a small group, but the results were encouraging.

Exercise and Bipolar Disorder

Exercise helps everyone keep healthier throughout life. However, it is especially important for the bipolar child to exercise because it helps reduce the possibility of depression and anxiety. Exercise increases naturally occurring endorphins. When endorphins spread through the child's brain he begins to get a sense of well-being and pleasure. It's hard for this student to be depressed or anxious when he feels so good. With this in mind, it is important that your child to identify how he can incorporate an ongoing exercise program in his life. Three areas will be addressed that may help your child exercise more. They are as follows:

- Reasons to Exercise
- Type of Exercise
- Self-Defeating Thoughts and Exercise
- Exercise Journal

Reasons to Exercise

There are numerous reasons to exercise. Your child needs to understand that exercise can improve his life state. As a parent you should review the benefits listed below and help your child understand how exercise could be helpful for him.

- Decreases manic episodes
- Improve Self-Esteem
- Relieves stress
- Ability to sleep improved
- Reduces addictive cravings
- Improves immune system
- Improves energy
- Improves self-confidence
- Weight loss
- Increases endurance
- Increases life span
- Decreases possibility of diabetes
- Decreases possibility of heart problems
- Increases strength
- Decreases blood pressure
- Improves complexion
- Can eat more and gain less
- Decreases depression
- Improves flexibility

See the appendices for the Reasons to Exercise form. Have the student review this form to help him see the benefits of exercising.

Types of Exercise

Everyone has a preference as to the type of exercise he likes. Some people prefer exercise that they can do by themselves, e.g., weightlifting, running, walking, Pilates, Yoga. Others prefer to exercise with others. They may enjoy playing basketball, practicing Karate, or Tennis. You need to help your child determine which type of exercise he is willing to participate in on an ongoing basis. He may be more consistent with his exercise if you exercise with him. Here are some examples of various exercises that your child may choose from. This is obviously not a complete list.

- Walking
- Running
- Riding a bike
- Karate
- Work out with weights

- Yoga
- Pilates
- Tennis
- Basketball

See the appendices for the Types of Exercise form. Have the student fill this form out to help him identify what he might want to do to exercise more often.

Self-Defeating Thoughts and Exercise

Even thought your child may understand why he should exercise, there will still be times when he will not want to. He will come up with every excuse in the world to avoid it. However, for his sake he needs to work through these self-defeating thoughts and identify why he really doesn't want to workout. Once he looks at the corrective thought, it may give him the encouragement to go ahead and exercise. In the appendices you will find a copy of the Removing Self-Defeating Thoughts form. Sit down and help your child complete this form when he finds that he is struggling with exercising.

Self-Defeating Thoughts and Exercise	
Name: Johnny	**Date:** 3/25

Instructions:
1. When you are finding that you are not wanting to exercise for some reason, it is important to work through the self-defeating thoughts that are triggering your lack of desire.
2. Write down the self-defeating thought. On the other side of the form write down the corrective thought.

Self-Defeating Thought	Corrective Thought
I'm too tired to exercise.	I will feel better and energized after I exercise.
I have too much homework to exercise.	I will be more alert after I exercise and will be able to accomplish more.
No one will exercise with me.	I have to depend on myself, not others to do what I know is best.

If needed, copy the Self-Defeating Thoughts and Exercise form from the appendices and have the student complete it.

Exercise Journal

Once your child has accepted that he needs to exercise, and how he is going to do it, it important that he schedule times when he will consistently follow through with his exercise program. Having a schedule can help anyone be more consistent with exercise. Rather than use an additional form, or document to keep track with exercise he may want to use the Daily Activity and Mood Chart. This chart has multiple areas that can be monitored. Having multiple areas on one form may help your child see how well he is doing from one perspective rather than having to look at a variety of forms. However, it he wants to focus on monitoring exercise he may want to use the Exercise Journal. Your support for exercise may be extremely important for your bipolar child. If you choose to participate in the exercise in some way, your child will have a much better chance at being successful on a consistent basis.

<table>
<tr><td colspan="3" align="center">Exercise Journal</td></tr>
<tr><td colspan="2">Name: Johnny</td><td>Date: 8/23</td></tr>
<tr><td>Day</td><td>Daily Exercise: What I did to exercise today!</td><td>Result: How did you feel when you were finished?</td></tr>
<tr><td>Sunday</td><td>Played basketball for an hour</td><td>Felt better…more energized.</td></tr>
<tr><td>Monday</td><td>Worked out with weights and ran</td><td>Felt much better.</td></tr>
<tr><td>Tuesday</td><td>Worked out with weights and ran</td><td>Felt much better.</td></tr>
<tr><td>Wednesday</td><td>Didn't exercise</td><td></td></tr>
</table>

If needed, copy the Exercise Journal form from the appendices and have the student complete it.

Your Child's Legal Rights

Beyond the elements that need to be addressed by parents as described above, it is important to note that the school also has some obligation to work with these children. There are many books on the market that discuss parent/student rights in school as found in ADA, Section 504, and Special Education (IDEA). These three laws are meant to assure that public schools provide special accommodations, or modifications for students who have a handicapping condition.

- Americans with Disabilities Act (ADA), which is a civil rights law
- Section 504 of the Rehabilitation Act of 1979
- Individuals with Disabilities Education Act (IDEA) of 1997….recently reauthorized in 2005

Americans with Disabilities Act (ADA)

Based on the Consumers Guide to Disability Rights Laws, the Americans with Disabilities Act prohibits discrimination on the basis of disability in employment, State and local government, public accommodations, commercial facilities, transportation, and telecommunications. In other words, this law ensures equal opportunity for people with disabilities, including school aged children. To be protected by the ADA, the individual must have a disability, or have a relationship or association with an individual with a disability. An individual with a disability is defined by the ADA as a person who has a physical or mental impairment that substantially limits one or more major life activities, a person who has a history or record of such an impairment, or a person who is perceived by others as having such an impairment. The ADA does not specifically name all of the impairments that are covered.

With this in mind it is important to note that ADA has a specific impact on a school aged children who have a disability. School districts across the United States have many responsibilities to implement ADA in the school setting. These responsibilities can become extremely complicated, especially when you must keep in mind that other laws and regulations, such as IDEA (Individuals with Disabilities Education Act), the Rehabilitation Act of 1973, and local laws that must also be followed.

ADA Title II is most specific for students. It includes requirements for public school districts to make their programs, facilities, and services accessible to students with disabilities. This not only includes the physical facility (the school building), but also includes any recreational facilities. The ADA requires that all recreational facilities (play grounds) be readily accessible to, and usable by, individuals with disabilities.

Section 504 of the Rehabilitation Act

This act requires that children with special needs or disabilities be given an appropriate education that is the same as children without disabilities. To receive benefit from this act the student must have a disability that significantly impairs his functioning. Those students who qualify are guaranteed special accommodations or services. However, the act does not indicate that the students who qualify should, or need to be separated from students who are in the regular classroom. In other words, they should be included in the regular classroom.

IDEA

IDEA is for students who have more severe disabilities. These student's disabilities are severe enough that they need Special Education support. The student must meet eligibility for a specific disability to qualify for services from Special Education. If your child is evaluated by special education staff and as a result meets eligibility requirements to be placed, the school and parents as a team must come up with a Individualized education Plan (IEP). Restrictiveness of placement, modifications, and IEP must be driven by the data found in the eligibility reports that the district completes, or accepts from outside sources. Based on law the student has to be re-evaluated every three years to determine ongoing eligibility.

If your child has Bipolar Disorder, severe ADHD, Depression, Anxiety or other severe emotional/behavioral conditions he may need the support that Special Education can provide. Your local school district can provide you with information regarding each of these laws and how they impact the school environment. In most cases the special education department will have information and/or sources where you can obtain further information.

Things to Consider

In summary, there are some very important things that you can do as a parent to help your child. It is extremely important to reduce both manic and depressive episodes to a minimum for your child. If this can't be done, you and your child will be in a constant state of frustration and he will struggle mightily at school. To accomplish this there are a number of things that both parents and school staff can do. Some of them are:

- Family and the school personnel should develop practical methods or strategies to better cope with both manic and depressive aspects of the disorder.
- Nutritional habits should be improved. Reduce empty carbs., sugar, caffeine, etc.
- He must learn how to identify signs and symptoms of episodes before they occur, and develop strategies to avert or minimize the effects of episode.
- Teach him to develop skills that will help avert or minimize the effects of the episode.
- Allow for adequate rest and activity.
- Promote and improve psychosocial functioning between episodes.
- He should never miss one dose of medication....it can trigger an attack and throws the brain into a chemical imbalance.
- Keep his day structured, e.g., the same time for getting out of bed, getting in bed, eating, etc. The more structure the less stress there will be.
- If he is having serious academic problems, and/or emotional/behavioral problems, get help from the school. Contact your child's campus counselor to find out who assists in beginning a referral for possible special education services, or contact the schools special education department.

Information regarding how to implement each of these suggestions can be found in this book. Strategies for improving manic or depressive mood swings can be implemented by parents as well as professionals. Additional strategies for each co-existing condition can also be implemented by the parents. Don't be afraid to try things that might help your child. If you feel uncomfortable using some of the more therapeutic strategies, find a therapist who is knowledgeable about Bipolar Disorder who can help. Caution: Just because someone is licensed to do counseling/therapy, doesn't mean that he has experience with Bipolar Disorder. Make sure that the person is knowledgeable...check around, ask questions. Find a therapist and/or psychiatrist who you are comfortable with, and who can show in some way that he has experience with this condition.

Discipline &
Management
of Bipolar Children
Chapter Twelve

When working with a bipolar student, it is extremely important that you treat his behavior based on the underlying causality. Basically, there are two reasons why bipolar students exhibit inappropriate behavior. First and foremost, many of the behaviors are caused by the student's biochemical disability. When these students become hypomanic, or manic, they will often be impulsive, talkative, and out of control verbally and sometimes physically. In such situations their behavior is not necessarily by choice. When this is the case, the use of discipline, or consequences are not very helpful or productive. Special Education Law (IDEA) actually states that you should not....must not discipline a child for behavior related to his disability. It would be like chastising a blind student for bumping into other kids, or putting a hearing impaired student in time out because he wasn't listening to you. A bipolar child who goes into a manic or rage state and is totally disruptive in the classroom should not be disciplined. At the very least he needs to have strategies in place that would provide alternative safe placements, stress management methods, and a person who could help talk him down. Needless to say, proactive strategies are of vital importance for these students.

The second type of behavior occurs as a result of choice. Just like their peers who do not have this disorder, bipolar students can simply make poor choices. Bipolar students are just like other kids their age. They make bad decisions, are immature, and as a result get into trouble. If this occurs the student must be held accountable for his actions, and appropriate consequences must follow. It is vital that he learn that there are consequences for his behavior. Providing consequences for these behaviors is a necessity, and most school staff are fully equipped to handle such situations. Teachers and parents have been through hours of training in how to discipline students when they behave inappropriately. Hundreds of books on the market can identify various methods

171

of dealing with students when inappropriate behavior occurs.   Dealing with this type of behavior problem is not addressed in this work because of the multitude of resources available to both teachers and parents.

A bipolar child who goes into a manic or rage state....needs to have strategies in place that would provide alternative placements, stress management methods, and a person who could help talk him down.

Disability or Poor Choice

The first task for the educator or parent is to identify if specific behaviors are a result of the disability, or is it a result of poor choice. The following chart gives you a quick look at some things you might consider as you attempt to determine which cause is evident.   If the behavior is a result of the disability, you must determine what kind of supports can be put into place to assist the student. If it is a result of choice, you need to determine the appropriate discipline or consequences that may need to occur.

Disability or Poor Choice	
Disability	**Poor Choice**
Student is out of control.	Student is in control.
Behavior is not planned.....is usually impulsive, or a reaction.	Behavior is planned or premeditated.
There is usually no gain from exhibiting the behavior.	The behavior is beneficial to the student....he gets something he wants from it.
The student has much emotion...sometimes rage.	Cold...calculating...little emotion.

Providing Supports for Behavior Related to Disability

There are multiple types of support that can be provided when a student is exhibiting behaviors as a result of his disability. The following type of supports can be implemented to assist the bipolar student in minimizing or reducing behaviors related to mood swings.

- Student Initiated Proactive Strategies
- Adult Initiated Proactive Strategies
- Motivation and Behavior Management
- Strategies for Crisis Management

Student Initiated Strategies

There are multiple strategies that a student can use that will help him deal with his bipolar behaviors. The following strategies may be helpful:

- General Proactive Strategies
- The Rage Freeze Technique
- Covert Modeling and Bipolar Disorder
- Self-Monitoring

General Proactive Strategies

The ultimate goal when working with bipolar student is to teach him self-management strategies so that he can take responsibility for his behavior. The student will be the first to know if he is starting to become depressed. He should also be the first to know when he is starting to experience some hypomanic tendencies. If he is consistently monitoring his behavior he will know when he is starting to exhibit symptoms of a mood swing. Once he identifies that he is beginning to experience symptoms, he needs to take initiative to go to the counselor, a safe room, etc. so that he can talk to someone or utilize one of the techniques that he has learned to address his mood swing. Here are some of the student initiated strategies that should be taught and ultimately utilized if the student is to self-manage his mood disturbances.

- Student must learn self-management skills (see chapter 9)
- Student must learn specific stress management skills that he can practice on an ongoing basis to reduce his general level of stress (see chapter 6)
- Student must utilize the stress management strategies when he starts to feel hypomanic in order to calm himself down (see chapter 6)
- Stress management strategies may also be used when he is beginning to feel depressed
- Teach coping skills that can help student cope more efficiently with the stressors that trigger his behavior (see chapter 6)
- Use the Rage Freeze Technique
- Use the Covert Modeling Technique

The Rage Freeze Technique

This technique is intended to be helpful in minimizing rage states. The student must be willing and able to catch himself as he is escalating into a rage state. This is difficult, but not impossible to do if he really is in tune with his body. The Rage Freeze technique was discussed by Lynn (2000) and adapted for use in this work. The technique is actually an adaptation of an NLP (neuro linguistic programming) strategy. It calls for the student to identify a Resource State. According to NLP this is simply a memory of a time when the student behaved appropriately or effectively as he dealt with a identified behavior problem. To use this technique the student must be sure that he is motivated to change, and willing to work with the adult who will help him work on reducing Rage states. Initially the technique should be taught to the student when he is in a relatively stable mood. There are four steps to using this technique.

- Identify a Rage Incident
- Identify a Rage Incident that was Stopped before it Began
- Anchor the Positive Image
- Practice Using Anchor

Step One: Identify a Rage Incident

The first step for using the Rage Freeze Technique is to have the student remember a time in which he had a rage attack. Have the student relax in a chair, or another comfortable place.

1. Have the student picture the rage event and the feelings he had when it occurred. Have him describe the event.
2. When he has finished describing the event, discuss with him how these feelings are non-productive, and often damaging to him and those he loves.

Step Two: Identify a Rage Incident that was stopped before it began

The second step is to identify a rage incident where he was able to stop the rage before it overcame him. This is an important step. Without this incident or memory it will be extremely difficult to use this technique.

1. Have the student identify a time when he was near a rage state, but was able to stop it before it got started.
2. Have him picture the aborted rage event and hold it in his mind.
3. Discuss what he did to stop it. How did it feel to control the rage?

Step Three: Anchor the Positive Image

Have the student close his eyes again and place the successful image in his mind. Once he has placed the image in his mind, he must anchor that image. You want him to be able to quickly and readily bring up the successful image showing him that he can and has controlled the rage. First, he must identify a somatic symptom that occurs just before he goes into the rage state. It may be a pulsing of his temple, his forehead starting to tense up, his brain may be on fire, his eyes may hurt or feel strange. The symptom that appears first is the one he needs to choose. Help the student identify which somatic symptom first occurs. This may take some work and may require reviewing rage states after the fact a few times to make sure you have a good idea as to what somatic symptoms occur. These symptoms will often be early warning signs that a rage attack is forthcoming. Use the Somatic Precursors to a Rage State form to help the student identify the specific somatic symptoms that may be occurring prior to the rage state. Once you have identified the most significant somatic symptom you can complete the anchor.

1. Have him touch the somatic spot (temple, eyes, forehead, etc.) with his finger or fingers.
2. At the same moment have him think about…visualize…the positive image that he identified in Step two. He should feel the success of controlling the rage…see himself feeling better about controlling it, watch the anger float away. He will immediately begin to relax knowing that he has controlled the rage, rather than let it control him. He will feel his body relax.
3. As he visualizes the success have him breathe deeply and slowly. Relaxing more with each breath.

Somatic Precursors to a Rage State		
Name: *Paula*		**Date:** *10/26*
Date	**Somatic Precursors**	
10/27	_X_ Pulsing in temple ___ Brain seems to burn ___ Tunnel vision _X_ Body tension ___ Other:	___ Forehead tensing up _X_ Eyes hurt ___ Grinding teeth ___ Shaking ___ Other:
	First Symptom:	*Pulsing in temple*
11/9	_X_ Pulsing in temple ___ Brain seems to burn ___ Tunnel vision _X_ Body tension ___ Other:	_X_ Forehead tensing up _X_ Eyes hurt ___ Grinding teeth ___ Shaking ___ Other:
	First Symptom:	*Pulsing in temple*

If needed, copy the Somatic Precursors to a Rage State form from the appendices and have the student complete it.

175

Step Four: Practice Using the Anchor

When using any technique like this it is important to practice it so much that it becomes automatic. To get to this automatic state, the student must practice this technique daily. A side benefit of this strategy is that it can be used to reduce other unwanted or problematic behaviors as they are identified. Practice using the anchor by visualizing a rage incident and by using the anchor to stop the rage feelings. Have the student practice this as often as possible so that he will become proficient at using the anchor. The goal is to practice using the anchor so much that when he feels the somatic symptom that is about to trigger the rage, he automatically will use the technique.

Covert Modeling and Bipolar Disorder

Covert Modeling is another technique that can be used to reduce rage states or other problematic behaviors. Joseph Cautela (1986) developed this technique. He determined that an individual can learn new behavior patterns by imagining other individuals, as well as self, performing the desired behavior successfully. Covert modeling provides a method by which a person can identify, refine, and practice in his mind the necessary steps for completing a desired behavior. As this new behavior is successfully practiced in the mind, it becomes easier to perform in real life. Covert modeling can take on a special role for bipolar students. The focus for behavior change for these students is a reduction in how he reacts to triggers. In other words, as a proactive technique, covert modeling can be used to minimize how the student reacts when others trigger him. As specific trigger events are identified the student can establish a preferred response.

Covert modeling is an effective way of altering an existing negative sequence of behavior and thinking….of learning a new pattern of behavior. In addition to manic or depressive issues, this technique can be used for anxiety issues, and any other problem behavior that may be troublesome. Some behaviors that might be altered using this technique are:

- Stress from specific triggers
- Performance at school
- Personal relationships
- Bad habits
- Social anxiety
- Rage states

The focus of using covert modeling for bipolar students is to help him learn to control his reactions to triggers or to reduce unwanted behaviors. A trigger may be a word, or behavior that another exhibits that causes the student to get anxious, angry, etc. As previously stated, when a bipolar student becomes anxious, stressed, angry, etc. he may be triggered into depression, mania or a rage state. If the student cannot visualize well, this technique will not work. The following is an adaptation of the Covert Modeling technique.

Steps to Using Covert Modeling

Step 1: Practice Using Imagery

Have the student practice imagery until he can do it well. If it too difficult to visualize and it produces frustration or stress, it may not be in the student's best interest to use this technique.

Step 2: Write Down Triggers

The student must identify the specific triggers that have produced depressive, manic or rage states (see Identifying Triggers or Antecedents form in appendices). For example, the trigger may be another student calling him an inappropriate name.

Step 3: Write Out the Desired Behavior

Have the student write down his desired response to the trigger.

Step 4: Imagining Context

Have the student practice imagining the context in which the triggering behavior occurs. Have him hold this image twice, for fifteen seconds each time.

Step 5: Imagining Desired Response

Have the student imagine himself performing the desired response with difficulty at first, then successfully. Visualize the successful response at least twice. The student should begin to see results after four fifteen-minute sessions.

Setting: The setting is in the hallway.
Desired Response: He will ignore the offending party and walk away.

Step 6: Role-Playing

Have the student role-play his desired response. This is an optional step. If you believe the student is ready to try the desired behavior in real life, go on to Step 8.

Step 7: Preparing Coping Statements

Even after practicing the desired behavior and positive thoughts, the student might experience some pessimistic thoughts that could inhibit him from applying what he has learned to real-life situations. That's why he will need to compose a couple of all-purpose cue cards (an index card will work). Have the student make a short coping statements that reminds him to relax, and instructs him to follow the plan.

Step 8: Performing Desired Behavior in Real Life

Perform the desired response when triggers occur.

Self-Monitoring

One of the most effective ways to manage behavior is to self-manage it. To self-manage the student must first be able to self-monitor behaviors that are problematic. Multiple methods of self-monitoring are discussed in previous chapters. The student must learn to self-monitor so that he can begin to take responsibility for his behavior. Ultimately, his ability to function in life will depend on how well he is able to monitor and personally manage his bipolar issues. Chapter nine specifically addresses multiple self-monitoring methods, while chapter two provides information where the student can find multiple strategies to manage his disorder.

Adult Initiated Proactive Strategies

In addition to the general proactive strategies listed below, there are three specific areas that teachers and parents can focus on to help alter behavior in bipolar students. Each of these are proactive in different ways. They help control behavior by proactively altering what is happening around the student in such a way that the unwanted behaviors can be reduced or discontinued.

- General Proactive Strategies
- Strategies for Sensory Issues
- Altering Antecedents to Reduce Inappropriate Behavior
- Strategies for Executive Functions

General Proactive Strategies

If the student is not able to self-manage, teachers, parents, counselors, etc. must identify specific strategies that they can implement that will help the student deal with problematic bipolar behavior. Some key strategies are listed below:

- Increase the structure of the environment. If a student is struggling with inappropriate behaviors, it may be due to the stress of attempting to function in an unstructured setting.
- Reduce the academic pressure. Minimize the amount of work, reduce items to be learned per concept. Provide alternative academic assignments that are less challenging, but related to the concept being taught.
- Reduce social stress in the classroom. Make sure that the student is able to handle speaking in front of the class or participating in groups. If he is not, find alternative ways for him to complete assignments,
- Provide a safe person who the student has some relationship with to help him calm down and who will help keep him safe.
- Address sensory issues. Some bipolar students have multiple sensory needs that if met, can help them control their behavior.

> *Urgent*
>
> *Don't give directions, tell the student to stop, or talk to the student in any way when he is in a rage state, or when he is trying to get or maintain control over his emotions. Give him space, time, and quiet!*

Strategies for Sensory Issues

Management of bipolar disorder includes modifying the student's surroundings so that he will not be overstressed by sensory issues. Sensory issues occur with many different conditions, e.g., Autism, Asperger, Non-verbal Learning Disability, and Bipolar Disorder. If a bipolar student has any form of sensory sensitivity it can produce stress when he experiences it. Stress, as has been previously stated, can trigger a mood state in the bipolar student. With this in mind, it is important to proactively identify specific sensory issues that the student may have so that you can reduce over-stimulation, and in turn help the student control his behavior or mood states. There are many senses, all of which can be overloaded. However there are two specific senses that are most often problematic for bipolar students. They are:

- Auditory
- Visual

Auditory

If a student is hyper-sensitive to sound it can produce stress. For instance, he may overreact to a school bell, a fire alarm, or loud announcements. Even background noises, e.g., the humming of fluorescent lights, someone tapping a pencil, or noise in the next room can trigger the hyper-sensitive student. Noise makes it difficulty to hear and focus.

- Be aware of auditory sensitivities and how the environment might be contributing to the child's marked increase in anxiety and challenging behaviors.
- Consider the use of headphones/ headband to muffle extraneous auditory stimuli.
- Use of headphones to listen to calming music when appropriate
- Forewarn the child of any fire drills, tornado drills, etc.
- Use of a quiet place in order to decrease sensory overload and increase self-calming.
- Use short precise messages with this student. Too much language can overload and confuse him. Give him time to internalize what you are saying before you say anything else.
- Avoid loud noisy places. If he is to transition where there is a lot of noise (cafeteria, hallway, fire drills, etc.), be sensitive to his reactions. He may need to be removed from the situation if it becomes too stimulating.
- Pre-warn the student when he will be facing a loud, noisy environment. It should be in his visual schedule and it should be reinforced verbally prior to the event.
- Attempt to muffle noises in the classroom for this student. You may want to use white noise or slow music (Mozart and Beethoven) to cover irritating noises that would be distracting or overwhelming to the student. Even so, be sensitive to the possibility that white noise or classical music may be too stimulating for the student.
- Exposure to noise is part of life. At some point in time the student must be desensitized to sound as much as he can be. Provide varied types of exposure to sound so that the student can gradually become adapted to it.
- Earphones to reduce auditory over-stimulation may need to be used.
- Reduce sound reverberation. If this is a problem, it is most likely causing some students to overload.
- Whisper when reading to help with understanding.
- Use a pvc pipe that is fashioned into the likeness of a phone that the student can use when reading. He can whisper and hear himself better while reading.

Visual

- If the student is visually sensitive you may need to reduce extraneous visual stimuli in the classroom.
- Reduce light refraction (glare/shine).
- Use natural lighting, e.g., the sun or full spectrum lighting.
- Reduce environmental movement.
- Keep furniture positions constant. By keeping furniture consistent there is less need for the child to keep a visual account of where the big pieces of furniture may be.
- Keep an orderly classroom. This can help decrease visual overload and by designating certain places for objects, the child can develop trust in routine and anticipate where things may be, thereby decreasing stress.
- Keep the walls and floors as plain as possible.
- Close the classroom door.
- Do not place the student in a position where has unlimited access to windows to the outside world.

Altering Antecedents to Reduce Inappropriate Behavior

Teachers and staff need to identify situations, settings, people, etc that trigger bipolar mood states. One very effective method for doing this is to change or remove the antecedent that provoked the behavior....or produced the stress that triggered the behavior. Simply stated, an antecedent is an environmental or intrapersonal event that occurs prior to the student exhibiting a behavior. Some antecedents are:

School-Based

- Conflicts
- Denial of something needed
- Something negative is inflicted
- Changes in routine
- Provocations
- Pressure
- Interruptions
- Ineffective problem-solving
- Academic errors
- Corrections
- Difficult academic work
- Peer problems

Non-School-Based

- Family disruption
- Health problems
- Abuse
- Nutrition
- Sleep
- Substance abuse
- Gang involvement
- Death of a pet
- Death of a family member

In the appendices there is a worksheet that will help the student identify specific triggers or antecendents that are causing problems for him (see the Identifying Triggers or Antecedents worksheet). After the antecendents are identified, it is up to the student, parent, and/or teacher to come up with ways to change the trigger, which in turn often causes the unwanted behavior to be discontinued. Here are two examples of how you could alter antecedents.

Antecedent Modification		
Name: *Mark*		**Date:** *8/24*
Behavior	**Antecedent: The Trigger**	**Changing the Antecedent**
Yells and screams	While in the lunch room Johnny steps up to Mark and says, "So retard, have you lost it yet today?" Mark goes into a rage state.	Do not let Mark go to lunch at the same time as Johnny, or monitor where Mark sits and make sure that Johnny has no access to him.
Throws books on floor	Teacher doesn't follow modifications and tells Mark that he has to finish the test without modifications. When Mark looks at the test he is overwhelmed and immediately gets angry.	Make sure that recommended modifications are used **every time**.

If needed, copy the Antecedent Modification form from the appendices
and have the student complete it.

Strategies for Executive Functions

Executive functions are in the frontal lobe of the brain and help control how efficiently a person accepts and utilizes information as it is filtered into the brain. Individuals with poor executive functioning can have a multitude of problems. Bipolar students, ADHD students, and Autism Spectrum students, to name a few, all have problems with executive function. The end result is that these students will often exhibit inappropriate or out of control behaviors when executive function difficulties are not modified for, or adjusted for in some way. Bipolar students can develop frustration as a result of difficulties regarding executive functions. This in turn can trigger manic, depressive, or rage state behaviors. It is important to identify which executive function issues the student is having trouble with. Once identified, the teacher and/or parent can help the student compensate by providing basic modifications, strategies, etc. that can help stabilize the student and reduce inappropriate behaviors. Here are some of the more commonly identified executive functions.

- Planning, prioritizing & time management problems
- Organizing materials and space
- Activating to work
- Focusing, regulating alertness & sustaining attention
- Processing speed
- Self-monitoring
- Flexibility & transitioning
- Emotional control
- Utilizing working memory
- Accessing recall
- Shifting attention
- Inhibition or response regulation

The more a teacher minimizes executive function issues, the greater the likelihood that the student will not stress and as a result exhibit manic, rage state, or depressed behaviors.

A quick checklist has been included that will help teachers and parents decide if the student has some executive function problems. This checklist is not an assessment that can tell you for sure which executive functions are problematic for a student. In depth testing may be needed to obtain that information. However, as his teacher or parent, you may be able to identify specific areas that appear to be causing problems for him. After checking to see which type of executive function problems you believe the student has, you can go to the section listed below that specifically provides helpful strategies for each executive function. This is not a complete list of strategies, but will give you some ideas as to what can be done for the student. It is important to note that the more a teacher minimizes executive function issues, the greater the likelihood that the student will not stress and as a result exhibit manic, rage state or depressed behaviors.

	Executive Functions		
Name: Jerry **Date:** 12/9			
		Yes	No
1	This student has planning, prioritizing & time management problems.	X	
2	This student has problems with organizing materials and space.	X	
3	This student has problems activating to work.	X	
4	This student has problems with focusing, regulating alertness & sustaining attention.	X	
5	This student has problems with processing speed.		X
6	This student has problems with self-monitoring.	X	
7	This student has problems with flexibility & transitioning.	X	
8	This student has problems with emotional control.		X
9	This student has a problem utilizing working memory.	X	
10	This student has a problem accessing recall.	X	
11	This student has a problem shifting attention.	X	
12	This student has a problem with inhibition or response regulation.		X

If needed, copy the Executive Functions checklist from the appendices and have the student complete it.

Problems with Planning, Prioritizing & Time Management

Some bipolar students have difficulty judging time, planning and prioritizing. As a result, large projects may be put off to the last minute. The following problems are often seen when a student has difficulty in this area:

- chronic problems with organization
- poor planning and time management skills

Strategies

- Actively involve the student in the development of planning his schedule. The use of a planning guide may be necessary to reduce the organizational and working memory difficulties that this student may have.
- Have this student write down his schedules with timelines and put them on his desk.
- Assign a peer study buddy who can model appropriate behavior.
    o A good student who can help 'teach'.
    o Someone who knows how to plan.
- Teach the bipolar student to accurately predict how much time it will take to complete a task or project. You can start doing this by asking the student how long a shorter task might take if he really focused on it. Use a reward to help the student maintain on task behavior.
- Give this bipolar student helper 'cards' that have steps for common routines or assignments. This can be used for math formulas, approaches to specific types of writing, etc.
- For bipolar students who are forgetful and are very visual you may want to use a daily picture schedule to help them remember what they should be doing. You may want to take pictures of daily/weekly events and put them on the visual calendar.

Problems with Organizing Materials & Space

Bipolar students often have difficulty finding materials when they need them. One of the reasons it is so difficult is because their space is chaotic around them. They are also extremely unorganized and often can't find work they have already done. The following problems are often seen when a student has difficulty in this area:

- Chronic problems with organizing materials
- Chronic problems with untidiness in work areas

Strategies

- Have this bipolar student keep everything in a specific place. If his desk area becomes untidy have him clean it up before he leaves that day.
- Bipolar students will benefit from working in a small groups with more organized peers who could serve as good role models.
- Have older bipolar students get out their assignment books and show them to you before you give them their assignments.
- Bipolar students need a home school communication tool to be put into place. Parents and teachers need to communicate with each other to make sure the organizational system will work properly.

- Bipolar students need to keep an extra set of books at home to assist with organizational difficulties.
- These students will inevitably forget supplies. With parents help you may want to keep an extra supply of paper, pencils, etc. that the student can get if he 'forgets' to bring what he needs for class.
- Due to the tendency to lose things, not keep supplies, etc., it may be helpful to keep a zippered supply pouch secured into a binder that is being utilized as an organizational system. With the parents help make sure that it is filled with extra school supplies.

Activating to Work

Activation to task is often difficult for bipolar students. They can't get started, sometimes don't understand what they are to do, and often seem to be distracted by other seemingly unimportant things that keep them from beginning their work. The following problems are often seen when a student has difficulty in this area:

- Chronically high level of anxiety that keeps them from activating to task
- Misinterprets what teachers meant them to do and fails to activate to identified task

Strategies

- Assist the bipolar student in starting the assignment.
- Make sure the bipolar student understands teacher instructions.
- Place this bipolar student around peers that can serve as models to help him get started on tasks.
- Bipolar students will benefit from working with a peer or in small groups. The intent if for his peer(s) to model appropriate behavior.
- When there is too many problems, etc. on a worksheet the bipolar student can easily become distracted and not activate. When you give the bipolar student work to do, it would be best if you added space between questions/tasks.

Problems with Focusing, Regulating Alertness & Sustaining Attention

Bipolar students often have difficulty sustaining attention. Both internal and external distracters are interesting if not more important than the task at hand. In addition, if the room is distracting it is extremely difficulty for the student to maintain his focus. As a result, maintaining alertness becomes increasingly difficult. The following problems are often seen when a student has difficulty in this area:

- Bipolar students have chronic problems in sustaining attention for tasks that are not self-selected.
- Bipolar students can get so preoccupied with their own thoughts or imagination that whatever else is going on around them becomes momentarily unimportant.
- Bipolar students have a problem regulating alertness unless the environment is stimulating.

- Bipolar students also have a tendency to get sidetracked. They may switch topics quickly causing confusion for those around them.
- Bipolar students also have problems with sustained attention.

Strategies:

- Make frequent eye contact with the student to assist him in staying focused. A simple glance can bring the student back from a daydream.
- Verbal redirection to task (preferably a whisper and in close proximity).
- Seat the bipolar student near your desk or wherever you are most of the time (proximity control). This reduces the tendency to drift off task.
- Project your voice, change tone, loudness, etc. Use your para-verbals.
- You may also use the above method and have the student self-monitor.
- Develop a prearranged cue to assist in redirection. The teacher may give a visual signal, e.g., touching he nose, ear, etc. or utilize a verbal phrase, e.g., "I'm watching for those who are on task."

Problems with Processing Speed

Due to executive function issues in the prefrontal cortex most bipolar students struggle with processing speed. In other words, it takes them longer to process new information and get it into the brain so that it can be utilized. The following problems are often seen when a student has difficulty in this area:

- Problems with slowness or in processing information

Strategies

- Summarize frequently in class to help give the student more time to process and review information.
- The rate of presentation for new material may need to be altered for some bipolar students. If too much is given at a time it will overload him and he will learn very little.
- Give this student additional processing time, or time to rehearse the new information before he is asked to share or use it.
- Give this student more time to formulate answers and respond to questions.
- Re-teaching may be necessary for students who have processing speed problems.
- Multimodal teaching may be beneficial for students who have processing speed problems.

Problems with Self-Monitoring

The ability to self-monitor requires that the student be able to identify behaviors that may have a negative impact on both him and those around him. It also suggests that he is capable of monitoring such behavior in order to favorably alter it. The following problems are often seen when a student has difficulty in this area:

- Difficulty self-monitoring specific behavior problems associated with executive function issues
- Difficulty seeing how behavior may have a negative impact on others

Strategies

- Bipolar students who have problems with self-monitoring may not understand the impact of their behavior on those around them. Discuss the behavior and how it impacts others in a private setting away from their peers.
- Encourage the bipolar student to self-monitor his own behavior. This helps build responsibility, and will often cause the student to watch his own behavior more closely, thus reducing inappropriate behaviors (see section that has worksheets for self-monitoring).
- Have this student chart his behavior in order to provide a visual record of the change in behavior. Build a reward into this as an incentive.
- Have the bipolar student set goals for accuracy rather than speed. This slower speed can help him increase attention to errors and improve his work.
- To improve self-monitoring you may want to reward the bipolar student when he accurately monitors his work.

Problems with Flexibility & Transitioning

The ability to change plans, adjust to new information, correct mistakes and handle transitional issues as they occur suggests that a student is flexible. The following problems may be seen when a student has difficulty in this area:

- Fails to adjust to new settings
- Has difficulty with adjusting to change in routines
- Inflexible in the face of new situations

Strategies

- Provide lots of structure. Post schedules and changes on the board, verbally remind the class what will be happening during the day and put the schedule on the student's desk if he has difficulty with transitioning.
- Prepare the bipolar student for any change in routine (preferably a day in advance if possible). Announce what is going to happen and give repeat warnings as the time approaches.
- Use cue cards that can be placed on the student's desk to aid in transition. The card would have the specific steps you would want to teach. For instance, the title would be, 'How to Make Transitions' The three steps to transition efficiently might be:
    1. Begin transition as soon as you are told to do so
    2. Put away unnecessary materials

3. Get what you need for the next activity
- Provide supervision during transitions – between subjects, classes, recess, lunchroom, assemblies, etc.
- Tell your students that it is important for their transitions to be both quick and quiet. For younger students ask them to repeat back the two elements of a good transition…."quick and quiet".
- Provide the student with situations where he must be more flexible. Take small steps at first to assure success. Gradually make the transitions more significant. This will increase flexibility.

Problems with Emotional Control

Bipolar students have difficulty controlling their emotional state at any given point in time. Emotional overreactions are often problematic with these students.   The following problems are often seen when a student has difficulty in this area:

- Bipolar students have problems regulating their emotions.
- Bipolar students are also extremely vulnerable and sensitive emotionally.
- Bipolar students are often easily annoyed, irritated, frustrated, etc. and do so at a rate and intensity that seems excessive for the situation.

Strategies

- Bipolar students should be taught response delay techniques. For instance, consider alternatives before you react, practice leaving a situation that is frustrating, counting before responding, etc.
- It is important that you teach this student to think about how people would feel, what they would think, etc., before he reacts emotionally.
- Establish clear rules and expectations for behavior in the classroom. This will help the bipolar student control his emotions.
- Students experience fatigue, pressure and stress that can test their self-control and lead to inappropriate behavior. As a result, it is important to provide the student with opportunities for rest and relaxation throughout the day.
- Allow for cool down or time out. This student will need a place where he can go that he sees as being safe.
- Teach and utilize relaxation methods to keep him at a low level of stress. This will keep him from exploding as much.

Problems with Utilizing Working Memory

Simply stated, working memory allows the student to put one or several things on hold while attending to other tasks. It works like a search engine in that it is in a constant act of integrating new information or thoughts with that which is already stored in the brain. Working Memory allows the student to manipulate multiple pieces of data at the same time. The following problems are often seen when a student has difficulty in this area:

- Bipolar students may often experience short-term working memory problems, e.g., forgetfulness in daily routines.
- Bipolar students may often forget to bring home papers or books needed for homework.
- Bipolar students may often forget to hand in homework assignments, notes from parents or teachers, permission slips, etc.
- Bipolar students will often have difficulty keeping one or several things in mind while doing something else.

Strategies

- Due to working memory issues bipolar students have difficulty keeping track of more than one or two steps at a time. He should be provided with a written checklist of steps required to complete a task.
- Teach the student to use outlines and underlining to help with learning and memory.
- Provide frequent short breaks when you are teaching new information to bipolar students. The breaks may only be one or two minutes in duration.
- bipolar students benefit from pre-teaching. Provide them with a basic framework of the new information prior to actually teaching it.
- Direct bipolar students to listen for important points. This can help reduce working memory difficulties.
- Preferential seating can be very beneficial for bipolar students with working memory problems.

Problems with Accessing Recall

Accessing recall calls for the student to be able to mentally call up different pieces of information without any visual, auditory, etc. cue. The following problems are often seen when a student has difficulty in this area:

- Bipolar students often have difficulty recalling what they have learned, e.g., learns something one day, but doesn't remember it the next day.
- Bipolar students may be able to recognize stored information, but struggles with remembering it in recall mode.

Strategies

- You may teach the bipolar student to use outlines and underlining as basic skills to help with learning and memory.
- Many bipolar students have difficult assessing recall. It's not that they don't have the information in their brain. It's that they have trouble with retrieval. Use recognition based assessments to obtain a true measure of what the student is learning.
- Have bipolar students look up when trying to remember something....not down.
- Teach a Memory System to Improve Retention and Recall.

- Make sure the bipolar student understands what you want. Have him repeat the directions or explain what you ask him to do.

Problems with Shifting Attention

Shifting calls for the student to be able to change from one task to another, or cognitively shift from one activity to another. The following problems are often seen when a student has difficulty in this area:

- Bipolar students will often have difficulty shifting from one physical task to another.
- Bipolar students will often have difficulty cognitively shifting from one mindset or topic to another.

Strategies

- Shifting from one task to another is difficult for this student. He should be gently led from one task to another to assure that a transition from one task to another has been accomplished. Materials from the previous task should be put up and be out of sight before he begins a new task.
- Provide a signal to indicate that it is time to transition from one activity to another. This would cue the student to put away materials get ready for the next task.
- Use the Two Minute Warning to help this student adjust to change in routine, task, or cognitive shift. Tell this student that one activity is about to end and another will begin. It would be good to give him a few minutes of leisure time between one activity and the beginning of the next. This will help him transition more smoothly.
- Utilize time limits for tasks. This will help the student shift from one task to the other. The use of a timer can help as he changes from one activity to another.
- Working in small groups of peers can help an bipolar student more effectively shift his focus or cognitive set. His peers can model when to change, how to change and what to change making it easier for the student to shift.

Problems with Inhibition or Self-Regulation (impulse control)

Self-regulation calls for the student to control the tendency to act without thinking without regard to how the behavior may have a negative impact on self or others. The following problems are often seen when a student has difficulty in this area:

Strategies

- Grabs things, or starts doing things without waiting for permission or directions.
- Difficulties self-regulating the pace of action, e.g., messy work, careless mistakes, not able to slow down.

- An inability to size up or monitor a situation adequately before acting, e.g., speaks without considering what might happen, doesn't stop soon enough when fooling around, teasing, etc., and too quick to react to what others say and do.
- Let the student know that you can't 'see' students who talk without raising their hand first.
- Positively acknowledge when students raise their hand to ask permission. "Johnny, thank you for raising your hand, what can I do for you?"
- Set up rules and guidelines for speaking in class, i.e., must raise hand and get permission from teacher before speaking. For bipolar students who have a significant problem with this, paste the skill set on his desk reminding him how to get the teachers attention.
- Teach this student to think out loud (whisper to self is helpful at times) when he is problem solving. This will help him think things through before speaking or acting.

Motivation and Behavior Management

Personal motivation can be a very powerful tool for change. If the bipolar student can identify something that is very important to him, he may very well work extremely hard to obtain it. He will work harder at monitoring his depressive, or hypomanic behaviors. He will work harder at learning specific strategies that will help him if he is going into a depressive, hypomanic or rage state. He will also be more apt to utilize strategies that he has learned in order to control his mood swings. These personal motivators can be a force that can help as a deterrent to behaviors that are problematic for the student. Here are some methods that can help determine what is reinforcing or motivating to the student, and how the reinforcers can be utilized once identified. They are:

- Reinforcement Survey: Elementary
- School Reward Survey: Secondary
- Reinforcement Schedule
- Reinforcement Board

Reinforcement Survey: Elementary

The reinforcement survey is predominantly used with elementary students. However, it can be used in certain situations with some secondary students. It consists of ten either or forced choices. There are five specific types of reinforcers that are measured. They are:

- **Consumables**: Consumables include candy, ice cream, drinks, favorite snacks, or anything else edible that is reinforcing to the student.

- **Tangibles:** Tangibles include art materials, pencils, pencil sharpeners, coloring books, or any other item that is reinforcing to the student.

- **Activity:** An activity might be free computer time, free time at a center, helping the teacher in class, game with friend, or any other activity that is reinforcing to the student.

- **Adult Approval:** Adult approval may be a smiley face on a paper, having a teacher comment about good work, having a teacher say how proud she is about something the student has done, or any other sign of approval that an adult might give.

- **Peer Approval:** Peer approval could be having an opportunity to be leader at recess, having friends tell you that you have done a good job, having friends ask you to be on their team, or any other sign of approval that a peer might give.

The age of the child would impact how the specific type of reinforcer would be applied in a positive way for the student. If there is a younger student who needs to have reinforcers given you may want to go to the appendices and help the student fill out the Reinforcement Survey. When finished there should be one or two specific types of reinforcers that seem to be the most preferred for the student. There are pages filled with reinforcers for each type listed above. For instance, if the student scored high for consumables and activities you would need to help the student complete the forms that specifically look at Consumables and Activities. When completed, it will give you multiple reinforcers that would be preferred by the student.

School Reward Survey: Secondary

This is a sentence stub survey that will provide information regarding what is most preferred as a reinforcer by older students. The five types of reinforcers are assessed again, but in a different way. The student's responses can provide any educator with multiple reinforcers that can be used hourly, daily, or weekly as needed. The School Reward Questionnaire can be found in the appendices.

Reinforcement Schedules

Once you have identified a variety of reinforcers that might be used with the student you now have to determine how you are going to effectively use them. There are multiple methods that can be used to reinforce a student. Some have been previously discussed in previous chapters. All of the reinforcers identified by either the Reinforcement Survey or the School Reward Survey can be used for any reinforcement schedule or purpose as long as it helps the student improve his behavior.

- Proactive Reinforcement Schedule
- Daily/Weekly Rewards Menu
- Reinforcement Board
- Reward Chart: Daily/Weekly

Proactive Reinforcement Schedule

The Proactive Reinforcement Schedule is a tool by which you can compile the students preferred reinforcers from all of the sources that you have utilized to gain information. Once you have information about what he likes, list the reinfocers on this worksheet so that you will have one place you can go to to find the reinforcers that he prefers. This sheet becomes a resource for all reinforcement schedules you may use for the student on a day to day basis.

Proactive Reinforcement Schedule

Name: *Johnny*   **Date:** *4/26*

Instructions:

1. With the data you have and the parent's help identify rewards that can be proactively used to help the student maintain control of his behavior.
2. Review all data before listing items that the student finds very rewarding.

Activity:

Spades, checkers, chess, free time on computer, Play cards.

Consumables:

Ice cream, a Mountain Dew, Hershey Bar, Popcorn, package of peanuts.

Adult Reinforcement:

Praise from teacher, telling my parents I did a good job on a project.

If needed, copy the Proactive Reinforcement Schedule from the appendices and complete it.

Daily/Weekly Rewards Menu

The Daily/Weekly Rewards Menu is one of the point sheets that can be used to implement a reward system for the student. It is simple to use and provides a visual for the student so that he can see what he is working for on a day by day basis. As with all rewards systems it would be best to have the student keep a copy of the rewards menu on h is desk, in his folder, etc. He needs to have access to it and be able to view it when ever he wants to. Making it that accessible provides the student with an ongoing motivation to work at keeping control of his behaviors. He will work harder at utilizing some of his strategies that will help him stay in control if he can constantly see what he may receive as a reward for maintaining control. This particular menu calls for different levels of rewards. The student and teacher should take his list of possible rewards and place them on the menu depending on their point value. Take time and make sure that each level of points has rewards that the student is interested in. Here is a partial sample of the Daily/Weekly Rewards Menu that can be implemented for any bipolar student.

Daily/Weekly Rewards Menu

Name: Jared   **Date:** 9/23

Instructions:

With the student's help identify four rewards that he can obtain at the end of the day if he receives 5, 10, 15, or 20 points in a day.

Daily Rewards

5 points for the day   =   Sticker, Balloons, Bookmark.

10 points for the day =   Coloring book and crayons, peanuts, beef jerkey.

15 points for the day =   Comic book, magazine, play Hackey Sack for 15 min, play card game with Friend, 15 minutes computer time.

20 points for the day =   Ice cream bar, popcorn, stuffed animal, listen to CD

Instructions:

If the student chooses he may bank his points in order to get a larger reward at the end of the week. With the student's help and help from the parent identify two rewards; one for 70 points and one for 90 points.

Weekly Rewards

70 points for the Week   = Cookies for class

90 points for the Week   = Cake and Drinks for class

If needed, copy the Daily/Weekly Rewards Menu from the appendices and have the student complete it.

Keep in mind that the rewards need to be adapted depending on the developmental age of the student. Older students will need more 'sophisticated' rewards.

Reward Chart

Another simple reward chart is shown below. This chart can be used by period, by day, or by week in order to provide a reinforcer for the student. There are two Reward Charts in the appendices. The first chart focuses on period by period reinforcers. The second chart as shown below is for end of day, or end of week reinforcers. It's important to note that some students may need reinforcers on multiple occasions during the period in order to maintain control of their behavior. If this is the case, the period by period chart can be adapted for that use. The Reward Chart also has a reinforcer built into it where the student can obtain a reward for his whole class if he does well during the week. This provides an opportunity for peer encouragement, which will often motivate the student to work hard to control his behavior. The chart below is an abbreviated version of the Daily/Weekly Reward Chart. The complete chart is in the appendices.

Daily/Weekly Rewards Chart	
Name: *Brandon*	Date: *11/28*
If I have less than 4 checks on my monitoring system I can choose from the following at the end of the day.	
Popcorn	Ice cream bar
Coloring book and colors	Card game with friend
If I have a minimum of 15 checks during from Monday through Friday I can choose a special activity, etc. for myself or my class.	
Movie for Class with popcorn	Cake and Drinks for class

If needed, copy the Daily/Weekly Reward Chart from the appendices and have the student complete it.

This reward chart must also have rewards that are developmentally appropriate. When the student identifies various reinforcers using the various forms in this book you will have a good list of possible reinforcers or rewards that you can use. To obtain the checks the student may use any number of self-monitoring devices found in this book or a teacher made point system may be used. Both teacher and student must decide what is fair regarding the amount of checks that can be allowed for various reinforcers. Remember to make sure that the intent is for the student to be successful so that he can improve his behavior.

Reinforcement Board

Many children are very visual in nature. This is true for many bipolar students. When they are going into a hypomanic state they are more apt to 'listen' with their eyes than they are with their ears. There is an old saying that says, 'A picture is worth a thousand words.' When you are working with a bipolar student who needs ongoing positive reinforcements to help him stay motivated and overcome inappropriate behaviors, you may want to use a reinforcement board. As you identify specific tangible items, activities, consumables, etc., that is rewarding to the student, place symbols of the identified items on a board. For instance, if he likes Oreo cookies you may cut out the front of an Oreo cookie box (or use a wrapper) and place it on the reinforcement board. You could also place a Hershey chocolate bar wrapper, an empty potato chip bag, a playing card, a picture of a computer, a picture of a book, a picture of various games, a picture of the teacher, etc. on the board. Any reward that the student may be interested in should be placed on the board. This board could have rewards that multiple students would be interested in receiving.

Strategies for Crisis Management

Before you consider strategies, it is important that both teachers and parents develop knowledge regarding crisis management. There are numerous programs that teach crisis management. Teachers, staff and parents should all participate in one of these programs. Training in crisis management can have a tremendous impact on how effective a student is dealt with. Sometimes, no matter what you do, the student will still have an episode that causes him to go out of control. When this occurs, both parents and educators must have strategies that they can use to help the student.

- Get the student to move
- Classroom Clear
- Restraint
- Call SRO or 911
- Hospitalization

Get the Student to Move

When a student is starting to get out of control, e.g., hypomania, mania, appears to be going into a rage state, it is important to take whatever measures you can to get him away from the other students. Although the safety of the student is important, it is also extremely important that you protect the other students in the classroom. One technique that has helped some teachers is fairly simple to use and should be attempted initially. Simply engage the student and begin to speak with him. As you do, lead him out of the classroom, encouraging him all the time. If he is engaged with you he may follow you into the hallway. The teacher should have a previously set up signal that she gives to a responsible student in the classroom. That student should immediately go to the office to get help. If he doesn't follow, ask him to go into the hallway so that you can have a private conversation with him.

Classroom Clear

If you cannot get the student out of the classroom and he appears to be harmful to self or others you may need to do a classroom clear. This technique is discussed in detail in chapter three as a method for dealing with a bipolar student who is in a rage state.

Communication

Attempt to communicate with the student. If he is able to talk attempt to get him out of the room and to a safer location. However, if he is not able to communicate in a rational way, allow him to rant, scream, or talk until he

Restrictive Setting

When a student is out of control he obviously cannot stay in the classroom. A safe, more restrictive setting needs to be available that the student can use until he can calm down or get control of his behavior.

Restraint

Restraint is defined as the use of physical force, or a mechanical device to restrict the free movement of all or a portion of the student's body. Restraint shouldn't only be used in an emergency with the following limitations:

- Limited to reasonable force necessary to address emergency
- Discontinued when emergency no longer exists
- Implemented to protect health/safety of student and others
- Shall NOT deprive student of basic human necessities (TAC 89.1053)

Restraint should be used as a last resort. In addition, it should be noted that restraint should not be used when the student is larger than the adults working with him. If he is taller, stronger, etc. it may not be wise to attempt a restraint. This is often the case in high school and sometimes the case in junior high or middle school. Regardless, it is important that you protect the student, or other students from significant harm. It may be that all you would be able to do is stop the student from hitting another with his hand. Just keep in mind that the degree of force you use is relative to the safety need of the student or another student. Keeping this in mind there are three conditions that would warrant a student being restrained.

1. The student exhibits imminent, serious physical harm to self
2. The student exhibits imminent, serious physical harm to others
3. The student exhibits imminent, significant property destruction

Imminent means that you have a reason to believe that the harm or destruction is about to occur. This could be based on history, action (balling fist, picking up a pencil and holding it is if it were going to be used in a destructive way, etc.) or any other factor that can be identified by others. Serious can mean many things. In relationship to harm, anytime blood is drawn intentionally it should be considered serious. It should also be considered serious if the person is in danger of causing unconsciousness, internal damage due to the force of the blows, etc. In relationship to property destruction, it is important for each district to identify what serious means monetarily. Some districts state that anything over $50 would be considered serious.

Call 911 or Get a Student Resource Officer (policeman) Involved

If the student goes into a rage at school it is important that everyone involved be given the greatest possibility of safety. The student must be kept safe, the staff must be kept safe, other students must be kept safe and it is important to control the amount of damage that may be done to school property. If things get out of control it may be essential to call the campus police to control the student and to possibly take him to the hospital.

On the other hand, parents must also be willing to call 911 to get assistance from the police when the rage becomes to violent to control at home.

Hospitalization

When should a student be hospitalized? Hospitalization is predominantly a parent decision, not the schools. The school is not intended to be a clinical setting where diagnosis and treatment is offered. If the student is so severe that he needs hospitalization it is important that the parents take appropriate action so that their child can get the medical support that he needs. If his behavior is that severe it may require a change in medication or additional medication to help stabilize him. The student should be stable before he returns to school. With proper treatment including medication many bipolar children never need hospitalization. However, some children become so severe that for safety purposes they will need to be hospitalized. Chances are if you have to take your child to the hospital it will be an emergency because of his mania or depression. If this is the case the doctors at the hospital will do an intake and determine what treatment is necessary for your child. Usually he will make a diagnosis, recommend medication or medications, and suggest a treatment plan that will possibly include:

- Individual counseling by a private counselor
- A day treatment program
- Ongoing inpatient hospitalization

Conclusion

Above all keep in mind that bipolar students need an extraordinary amount of proactive strategies to help them maintain appropriate behavior. Whether the behavior is extremely problematic for others or just for the student himself, it is essential to give him the tools that he heeds so that he can learn to monitor and manage his own behavior. Even so, there will be times that he will require assistance from parents and teachers in the form of structure, positive supports and personal support in order to make it on a day to day basis. Don't give up....with your help these students can and will make it.

APPENDICES

Mania Reduction

Name: Date:

Instructions:
1) Write down the hypomanic symptom.
2) Using a 1-5 scale, mark the number that describes your current mood.
3) Use a strategy that will help control the manic tendency.
4) Using a 1-5 scale, mark the number that describes your mood after using the strategy.

1 = Normal for me   3 = Very Agitated   5 = About ready to go manic

Date/ Time	Symptom	How hypomanic initially?	Strategy Used	How hypomanic after strategy?
		1 2 3 4 5		1 2 3 4 5
		1 2 3 4 5		1 2 3 4 5
		1 2 3 4 5		1 2 3 4 5
		1 2 3 4 5		1 2 3 4 5
		1 2 3 4 5		1 2 3 4 5
		1 2 3 4 5		1 2 3 4 5
		1 2 3 4 5		1 2 3 4 5
		1 2 3 4 5		1 2 3 4 5
		1 2 3 4 5		1 2 3 4 5
		1 2 3 4 5		1 2 3 4 5
		1 2 3 4 5		1 2 3 4 5
		1 2 3 4 5		1 2 3 4 5
		1 2 3 4 5		1 2 3 4 5
		1 2 3 4 5		1 2 3 4 5
		1 2 3 4 5		1 2 3 4 5

May be reproduced for Therapy, Home, or School use only!

Debriefing the Student

Name: Date:

Event:
If he can remember the event, discuss what happened. If he can't, tell him what he did during the rage. Write down his perceptions of the event.

When he has processed what has happened go to 'Trigger'.

Trigger:
Explore what triggered the rage state. Was there an antecedent? If so, what was it?

Patterns:

Look to see if there has been a pattern. Is the antecedent an event, a time of the day, a place, a person who consistently triggers the rage state?   Try to find the pattern if there is one.

Training: Identify the method that would best handle the triggering event.

Some possible methods are:

Desensitization Training (ERP):

Conflict Management Skills:

Cue Cards:

Stress Management Techniques:

Stress Inoculation Training:

Self-Monitoring Technique:

Other:

Contract

Name:_____

Situation:_____

_____

_____

Condition: _____

_____

_____

Rewards:_____

_____

_____

_____   _____
Child/Adolescent   Parent or Teacher

Depression Reduction

Name: **Date:**

Instructions:
1) Identify the depressive symptom.
2) Using a 1-5 scale, mark the number that describes your current mood.
3) Use a strategy that will help control the depressive tendency.
4) Using a 1-5 scale, mark the number that describes your mood after using the strategy.

1 = Normal for me		3 = Very Agitated		5 = Depressed
Date/ Time	Symptom	How depressed initially?	Strategy Used	How depressed after strategy?
		1 2 3 4 5		1 2 3 4 5
		1 2 3 4 5		1 2 3 4 5
		1 2 3 4 5		1 2 3 4 5
		1 2 3 4 5		1 2 3 4 5
		1 2 3 4 5		1 2 3 4 5
		1 2 3 4 5		1 2 3 4 5
		1 2 3 4 5		1 2 3 4 5
		1 2 3 4 5		1 2 3 4 5
		1 2 3 4 5		1 2 3 4 5
		1 2 3 4 5		1 2 3 4 5
		1 2 3 4 5		1 2 3 4 5
		1 2 3 4 5		1 2 3 4 5
		1 2 3 4 5		1 2 3 4 5

May be reproduced for Therapy, Home, or School use only!

Thought Distortion Checklist

Name:	Date:			
Instructions: Read the definition for each distortion and rate if it occurs.				
1 = Rarely 2 = Sometimes 3 = Often				
Thought Distortions	**Definition**			
All or Nothing Thinking	Events are really only black or white, good or bad. There is no middle ground. This distortion often leads to perfectionism and ongoing frustration. For instance, if the student is turned down for a date, he may feel that no one will ever say, 'Yes.' If he fails his Language Arts test, he is convinced that he will not pass any test. This distortion leads to negative thinking which in turn has a negative impact on the brain.	1	2	3
Mind Reading or Jumping to Conclusions	Illogic is the key problem with this distortion. The student may predict what another person thinks without having evidence or information that would support his conclusions. For instance, the student may feel bad because he believes a fellow student is thinking something negative about him, even though nothing has been said or done to suggest it.	1	2	3
Maximization or Minimization	These distortions occur when the student blows things out of proportion, or when he minimizes things, e.g., he may minimize/maximize qualities, or characteristics about himself. Both distortions cause problems for the student in how he feels about himself and in how he relates to others.	1	2	3
Fortune Telling	This distortion occurs when the student predicts a bad outcome to a situation before it has even happened. The mind is a very powerful organ. If the student feeds his mind enough information suggesting that there will be a bad outcome, it will go out of the way to assure that it happens. For example, the student may say, "I know I will fail my math test." His mind will then do what it can to help him accomplish that belief. One way it might accomplish this is by making him believe that since he is going to fail anyway, there is no use in studying hard.	1	2	3

Emotional Reasoning	This distortion calls for the student to believe what he feels. In other words if he feels something is true, it is true. It doesn't matter what the facts say, his feelings rule. For instance, if he feels that others don't care, then it is true. Emotional reasoning can easily produce depression.	1	2	3
Shoulds or Musts	This distortion calls for the student to set strict rules or expectations that are not always realistic. He feels guilty if he doesn't live up to the rules or expectations. When others don't live up to his 'shoulds' or 'musts' he feels angry, upset	1	2	3
Personalization	This distortion occurs when he believes that the things that people do or say are a direct reaction to him. He may assume the responsibility for something negative that happens even though he had nothing to do with it. For instance, he notices the girl he's sitting next to takes a look at her watch. As a result, the student believes that he is boring.	1	2	3
Negative Filtering	This distortion occurs when the student focuses on the negative, while he ignores the positive. The student may seem to be a negative person because he finds something negative about everything he looks at.	1	2	3
Catastrophizing	This distortion occurs when the student expects things to turn out badly. For instance, if he asks a teacher to help, he believes that she will make things hard on him. So he doesn't ask and as a result, he doesn't get help.	1	2	3

May be reproduced for Therapy, Home, or School use only!

Dissecting Cognitive Distortions

Name: Date:

Negative Thought	Cognitive Distortion	Rational Response

May be reproduced for Therapy, Home, or School use only!

Negative vs Positive Thoughts

Name: Date:

Negative Thoughts	Positive Counters

Negative Thought Tracking

Name: Date:

Negative Thought	Number of Times
	1 2 3 4 5 6 7 8 9 10
	1 2 3 4 5 6 7 8 9 10
	1 2 3 4 5 6 7 8 9 10
	1 2 3 4 5 6 7 8 9 10
	1 2 3 4 5 6 7 8 9 10
	1 2 3 4 5 6 7 8 9 10
	1 2 3 4 5 6 7 8 9 10
	1 2 3 4 5 6 7 8 9 10
	1 2 3 4 5 6 7 8 9 10
	1 2 3 4 5 6 7 8 9 10
	1 2 3 4 5 6 7 8 9 10
	1 2 3 4 5 6 7 8 9 10
	1 2 3 4 5 6 7 8 9 10
	1 2 3 4 5 6 7 8 9 10
	1 2 3 4 5 6 7 8 9 10
	1 2 3 4 5 6 7 8 9 10
	1 2 3 4 5 6 7 8 9 10
	1 2 3 4 5 6 7 8 9 10
	1 2 3 4 5 6 7 8 9 10
	1 2 3 4 5 6 7 8 9 10
	1 2 3 4 5 6 7 8 9 10
	1 2 3 4 5 6 7 8 9 10
	1 2 3 4 5 6 7 8 9 10
	1 2 3 4 5 6 7 8 9 10

Fun Outdoor Activities

Name: Date:

Instructions:
1. Place a check next to anything listed below that you believe would be fun or enjoyable.
2. Out of the items listed below pick your top five outdoor activities that you would like to do for fun.

	Being in the country		Playing miniature golf
	Playing baseball or softball		Driving go carts
	Being at the beach		Snow skiing
	Rock climbing or mountaineering		Exploring (hiking away from known routes, etc.)
	Playing golf		Playing tennis
	Going to a sports event		Being with animals
	Going to the races (horse, car, boat, etc.)		Watching the sky, clouds, or a storm
	Boating (canoeing, kayaking, Motor-boating, sailing, etc.)		Camping
	Competing in a sports event		Going on outings (to the park, a picnic, a barbecue, etc.)
	Playing basketball		Going to a museum or exhibit
	Gathering natural objects (rocks, driftwood, etc.)		Sitting/laying in the sun
	Being in the mountains		Riding a motorcycle
	Seeing beautiful scenery		Going to a beach/water park
	Waterskiing		Going to a fair, carnival, circus, zoo, or amusement park
	Hiking		Other:
	Doing yard work		Other:

1._____

2._____

3._____

4._____

5._____

May be reproduced for Therapy, Home, or School use only!

Fun Indoor Activities

Name: Date:

Instructions:
1. Place a check next to anything listed below that you believe would be fun or enjoyable.
2. Out of the items listed below pick your top five outdoor activities that you would like to do for fun.

	Going to a concert		Having a party
	Planning trips or vacations		Playing pool or billiards
	Doing art work (painting, drawing, movie-making, etc.)		Being with relatives
	Rearranging or redecorating your room		Doing craft work (pottery, jewelry, beads, weaving, etc.)
	Going to a sports event		Playing cards
	Going to a fun party		Playing chess or checkers
	Going to lectures or hearing speakers		Putting on makeup, fixing my hair, etc.
	Thinking up or arranging songs or music		Drawing
	Playing a musical instrument		Having lunch with friends
	Taking pictures		Lifting weights
	Hearing or telling jokes		Bowling
	Going to a museum or exhibit		Listening to the radio/cd
	Playing a video game		Having friends come to visit
	Watching humorous videos		Playing basketball
	Playing a game with friends		Other:
	Watching television		Other:

1._____

2._____

3._____

4._____

5._____

May be reproduced for Therapy, Home, or School use only!

Building a Healthy Social Support System

List four things you could do to improve or strengthen your current social support system.

1. _____

2. _____

3. _____

4. _____

List activities where you currently enjoy what you do and get to meet other people.

1. _____

2. _____

3. _____

4. _____

List other activities that you enjoy doing that might offer an opportunity to meet other people.

1. _____

2. _____

3. _____

4. _____

May be reproduced for Therapy, Home, or School use only!

Daily or Weekly Rewards List

Name: Date:

Instructions:

1. List ten rewards that you would be willing to work for on a daily basis. You are not limited to these rewards. They can be added to, or altered whenever you like. This just gives you a working list to help you get started on a reward program.
2. List six rewards that would be given at the end of the week. You would have to trade in five daily rewards to get the weekly reward. These too can change as you identify other things that you might like to have as larger weekly rewards.

List ten daily rewards that you would really like.

1.	6.
2.	7.
3.	8.
4.	9.
5.	10.

List six weekly rewards that you would really like.

1.	4.
2.	5.
3.	6.

Fun Activities

Name: Date:

	SU	M	T	W	Th	F	SA	T O T A L
Week #1								
Week #2								
Week #3								
Week #4								
Week #5								

Possible Daily Rewards
If you have completed your activity for the day you may choose one of the rewards listed below, or accumulate five for the week to get a weekly reward.
1.
2.
3.
4.
5.
6.
7.

End of Week Reward
You must have refused five daily rewards in order to get the weekly reward on Saturday. The reward week stars on a Sunday and Ends on Saturday.

May be reproduced for Therapy, Home, or School use only!

Visualizing a Fun Activity Strategy

Name: Date:

Step One: Find a location where you can sit and relax for a bit. This could be the counselor's office, or any other room where you can have some time alone to use this strategy.

Step Two: Pick an activity that you would find very enjoyable, or a time when you were participating in an activity or situation when you felt very good....when you were having a lot of fun.

Step Three: Do deep breathing for a few minutes.

Step Four: Visualize yourself doing what you have chosen in step one for about five minutes or longer.

May be reproduced for Therapy, Home, or School use only!

Stress Monitor

Name:	Date:

Instructions:
1. Identify the event that is causing stress for you.
2. Rate how stressed you are the next time the event occurs.
3. Use a stress technique that you have chosen that will help you relax.
4. When you have finished relaxing using the technique, rate your level of stress again. If it is not any lower you may want to use the technique again or use another technique.

Rating Scale: 1 = No Stress 2 = Mild Stress 3 = Moderate Stress 4 = Major Stress

Event	Level of Stress	Method for De-stressing	Post Stress Reduction Level

May be reproduced for Therapy, Home, or School use only!

Anger Reduction

Name: Date:

Instructions:
1) Write down situations where you experience anger.
2) Rank the anger experiences from most angry to least angry.
3) Rate your level of anger on a scale from 1-10 (1= No anger 10 = Rage).
4) Identify a counter for each anger issue.
5) Combine a relaxation technique with the counter and use them (chapter 6).
6) Rate your level of anger using the above scale after you complete step 5.

Rank	Anger Situations	Initial Anger Rating	Counters	Post Anger Rating

Agreement to Heal

If you have OCD, you must want to get better if things are to change. You must also be willing to do whatever it takes to reduce the obsessive or compulsive issues that are stressing your life. The following is a list of things that you should keep in mind as you seeks to address your OCD issues.

- You must commit to doing what it takes to overcome OCD issues. That means you must be willing to be uncomfortable to get better. When you practice exposure and ritual prevention exercises it will be easy to say, "That's too hard." "I can't do that." It will be uncomfortable! It will be difficult! However, if you continue to press forward and use the techniques you will gradually reduce your obsessive and compulsive tendencies. Commit to doing what it takes to get better.

- Don't be afraid to get angry at the specific OCD issue. Give it a name....specifically, give it a funny name that is as powerless as you can make it, e.g., Dumbo, Dizzy, Toto, Diddles, or Bugger. When the specific OCD issue starts to cause a problem for you call it by name...tell it you are angry with it and don't want to play.

- When confronted with a compulsion, make a distinction between behaviors that, 1) are probably not harmful or dangerous to you, or 2) are probably harmful or dangerous to you. Touching a doorknob and not washing your hands is probably not a harmful or dangerous activity. However, counting signposts while you drive (ride a bike) could be potentially dangerous. You need to get a handle on these potentially dangerous compulsions first.

- Don't go into an avoidant mode. Any avoidance you use to deal with your OCD will simply make it worse. Utilize ERP (Exposure, and Ritual Prevention) techniques as part of your day to address OCD issues.

Identifying Obsessive Thoughts

Name: Date:

Rating Scale:
1 = Minor Irritant 2 = Periodically Causes Problems 3 = Causes Moderate Problems
3 = Causes Significant Problems 4 = Dangerous Thought/Possible Serious Problems

	Rating
	1 2 3 4 5
	1 2 3 4 5
	1 2 3 4 5
	1 2 3 4 5
	1 2 3 4 5
	1 2 3 4 5
	1 2 3 4 5
	1 2 3 4 5
	1 2 3 4 5
	1 2 3 4 5
	1 2 3 4 5

May be reproduced for Therapy, Home, or School use only!

Obsessive Thoughts

Name: Date:

Step One: Evaluate Obsessive Thought
Identify the specific thought. Was there an antecedent? List the coping strategies that you use to avoid thinking about this specific thought. See Chapter 6!

Obsessive thought	Antecedent	Coping Strategy

Step Two: Thought vs Action
Rate how much you believe that you would actually act on this particular obsessive thought. 1 = would not act on it   5 = would act on it almost every time.

1   2   3   4   5

Step Three: Accept the thought knowing that you usually won't act on it.
If this obsession is one that would cause you to exhibit a compulsive act and it is troublesome to you go to step four (anything rated a 4 or 5). If it is merely a thought that rarely produces problems for you (anything rated 1 or 2), pick another obsessive thought and evaluate it.   If you rated the obsession a three you have to decide if it is problematic enough to go to step four.

Step Four: Confront the thought and do exposure exercises to habituate to the thought.

The goal of exposure exercises is meant to help you accept the thought in your mind without it causing discomfort or triggering you to a compulsive action. Chances are you will not get rid of the unwanted thought. However, you can learn to control it. Here are a few Exposure Exercises that may be helpful.

1. Imaging, Exposure and Response Prevention Technique
2. Verbal Exposure and Response Prevention Technique
3. Taped Exposure and Response Prevention Technique
4. Written Exposure and Response Prevention Technique

Personal Warning Signs for Mood Shifts

Name:	Date:

Instructions:
1) With help from parents, teachers and friends identify the early warning signs that suggest you may be in the early states of a mood switch.
2) List early warning signs for depression, and hypomania or mania.
3) Once you have this list it may become a very individualized self-monitoring device for you mood switches. Check daily to see if you are exhibiting any of the early warning signs.

Early Warning Signs	Sun	Mon	Tues	Wed	Thurs	Fri	Sat
Hypomanic/Manic							
Depressive							

May be reproduced for Therapy, Home, or School use only!

Daily Mood Diary

Name: **Date:**

Instructions:
Using a 1-5 scale, mark the number that describes your mood for the day.

1 = sad, depressed   3 = average feeling alright   5 = very happy, manic like

Sunday	1	2	3	4	5

Specific comments about how you were either low (1) or high (5)

Monday	1	2	3	4	5

Specific comments about how you were either low (1) or high (5)

Tuesday	1	2	3	4	5

Specific comments about how you were either low (1) or high (5)

Wednesday	1	2	3	4	5

Specific comments about how you were either low (1) or high (5)

Thursday	1	2	3	4	5

Specific comments about how you were either low (1) or high (5)

Friday	1	2	3	4	5

Specific comments about how you were either low (1) or high (5)

Saturday	1	2	3	4	5

Specific comments about how you were either low (1) or high (5)

Warning Signs for Depression Self-Monitoring

Name: Date:

Instructions:
1) Put a checkmark each time one of the warning signs occurs on a day by day basis.
2) If you have a depressive behavior that is not listed you may want to write it into one of the spaces provided so that you can monitor it also.

Depression Warning Signs	Sun	Mon	Tues	Wed	Thurs	Fri	Sat
Extremely Fatigued							
Hard Time getting out of bed							
Sleep Disturbance							
Avoiding Crowds							
Insecurity							
Negative Attitude							
Difficulty Concentrating							
Difficulty Experiencing Pleasure							
Feeling Down about Self							
Change in Appetite							
Procrastination							
Poor Judgment							
Extreme Difficulty Concentrating							
Poor Self-Confidence							
Thoughts of Suicide or Self Harm							

May be reproduced for Therapy, Home, or School use only!

Warning Signs for Mania
Self-Monitoring

Name: **Date:**

Instructions:
1) Put a checkmark each time one of the warning signs occurs on a day by day basis.
2) If you have a manic like behavior that is not listed you may want to write it into one of the spaces provided so that you can monitor it also.

Manic Warning Signs	Sun	Mon	Tues	Wed	Thurs	Fri	Sat
Argumentative							
Insomnia							
Failure to Take Medications							
Sexually High Energy							
Overactive							
Controlling							
Unnecessary Risk Taking							
Change in Appetite							
All-Knowing							
Self-Medicating							
Poor Judgment							
Very Talkative							
Thrill Seeking							
Drug/Alcohol Use							
Racing Thoughts							
Sleeping Less							

May be reproduced for Therapy, Home, or School use only!

Self-Monitoring
Multiple Behaviors by Period

Name: Date:

Instructions:
1. Identify one to three behaviors that need to be monitored. List them across
the top of this form. The student is to put a check in each box each time he exhibits
that behavior during each period.
2. Have him add the number of tallies that he has from behavior one, two and three to
get the total number for the day. Quality and quantity of rewards are dependent on
the number of overall tallies for the day. The fewer tallies the greater the reward.

Period	Behavior #1	Behavior #2	Behavior #3
Number of Tallies			

May be reproduced for Therapy, Home, or School use only!

Self-Monitoring
Multiple Behaviors by Day

Name: Date:

Instructions:
1. Identify the behaviors that need to be monitored. List them in the space provided below. Put a mark across the number each time you exhibit an appropriate behavior.
2. The fewer marks made for each behavior the greater the reward.

Behavior

	1	2	3	4	5	6	7	8	9	10
	1	2	3	4	5	6	7	8	9	10
	1	2	3	4	5	6	7	8	9	10

May be reproduced for Therapy, Home, or School use only!

Monitoring Communication

Name: Date:

I will check how many times I am negative or positive from:

until

Positive Communication	1	2	3	4	5	6	7	8	9	10
Negative Communication	1	2	3	4	5	6	7	8	9	10

May be reproduced for Therapy, Home, or School use only!

Personal Time Outs

Time Out Card

Hall Pass

Personal Pass

Monthly Medication Management

Name:	Date:											
Month:	**List of Medications to be Taken**											
Week One:	AM	PM	AM	PM	AM	PM	AM	PM	AM	PM	AM	PM
Sunday												
Monday												
Tuesday												
Wednesday												
Thursday												
Friday												
Saturday												
Week Two:												
Sunday												
Monday												
Tuesday												
Wednesday												
Thursday												
Friday												
Saturday												
Week Three:												
Sunday												
Monday												
Tuesday												
Wednesday												
Thursday												
Friday												
Saturday												
Week Four:												
Sunday												
Monday												
Tuesday												
Wednesday												
Thursday												
Friday												
Saturday												

May be reproduced for Therapy, Home, or School use only!

Daily Medication Side Effects Chart

Name:	Date:

Instructions:
1. Circle each side effect you have daily in the space provided.
2. If desired, you chart the results on the Weekly Drug Side Effect Chart to see which side effects are consistently causing the most difficulty.

Medication	Circle the Side Effects You Believe You are Having
Antipsychotic or Neuroleptic	Grogginess, Constipation, Dry Mouth, Dizziness, Weight Gain, Upset Stomach, Headaches, Difficulty Sleeping. More Serious Side Effects That Can Potentially Occur: Uncontrollable Chewing Movements, Tightness Of Muscles in the Face, Neck or Back, Tremors in Hands and Fingers, Tightness of Muscles, and Smacking Of Lips Other:
Antidepressant	Headaches, Nausea, Dry Mouth, Insomnia, Nervousness, Sexual Dysfunction, Diarrhea, Tiredness, And Agitation. Dizziness, Blurred Vision, Skin Rash, Drowsiness, Weight Gain, Urinary Retention, Constipation, Confusion Or Trouble Thinking Or Concentrating, Profuse Sweating, Muscular Twitches, Tiredness, Nausea, Increased Heart Rate, And Irregular Heart Rhythm (Uncommon) Other:
Mood Stabilizer	Tremors, Weakness or Muscles, Diarrhea or Upset Stomach, Frequent Urination, Increased Thirst, Difficulty When Trying To Concentrate, Weight Gain, Changes In Complexion (Acne), Sleepiness, Dizziness, Tremors, Thinning Hair, Vomiting, Rash, Double Vision Other:
Other Medication	
Other Medication	
Other Medication	
Reactions that don't seem to fit the medications listed above.	

May be reproduced for Therapy, Home, or School use only!

Weekly Drug Side Effect Chart

| Name: | | | | | | Week of: | | |

Instructions:
1. Review a week of data from the **Daily Medication Side Effects Chart** and chart it below to determine if the side effects happen daily or if it (they) are ongoing in nature.
2. If there is a pattern report this to the parent so the parent can report it to the doctor.

Side Effect	Sunday	Monday	Tues	Wed.	Thurs	Friday	Saturday
Grogginess							
Constipation							
Dry Mouth							
Dizziness							
Weight Gain							
Upset Stomach							
Headaches							
Difficulty Sleeping							
Nausea							
Insomnia							
Nervousness							
Sexual Dysfunction							
Diarrhea							
Tiredness							
Agitation							
Blurred Vision							
Skin Rash							
Drowsiness							
Urinary Retention							
Frequent Urination							
Confusion Or Trouble Thinking Or Concentrating							
Profuse Sweating							
Muscular Twitches							
Increased Heart Rate							
Irregular Heart Rhythm (Uncommon)							
Tremors							
Muscle Weakness							
Increased Thirst							
Changes in Complexion							
Sleepiness							
Vomiting							
Other:							

May be reproduced for Therapy, Home, or School use only!

Daily Activity and Mood Chart

Name:		Date:	
			Day of the Week:
Early Morning Rate Your Mood	-3 -2 -1 0 1 2 3 Very Depressed normal Very Elated		
	Time	Identify any routine changes or events.	Did you relate with anyone socially at this time? If so, who?
Time you are out of bed			
Morning Breakfast			
On time for class			
On time for class			
On time for class			
On time for class			
Lunch		List what you ate: Hot dog and fries and water Who did you eat with? Visited with Mary, no problems.	
Mid Day Rate Your Mood	-3 -2 -1 0 1 2 3 Very Depressed normal Very Elated		
	Time		
On time for class			
On time for class			
On time for class			
Schools out			
Dinner time			
Homework			
Time to bed			
End of Day Rate Your Mood	-3 -2 -1 0 1 2 3 Very Depressed normal Very Elated		
Have there been any changes that have caused you a problem? If so, write it down in the space provided.			

May be reproduced for Therapy, Home, or School use only!

Reasons to Exercise

Name: Date:

Instructions:

Check any of the following reasons that would encourage you to exercise.

☐	Decreases manic episodes.	☐	Increases life span.
☐	Improves Self-Esteem	☐	Decreases possibility of diabetes.
☐	It relieves stress.	☐	Decreases possibility of heart problems.
☐	Improves my ability to sleep at night.	☐	Decreases blood pressure.
☐	Reduces addictive cravings.	☐	Improves complexion.
☐	Improves immune system.	☐	Allows you to eat more and gain less.
☐	Improves energy.	☐	Decreases depression.
☐	Improves self-confidence.	☐	Increases strength.
☐	Weight loss.	☐	Improves flexibility.
☐	Increases endurance.	☐	Other:
☐	Other:	☐	Other:

List your top five reasons why you should exercise!

1._____

2._____

3._____

4._____

5._____

May be reproduced for Therapy, Home, or School use only!

Types of Exercise

Name:		Date:	

Instructions:

1. Place a check mark next to any exercise that you would be willing to do on a weekly or daily basis. If there is an exercise that you would prefer that is not listed you can add it.
2. Once you have decided which forms of exercise you are willing to use you must commit to using one of the forms daily if at all possible.

	Walking before school.		Walking immediately after school.
	Running before school.		Running immediately after school.
	Riding a bike after school.		Go dancing.
	Take a karate class.		Take a Yoga, or Pilates class.
	Work out with weights.		Play tennis, basketball, etc for fun.
	Other:		Other:

What days will you commit to exercising for at least fifteen minutes?

Self-Defeating Thoughts and Exercise

Name: Date:

Instructions:

1. When you are finding that you are not wanting to exercise for some reason it is important to work through the self-defeating thoughts that are triggering your lack of desire.
2. Write down the self-defeating thought. On the other side of the form write down the corrective thought.

Self-Defeating Thought	Corrective Thought

May be reproduced for Therapy, Home, or School use only!

Exercise Journal

Name: Date:

Day	Daily Exercise: What I did to exercise today!	Result: How did you feel when you were finished?
Sunday		
Monday		
Tuesday		
Wednesday		
Thursday		
Friday		
Saturday		

May be reproduced for Therapy, Home, or School use only!

Somatic Precursors to a Rage State

Name:	Date:

Date	Somatic Precursors	
	___ Pulsing in temple ___ Brain seems to burn ___ Tunnel vision ___ Body tension ___ Other:	___ Forehead tensing up ___ Eyes hurt ___ Grinding teeth ___ Shaking ___ Other:
	First Symptom:	
	___ Pulsing in temple ___ Brain seems to burn ___ Tunnel vision ___ Body tension ___ Other:	___ Forehead tensing up ___ Eyes hurt ___ Grinding teeth ___ Shaking ___ Other:
	First Symptom:	
	___ Pulsing in temple ___ Brain seems to burn ___ Tunnel vision ___ Body tension ___ Other:	___ Forehead tensing up ___ Eyes hurt ___ Grinding teeth ___ Shaking ___ Other:
	First Symptom:	

May be reproduced for Therapy, Home, or School use only!

Cue Cards for Behavior

Students under stress may need a Cue Card to help them remember what to do for specific situations. Obviously, you cannot have a dozen Cue Cards. However, a student may have one to three that he can keep in his day timer or shirt pocket that will help him remember what to do when he is triggered by another student, teacher, or situation. Here are some examples of cue cards.

Cue Card I will ignore Josh when he calls me a name, and walk away.	**Cue Card** I will go to my time out room when I get stressed.
Cue Card I will go get a drink when I feel stressed out.	**Cue Card** I will use my quick stress technique when I get agitated in class.
Cue Card I will go to the counselor when I get upset.	**Cue Card** I will go back to my task when others start to bother me in class.

Identifying Triggers or Antecedents

Name: Date:

Instructions:
1). With the help of your family, teachers and trusted friends list the situations, people, etc. that seem to trigger you. It may cause you to be agitated, angry, manic, depressed, etc.
2) After you get a good list, rate each trigger or antecedent based on how much they cause problems for you. See the rating scale below.

Rating Scale:
1 = Minor Irritant 2 = Periodically Causes Problems 3 = Causes Moderate Problems
3 = Causes Significant Problems 4 = Dangerous Thought/Possible Serious Problems

	Rating
	1 2 3 4 5
	1 2 3 4 5
	1 2 3 4 5
	1 2 3 4 5
	1 2 3 4 5
	1 2 3 4 5
	1 2 3 4 5
	1 2 3 4 5
	1 2 3 4 5

May be reproduced for Therapy, Home, or School use only!

Antecedent Modification

Name:		Date:
Behavior	**Antecedent: The Trigger**	**Changing the Antecedent**

May be reproduced for Therapy, Home, or School use only!

Executive Functions

Name: Date:

		Yes	No
1	This student has planning, prioritizing & time management problems.		
2	This student has problems with organizing materials and space.		
3	This student has problems activating to work.		
4	This student has problems with focusing, regulating alertness & sustaining attention.		
5	This student has problems with processing speed.		
6	This student has problems with self-monitoring.		
7	This student has problems with flexibility & transitioning.		
8	This student has problems with emotional control.		
9	This student has a problem utilizing working memory.		
10	This student has a problem accessing recall.		
11	This student has a problem shifting attention.		
12	This student has a problem with inhibition or response regulation.		

May be reproduced for Therapy, Home, or School use only!

Reinforcement Survey

Name:_____ Grade:____ Teacher:_____ Date:_____

Instructions: Read the following to the student and have him pick between the two choices.   Place a check mark under the column that the student chooses. Rank the student's most preferred to the least preferred in the space provided.

Out of the two items I will name, which would you like to have the most,	Consumable	Tangible	Activity	Adult Approval	Peer Approval
1.) To be given art materials to use (Tangible) or		☐			
2.) To be given your favorite candy bar (Consumable)	☐				
3.) To receive an ice cream treat that you like (Consumable) or	☐				
4.) To have your teacher put a smiley face on your paper. (Adult Approval)				☐	
5.) To be given your favorite drink, e.g., milk, soft drink, sports drink, etc. (Consumable) or	☐				
6.) To have fellow students ask you to be their leader during recess (Peer Approval)					☐
7.) To have your fellow students ask you to play with them (Peer Approval) or					☐
8.) To be given a pencil from your teacher (Tangible)		☐			
9.) To have some free computer time (Activity) or			☐		
10.) To have friends tell you that you did a good job (Peer Approval)					☐
11.) To have your teacher comment on how good our work is in front of class (Adult Approval) OR				☐	
12.) To be given a pencil sharpener (Tangible)		☐			
13.) To have your teacher tell you how proud she is of you (Adult Approval) Or				☐	
14.) To have friends ask you to be on their team (Peer Approval)					☐
15.) To have free time at a center or in the library (Activity) or			☐		
16.) To be given your favorite snack (Consumable)	☐				
17.) To help your teacher in class in class, (Activity) or			☐		
18.) To have your teacher pat you on the back for good work. (Adult Approval)				☐	
19.) To have five minutes of free time at your desk in class, (Activity) or			☐		
20.) To be given a coloring book or pages to color (Tangible)		☐			
Totals:	____	____	____	____	____
Rank:	____	____	____	____	____

If there is a tie between two or more reinforcers, have the student pick which is 1st, 2ⁿᵈ or 3rd.
Adapted from an unknown resource.
May be reproduced for Therapy, Home, or School use only!

Consumables

Name:_____ Grade:____ Age:____Date:_____

Read the following statements check the ones that are things you really like. Before you do fill in the blanks.

___Potato chips   ___M&M's
___Popcorn   ___Raisins
___Peanuts   ___Crackers
___Crackerjacks   ___Lemon Drops
___Milk
___Other:

___Favorite Candy:
___Favorite Juice Drink:
___Favorite Sport Drink:
___Favorite Soft Drink:
___Favorite Pie:
___Favorite Cake:
___Favorite Snack:
___Favorite Ice Cream:
___Favorite Cookie:
___Other:

Pick your top three and list them below:

1._____

2._____

3._____

May be reproduced for Therapy, Home, or School use only!

Tangibles

Name:_____ Grade:___ Age:___Date:_____

Tangibles are items that a student prefers that can be a strong reinforcer. To determine the tangible items that are most preferred by this student have him complete this form.

Put a check next to the four things that you would most like to get as a reward:

____Coloring book   ___Chalk

___Marbles   ___Ball

___Pencil   ___Balloon

____Silly Putty   ___Book marker

___Jacks   ___ Other:

Pick your top three and list them below:

1._____

2._____

3._____

Activity

Name:_____ Grade:___ Age:___Date:_____

Read the following statements check the ones that are true for you.

___Working on a puzzle   ___Running errands

___Taking care of a class pet   ___Drawing, painting, etc.

___Using a radio w/ earphone   ___Free computer time

___Helping the teacher   ___Reading to a friend

___Other: ___Other:

Pick your top three and list them below:

1._____

2._____

3._____

Adult Approval

Name:_____ Grade:___ Age:___Date:_____

Read the following statements check the ones that are true for you.

___1. I would like my teacher to say something special to me in front of the other kids.

___2. When I do a good job I would like my teacher to tell my parents about it.

___3. I would like to spend time with my teacher at lunch.

___4. I would like for one of my parents to come up and have lunch with me.

___5. I would like for my teacher to say something special to me in front of other teachers.

___6. Other:

___7. Other:

Put the number of two of the above that you would like to happen the most in the spaces provided below.

1.___   2.___

Peer Approval

Name:_____ Grade:____ Age:____ Date:_____

Read the following statements check the ones that are true for you.

____1. Be asked to play by your best friend.

____2. Have your class clap for you when you do something well.

____3. Be able to earn your class a field trip

____4. Be able to earn your class extra recess or activity time

____5. Be elected a class officer

____6. Other:

____7. Other:

Put the number of two of the above that you would like to happen the most in the spaces provided below.

1.____   2.____

School Reward Questionnaire
Secondary

Name:_____ Grade:_____ Date:_____

1. The reward I would like best at school is

2. The names of my best friends at school are

3. The thing I like best about school is

4. The thing that I would most like to do at school with a friend is

5. The friend I would most like to have free time at school with is

6. I have the most fun in school when I

7. The teacher I like the most is

8. I would like my teacher to say to me

9. I would like to be allowed to quietly do this at school when I have extra time

10. The thing I need most in school is

11. The best thing my teacher can say to me is

12. The activity I like to do the most when I have free time at school is

13. During free time at school the thing I would like to do most is

14. The school period I like best is

15. My three favorite snacks at school are

16. When I have free time and I am alone at school the thing I would most like to do is

17. My favorite soft drink, sport drink, or juice is

18. The three things I would most want to do during free time at school are

19. When I do well at school I would like my teacher to

20. When I finish class work at school I would like to

May be reproduced for Therapy, Home, or School use only!

Proactive Reinforcement Schedule

Name: **Date:**

Instructions:

   1. With the data you have and the parent's help identify rewards that can be
      proactively used to help the student maintain control of his behavior.
   2. Review all data before listing items that the student finds very rewarding.

Activity:

Peer Reinforcement:

Adult Reinforcement:

Tangibles:

Consumables:

Other:

May be reproduced for Therapy, Home, or School use only!

Daily/Weekly Rewards Menu

Name:	Date:

Instructions:

With the student's help identify four rewards that he can obtain at the end of the day if he receives 5, 10, 15, or 20 points in a day.

Daily Rewards

5 points for the day   =

10 points for the day =

15 points for the day =

20 points for the day =

Instructions:

If the student chooses he may bank his points in order to get a larger reward at the end of the week. With the student's help and help from the parent identify two rewards; one for 70 points and one for 90 points.

Weekly Rewards

70 points for the Week   =

90 points for the Week   =

May be reproduced for Therapy, Home, or School use only!

Period/Daily Reward Chart

Name: _____   Date: _____

If I have less than _____ checks on my monitoring system I can choose from the
following rewards at the end of the period.

If I have less than _____ checks on my monitoring system I can choose from the
following rewards at the end of the period.

If I have less than _____ checks on my monitoring system I can choose from the
following rewards at the end of the period.

If I have less than _____ checks on my monitoring system I can choose from the
following rewards at the end of the period.

If I have less than _____ checks on my monitoring system I can choose from the
following rewards at the end of the period.

If I have a minimum of _____ checks during the day I can choose a special reward for
myself.

May be reproduced for Therapy, Home, or School use only!

Daily/Weekly Reward Chart

Name: Date:

If I have less than _____ checks on my monitoring system I can choose from the
following rewards at the end of the day.

If I have less than _____ checks on my monitoring system I can choose from the
following rewards at the end of the day.

If I have less than _____ checks on my monitoring system I can choose from the
following rewards at the end of the day.

If I have less than _____ checks on my monitoring system I can choose from the
following rewards at the end of the day.

If I have less than _____ checks on my monitoring system I can choose from the
following rewards at the end of the day.

If I have a minimum of _____ checks during from Monday through Friday I can choose
a special reward for myself or my class.

May be reproduced for Therapy, Home, or School use only!

250

References

- Akiskal, H.S., The Prevalent clinical spectrum of Bipolar Disorders: Beyond DSM-IV. Journal of Clinical Psychopharmacology 16 (2 Suppl. 1): 4-14.
- Alpert JE. SAMe, folate, and B12: one-carbon metabolism and depression Program and abstracts of the American Psychiatric Association 2004 Annual Meeting; May 1-6, 2004; New York, NY. Symposium 19C.
- Alpert JE, Mischoulon D, Nierenberg AA, Fava M. Nutrition and depression: focus on folate. Nutrition. 2000;16:544-546.
- Alpert JE, Mischoulon D, Rubenstein GE, Bottonari K, Nierenberg AA, Fava M. Folinic acid (leucovorin) as an adjunctive treatment for SSRI-refractory depression. Ann Clin Psychiatry. 2002;14:33-38.
- American Psychiatric Association. Diagnostic and statistical book of mental disorders (4th ed.) Washington, DC., 1994a.
- Benson, H. The Relaxation Response. New York: William Morrow and Company, 1975.
- Blum, K. and Comings, D. (1996) Reward Deficiency Syndrome. American Scientist 84, 2, 16-23
- Burns, D. Feeling Good. New York: Avon Books, 1980.
- Carlson GA, Jensen PS, Nottelmann ED, eds. Special issue: current issues in childhood bipolarity. Journal of Affective Disorders, 1998; 51: entire issue.
- Cautela, J. R., & Kearney, A. J. The Covert Conditioning Handbook. New York, NY: Springer, 1986.
- Coppen A, Bailey J. Enhancement of the antidepressant action of fluoxetine by folic acid: a randomized, placebo controlled trial. J Affect Disord. 2000;60:121-130
- Davidson JR, Abraham K, Connor KM, McLeod MN. Effectiveness of chromium in atypical depression: a placebo-controlled trial. Biol Psychiatry. 2003;53:261-264.
- Fawcett, J., Busch, K.A., and Jacobs, D. Suicide: A four-pathway clinical-biochemical model. Annals of the New York Academy of Science 836, 288-301, 1997.
- Fava M, Borus JS, Alpert JE, Nierenberg AA, Rosenbaum JF, Bottiglieri T. Folate, vitamin B12, and homocysteine in major depressive disorder. Am J Psychiatry. 1997;154:426-428.
- Feinman JA, Dunner DL. The effect of alcohol and substance abuse on the course of bipolar affective disorder. J Affect Disord. 1996;37:43-49.
- Geller, B. Delbello, M.P., and Frome, M.P. Bipolar Disorder in Childhood and Early Adolescence. New York: Guilford, 2003.
- Geller B, Luby J. Child and adolescent Bipolar Disorder: a review of the past 10 years. Journal of the American Academy of Child and Adolescent Psychiatry, 1997; 36(9): 1168-76.
- Geller, B., Williams, M., Zimerman, B., Frazier, J., Beringer, L., and Warner, K. L. Prepubertal and early adolescent bipolarity differentiate from ADHD by manic symptoms; grandiose delusions; ultra-rapid or ultradian cycling. Journal of Affective Disorders , 1998.
- Geller B, Sun K, Zimerman B, Luby J, Frazier J, Williams M (1995), Complex and rapid-cycling in bipolar children and adolescents: a preliminary study. J Affect Disord 34:259-268.

- Himmelhoch JM, Mulla D, Neil JF, Detre TP, Kupfer DJ. Incidence and significance of mixed affective states in a bipolar population. Arch Gen Psychiatry. 1976;33:1062-1066.
- Kessler RC, Chiu WT, Demler O, Walters EE. Prevalence, severity, and comorbidity of 12-month DSM-IV disorders in the national comorbidity survey replication. Arch Gen Psychiatry. 2005;62:617-627.
- Kovacs, M & Pollock, M. Bipolar Disorder and Co-morbid Conduct Disorder in Childhood and Adolescence. Journal of the American Academy of Child and Adolescent 34, June, 1995, 715-723.
- Krishnan KR (2005), Psychiatric and medical comorbidities of Bipolar Disorder. Psychosom Med 67(1):1-8.
- Lynn, G. Survival Strategies for Parenting Children with Bipolar Disorder. Philadelphia: Jessica Kingsley, 2000.
- Malkoff-Schwartz, S., Frand, E., Anderson, B., Sherrill, J.T., Seigel, L., Patterson, D., & Kupfer, D.G., (1998). Stressful life events and social rhythm disruption in the onset of manic and depressive bipolar episodes: A preliminary investigation. Archives of General Psychiatry, 55, 702-707.
- Maltz, M Psycho-Cybernetics. New York: Pocket Books, 1960.
- Markou A, Kosten TR, Koob GF. Neurobiological similarities in depression and drug dependence: a self-medication hypothesis. Neuropsychopharmacology. 1998;18:135-174.
- McKnew, D.G., Cytgryn, L., & Yahraes, H. Why isn't Johnny Crying? Coping with Depression in Children. New York: Norton & Company, 1983.
- Meichenbaum, D. A clinical Handbook/Practical Therapist Manual: For assessing and treating Adults with Post-Traumatic Stress Disorder. Waterloo, Ont.: Institute Press, 1994.
- Miklowitz The Bipolar Disorder Survival Guide. New York: Guilford, 2002.
- Moeller FG, Dougherty DM (2002), Impulsivity and substance abuse: what is the connection? Addict Disorder Treat 1:3-10.
- Novaco, R. Anger Control: The Development and Evaluation of an Experimental Treatment, Lexicon Books, 1975.
- Papolos and Papolos, The Bipolar Child. New York: Broadway Books, 2002.
- Pennebaker, J.W. Opening Up: The Healing Power of Expressing Emotions. New York: Guilford Press, 1997.
- Popper, C. Diagnosing Bipolar vs ADHD: A Pharmacological Point of View. The Link 13: 1996.
- Sonne SC, Brady KT, Morton WA. Substance abuse and bipolar affective disorder. J Nerv Ment Disease. 1994;182:349-352.
- Strakowski SM, Sax KW, McElroy SL, Keck PE, Hawkins JM, West SA. Course of psychiatric and substance abuse syndromes co-occurring with bipolar disorder after a first psychiatric hospitalization. J Clin Psychiatry. 1998;59:465-471.
- Strakowski SM, DelBello MP. The co-occurrence of bipolar and substance use disorders. Clinical Psychology Review, 2000; 20(2): 191-206.
- Strober, M., Morrell, W., Lampert, C., and Burroughs, J. Relapse following discontinuation of lithium maintenance therapy in adolescents with bipolar I illness: A naturalistic study. Am J Psychiatry 147, 457-461, 1990.
- Stoll AL, Severus WE, Freeman MP, et al. Omega 3 fatty acids in bipolar disorder: a preliminary double-blind, placebo-controlled trial. Arch Gen Psychiatry. 1999;56:407-412.
- Swann AC, Dougherty DM, Pazzaglia PJ et al. (2004), Impulsivity: a link between Bipolar Disorder and substance abuse. Bipolar Disorder 6(3):204-212.

- Swedo, S., Leonard, H., Garvey, M., Mittleman, B.., Allen, A., Perlmutter, S., Dow, S., Zamkoff, J., Dubbert, B., and Lougee, L. Pediatric Autoimmune Neuropsychiatric Disorders Associated With Streptococcal Infections: Clinical Description of the First 50 Cases Am J Psychiatry 155:264-271, February 1998.
- Tohen M, Waternzux CM, Tsuang MT. Outcome in mania: a 4-year prospective follow-up of 75 patients using survival analysis. Arch Gen Psychiatry. 1990;47:1106-1111.
- Tohen M, Zarate CA, Zarate SB, Gebre-Medhin P, Pike S. The McLean/Harvard First Episode Mania Project: pharmacologic treatment and outcome. Psychiatric Ann. 1996;26(suppl):S444-S448.
- Vainionpaa LK, Rattya J, Knip M, et al. Valproate-induced hyperandrogenism during pubertal maturation in girls with epilepsy. *Annals of Neurology*, 1999; 45(4): 444-50.
- Wehr, T.A., Sack, D.A., & Rosenthal, N.E., (1987). Sleep reduction as a final common pathway in the genesis of mania. American Journal of Psychiatry, 144, 210-214.
- Weiss RD, Ostacher MJ, Otto MW, et al. Does recovery from substance use disorder matter in patients with bipolar disorder? J Clin Psychiatry. 2005;66:730-735.
- Welner, A., Welner, Z., and Fishman, R. Psychiatric adolescent inpatients: Eight to ten-year follow-up. Arch Gen Psychiatry 36[6], 698-700, 1979.
- Williams, M.GB., Poijula, S The PTSD Workbook. Oakland: New Harbinger, 2002.

Index

Ordering

For more information, multiple book prices, contact cpc@cpccom.com. Leave your name, phone number and message. Discounts available for bulk purchases.

ITEM	Cost	Tax	Cost +Tax	Shipping Cost	Total
Bipolar or ADHD Book	$34.95	8.25%			
Bipolar or ADHD Book plus CD Supplement*	$49.95	8.25%			
Bipolar or ADHD CD Supplement*	$24.95	8.25%			
Bipolar Checklist with Strategy Locator (25 sheets)	$ 9.00	8.25%			
Bipolar or ADHD Checklist with Strategy Locator (25 Sheets)	$12.00	8.25%			
Total Package: 1 book, CD supplement, one pad of Bipolar Checklist with Strategy Locator, and one pad of Bipolar or ADHD Checklist with Strategy Locator	$64.95	8.25%			
				Total Cost	

* The CD supplement includes all worksheets in the book and can be individualized or adapted for personal use. Checklists found in the book are also included, along with multiple narrative strategies that can be utilized to help the student deal with stress/anxiety, anger, OCD issues, etc.

Shipping Costs	
Item	**UPS Ground 4 Days**
Bipolar/ADHD Book	$8.00
Bipolar/ADHD book + CD	$9.00
Bipolar or ADHD CD Supplement	$7.00
Bipolar Checklist with Strategy Locator	$8.00
Bipolar or ADHD Checklist with Strategy Locator	$8.00
Total Package (Described above)	$12.00
Only for continental United States	

UPS shipping fees are subject to any changes UPS makes in actual shipping costs.

___ Check enclosed
___ Purchase Order Attached (Bill my institution)
___ Please charge my credit card: ☐ Visa ☐ Mastercard

Send to:
Crites Psychoeducational Consultants
106 N. Denton Tap Rd. Ste. 210-216
Coppell, Texas   75019

Credit Card #:_____ Expiration Date:_____

Signature required with credit card use: _____

Name:_____ School /Institution:_____

Address:_____ Phone:_____

_____
City   State   ZIP

E-mail address:_____

For additional products, workshops, etc. you may go to www.cpccom.com